The Politics of Child Abuse

The Politics of Child Abuse

Nigel Parton

**MACMILLAN
EDUCATION**

First published 1985
Reprinted 1986, 1987, 1988

Published by
MACMILLAN EDUCATION LTD
Houndmills, Basingstoke, Hampshire RG21 2XS
and London
Companies and representatives
throughout the world

Filmset by Latimer Trend & Company Ltd, Plymouth

Printed in Hong Kong

British Library Cataloguing in Publication Data
Parton, Nigel
The politics of child abuse.
1. Child abuse
I. Title
362.7'044   HV713
ISBN 0—333—36316—7
ISBN 0—333—36317—5 Pbk

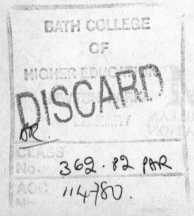

For Laura and Kate

Contents

List of Figures and Tables

FIGURES

TABLES

Preface

My interest in writing this book has grown out of my experiences as a generic social worker in a social services department in the early to mid 1970s. The department was undergoing various traumas and readjustments resulting from the double reorganisation following Seebohm and local government reorganisation. My colleagues and I were attempting to cope with the rapid changes in our role and workload and the changing demands and expectations made of us by both our clients and the wider community.

However, the period was punctuated by an event which generated enormous interest in, and debate about, social work and social workers, and which seemed of a different order to anything that had happened before – certainly in recent history. It felt as if the death of Maria Colwell and the subsequent inquiry had an impact on social work well beyond the more specific concerns about protecting children from cruel parents, a responsibility which child care officers were well accustomed to.

Not only did it seem that social workers were being pilloried – particularly in the media – but that we were being asked to get involved in and take responsibility for a problem which was called variously 'battered babies', 'non-accidental injury', or 'child abuse', and which was qualitatively different from anything that social workers had dealt with before. It seemed that a new social problem had been discovered which required new skills, new forms of intervention and new organisational arrangements to deal with it. Throughout there was a pervasive fear that the circumstances surrounding the death of Maria Colwell could have happened to any of us. It was as if the optimism that had been so evident at the beginning of the decade was dealt a fatal blow by one dramatic event, and that we were being asked to re-think our priorities and practice in fundamentally different ways.

However, I had an uneasiness about what was happening to both clients and social workers. I was especially concerned that the nature of this new problem did not seem as clear-cut and straightforward as was suggested in most of the training manuals and guidelines. Nor was I convinced that many of the new policies and practices introduced were as humane as was assumed. They seemed to have unintended consequences which were deleterious for everyone involved.

Increasingly I felt the need for a more critical analysis of what was happening in a period of rapid change and high anxiety, in the hope of formulating new perspectives. First, it seemed important to look behind these events in order to understand my own experiences. Then, if we could establish why and how we came to this situation, we could begin to develop new ideas and practices.

Part One is primarily concerned with looking at the way in which child abuse was discovered, and the political processes whereby it was defined, brought to public attention and made the subject of state intervention. Briefly the argument is that the way the problem has been socially constructed has been based on a very particular set of assumptions and explanations. The medical model with its emphasis on individual 'disease', 'treatment', 'identification' and 'prevention' has been dominant. This has been crucial in influencing what we do about the problem and the manner in which we do it. Nor has this been a chance development, for changes in the economy, the state and the wider society have been central, together with the intervention of certain professional, organisational and political interests.

Part Two critically analyses this model and demonstrates how it offers a very partial and inadequate explanation and consequently an inappropriate framework for policy and practice. Other explanations are offered, based on an explicitly social-structural position, which then inform an alternative model for policy and practice.

Perhaps because the problem of child abuse has only

emerged in the last twenty years, most of the literature and policy and practice recommendations have been concerned to encourage welfare practitioners to act where previously they may not have done. In the process, the assumptions inherent in such developments have been left implicit, the theoretical underpinnings left untested and practice rarely evaluated. It is generally assumed that everyone agrees and knows what the problem is, it is just a question of identifying and doing something about it. In contrast, however, I argue that debates about the nature of child abuse and what to do about it are in essence not technical but political debates about the good society, and the relationship between the family and the state.

Chapter 1 sets out the theoretical framework on which the book is organised and explores the application of a sociological understanding of social problems to child abuse. Those less interested in the theoretical framework of the book could move on to the remainder without any great loss. Similarly, those most interested in the current policy issues and the application of this perspective to practice may wish to turn directly to Chapters 5 and 8.

The book has been trying to get out for a number of years and during that time and previously I have benefited from all kinds of advice and discussions from practitioners and academics. There are many I cannot mention because of space, but I would particularly like to thank Joan Court, Linda Davies, Robert Dingwall, Alfred White Franklin, Christine Hallett, Bill Jordon, Gerry Lavery, Chris Melotte, Revd Arthur Morton, Terry Norris, Jean Packman, Ken Plummer and Terry Thomas.

I have drawn on the energies of various library staff – particularly those at Huddersfield Polytechnic, who have always remained good humoured for all my continual demands. Linda Barker, Sandra Lewis and Liz Tunaley have provided excellent typing help and students and colleagues in the social work section at the Polytechnic have always been supportive. More particularly they allowed me the time to write: without them the book would never have been completed. However, more than anyone Chris Parton has ensured that the book is as good as it is. She has lived with it from the outset, provided encouragement when times were bad and intellectual stimulation throughout, as well as critically commenting on every chapter. Similarly, she has taken far more than her fair share of household and child care responsibilities so that I could make progress.

I am very aware that the subject is an emotive one and that much of what I write may be seen as contentious. I am also aware that many issues are left untouched or dealt with only in the context of the general argument. It is therefore important to underline that I am fully responsible for what follows.

March 1984   NIGEL PARTON

PART ONE
THE HISTORY

1

Child Abuse and the Sociology of Social Problems

My main concern in Part One is to demonstrate and explain why the problem of child abuse has emerged as such a crucial one for welfare practitioners, what the nature of that problem is, how it has changed, and what have been the implications for policy and practice. The analysis will draw upon perspectives and concepts that have been developed in the sociology of deviance and social problems. It is perhaps ironic that an area of sociology that has been subject to so much rapid development, theoretical argument and heated discussion[1] should have made such little impact on our thinking and analysis of child abuse.[2] Even more ironic when it is often argued that sociology in general[3] and the sociology of deviance in particular has played such a central role in the radicalisation and increasing disillusionment of social workers.[4]

What is the distinctive analytical framework of the sociology of deviance and social problems and how does it help answer the questions posed about child abuse? In 1973 Stanley Cohen commented that in the previous decade the sociological study of deviance had undergone a radical re-orientation:

This orientation is part of what might be called the sceptical revolution in criminology and the Sociology of Deviance. The older tradition was canonical in the sense that it saw the concepts it worked with as authoritative, standard, accepted, given and unquestionable. The new tradition is sceptical in the sense that when it sees terms like 'deviant', it

asks 'deviant to whom?' or 'deviant from what?'; when told something is a
social problem, it asks 'problematic to whom?'; when certain conditions or
behaviour are described as functional, embarrassing, threatening or
dangerous, it asks 'says who'? and 'why?'. In other words, these concepts
and descriptions are not assumed to have a taken-for-granted status.[5]

Certainly since the late 1960s in Britain the older conceptions
of and explanations of deviance have come increasingly under
attack and a variety of social problems have been subject to
critical analysis. However, while it is possible to talk about the
emergence of a new orientation it is important to recognise that
it includes a number of often sharply divergent schools of
thought, which include phenomenology, symbolic interac-
tionism, functionalism, control theories and radical or marxist
variants.[6] Thus to talk of an internal consistency or new
consensus in these developments is quite erroneous – as the
heated debates of the 1970s testify. However, the orientation
focuses on some central concerns for developing our understanding of child abuse and provides an important basis for
critically analysing and explaining the problem. What have
been these central concerns?

First, there was a concern that the study of deviance had
become dissociated from the workings of the control processes,
including the State. It was argued that research and theories
should not simply chart the characteristics and causes of
deviant individuals but should also analyse the nature of the
social control processes. Crucially, no adequate understanding
of deviance was possible without considering the interdepen-
dence between the control processes (or reactions), the deviant
behaviour (or actions) and the nature of laws, rules and norms.
Increasingly it was argued that the nature and general shape of
the deviance could not be understood by considering the
deviant and his behaviour in isolation from the way it was
defined and reacted against.

Secondly, there was a reaction against the assumption that
the conventional approach was 'value free'. The literature
paraded extraordinary value positions under the guise of
objectivity, so that highly evaluative terms such as 'immaturity', 'disordered', 'disorganised', 'undersocialised' were common. It was seen as crucial to make value discussions explicit.

Thirdly, and related to this, there was a reaction against a spurious 'scientism' or positivism whereby, using the scientific standards of natural science, attempts were made to discover scientific laws which might explain the deviance and, if discovered, might lead to its eradication. What seemed to get lost was any sense of history or process or any understanding of the impact of the social situation.

Thus, fourthly, the traditional concern was with explaining the aetiology of the individual deviant in order to prevent or predict future occurrences. The explanations were deterministic in nature and again failed to appreciate the perspective of the deviant or the significance of social processes. It is not surprising therefore if the new deviancy theorists rejected the old absolutism in favour of a more relative and socially situated orientation.

Initially this re-orientation was associated with the processes of labelling, and demonstrated that the social processes whereby deviant behaviour is controlled and defined cannot be treated as unproblematic. Laws and rules, rather than simply defining the boundaries of investigation, need to be included in any explanation. It underlined the need to examine the political nature of deviance and its control and the relationship between theory and ideology. As Plummer suggests,[7] the labelling perspective 'constitutes neither theory nor proposition' but asks a series of questions designed to consider the 'nature', 'emergence', 'application' and 'consequences' of deviancy labels. For our purposes in Part One, we are concerned with asking: what are the characteristics of child abuse labels, their variations and forms? What are the sources of the labels, historically, and societally? More centrally we are concerned with asking why child abuse emerged as a social problem in Britain when it did and in the form in which it did?

We cannot begin to understand child abuse without an analysis of the nature of the category and how this has been constructed and recognised as a social problem requiring State intervention. The work of Fuller and Myers provides a useful starting point. They suggest that:

A social problem is a condition which is defined by a considerable number of persons as a deviation from some social norm which they cherish. Every social problem thus consists of an *objective condition* and a *subjective definition*. The objective condition is a verifiable situation which can be checked as to existence and magnitude (proportions) by impartial and trained observers. The subjective definition is the awareness of certain individuals that the condition is a threat to certain cherished values.[8]

However, while they suggest that objective conditions are not sufficient for the existence of social problems, they stop short of arguing that objective conditions are neither necessary nor sufficient. Yet as Blumer[9] and Spector and Kitsuse[10] suggest, a concern for what constitutes the objective conditions may deflect attention from what should be the central focus of analysis[11] – to account for the emergence, maintenance, history and conceptualisation of what is defined as a social problem and what should be done about it. For, according to Rubington and Weinberg: 'Sociologists usually consider a social problem to be an alleged situation that is incompatible with the values of a significant number of people who agree that action is needed to alter the situation.'[12]

It follows from this that it is the *allegation* that is crucial. Similarly it places the issue of values and possible value conflict at the centre of discussion. Values are crucial not only in whether and how a situation is defined as a problem but also in what is seen as appropriate to do about it. These are closely interrelated, as calls for action are heavily influenced by the way the problem is defined. Thus the emergence of 'child abuse' depends on the collective activities that have become organised around the assertion that some putative condition is a problem which needs eradicating, ameliorating or otherwise changing.

A number of writers have applied this approach in relation to empirically based case studies and identified different explanatory concepts. In America much of this has evolved to account for the regulatory policies by narcotics enforcement agencies. The issues they try to explain are: why these agencies sought to proscribe the supply of narcotic substances to addicts; and why they sought and secured the passage of additional legislation proscribing the consumption of other dangerous drugs.

Howard Becker[13] has argued that the main force was the Treasury Department's director, J. H. Anslinger, and his central explanatory concepts are 'moral enterprise' and the 'moral entrepreneur'. According to Becker: 'Wherever rules are created and applied we should be alive to the possible presence of an enterprising individual or group. Their activities can properly be called "moral enterprise" for what they are enterprising about is the creation of a new fragment of the moral constitution of society, its code of right and wrong.'[14]

He suggests that the prototype of the rule creator is the 'crusading' reformer who is not happy with the present situation as there is some 'evil' which they find disturbing and about which something needs to be done. Such crusaders operate with an absolute ethic, are 'fervent and righteous', and are often humanitarian, for they feel that if people do what is 'right' it will do them good. Therefore, according to Becker, an adequate explanation is provided once an entrepreneur who was involved in promoting the problem has been identified.

An alternative explanation has been suggested by Dickson.[15] He argues that the narcotics enforcement agencies had a natural tendency to extend their power so that the moral enterprise arises from and is secondary to 'bureaucratic' imperatives. Rather than the moral entrepreneur mobilising the agency, according to Dickson the agency mobilises the individual or group.

Galiher and Walker[16] offer another explanation, for they argue that the legislative changes and reactions to narcotics are primarily symbolic. The laws were introduced not on the assumption that vigorous enforcement would ensue but primarily to affirm certain values. It was essentially 'symbolic'.

A number of writers have used this notion of symbolic action.[17] For example, Joseph Gusfield uses the model in his analysis of the early twentieth-century temperance movement.[18] He distinguishes between instrumental and symbolic action, where the latter refers to an object which has a range of meaning well beyond itself. Thus 'disinterested reform' occurs when an issue appears as a moral one, divorced from any direct economic interests, and symbolically enhances the prestige and self-esteem of the victors and degrades the culture, values and life-style of the losers.

Tony Platt's[19] historical analysis of the role of the 'child saving movement' in inventing delinquency and introducing the juvenile court to Illinois at the end of the nineteenth century, draws on a number of these concepts. He argues that the movement was related to the changing role of middle-class women who were attempting to re-build the moral fabric of the society. While the changes were of instrumental significance in that they legitimated new career openings for such women, they were also symbolic in that they preserved their prestige in a rapidly changing society and institutionalised certain values and ways of life for women, children and the family. He characterises the 'child savers' as disinterested reformers because they regarded their cause as a matter of conscience and morality, and not one which would improve their economic or class interests.

These empirical studies suggest some important questions and explanatory concepts in relation to analysing child abuse, for we need to consider how far the concepts of moral enterprise, bureaucratic imperatives and symbolic action help to explain why the issue was recognised as a problem when it was.

Two recently published case studies[20] have demonstrated how, in the process of recognising a problem, the way it is defined and conceptualised has direct implications for what is seen as the best way of dealing with it. Gusfield and Wiener argue that the concepts of 'ownership' and 'responsibility' are central for specifying the structure of social problems. The concept of 'ownership of public problems' derives from the recognition that not everyone has equal power and authority to define the reality of the problem. 'Ownership' refers to a group's ability to create and influence the public definition of a problem. The owners of the problem are seen to have credibility and command public attention, trust and influence. They are asked for their opinion, often as experts, and are reported by others, who are keen for explanations and solutions of the problem. The owners of the problem are crucial for establishing the 'facts' of the problem.

However, establishing who owns the problem does not specify the content of these facts and the solutions implied or recommended. 'Causal responsibility' refers to the nature of the explanation that is offered, 'an assertion about the sequence that factually accounts for the existence of the problem'. It draws attention to the factors or events which give rise to the problem. Thus many argue that a major factor in causing child abuse is that the parents themselves were abused as children.

The second meaning of responsibility, 'political responsibility', is a matter of policy and tries to answer the question, What is to be done? It asserts that some person or office is responsible for controlling, preventing or eradicating the problem. Often it has been seen as primarily the responsibility of social workers to do something about child abuse, so that when things go wrong they are held to blame. As Gusfield points out, quite often ownership and political responsibility may not reside with the same people or occupation. In fact, quite often those who own the problem are trying to make sure that others take responsibility and behave 'properly'.

The way the problem is defined, then, has central implications for what we then do about it. The 'facts' of social problems are socially constructed. As Gusfield writes:

> At every stage in this process human choices of selection and interpretation operate. Events are given meaning, and assumptions and values guide the selection. Public 'facts' are not like pebbles on the beach, lying in the sun and waiting to be seen. They must be picked, polished, shaped and packaged. Finally ready for display, they bear the marks of their shapers.[21]

We are not therefore simply concerned with the process whereby child abuse was recognised as a social problem, but also tracing the way the facts regarding the problem have been shaped. Here the concepts of ownership, causal responsibility and political responsibility will help specify the way the problem has been constructed. The relationship between causal responsibility and political responsibility is central to understanding how child abuse is shaped and changed. The core of the politics and practice of child abuse lies in the choices of one or another theory or cause and one or another locus of political responsibility.

Current Theoretical Debates

The concepts of symbolic action, moral enterprise and bureaucratic imperatives may prove very helpful in our analysis of child abuse. But there are difficulties in the way these concepts have been used in other case studies.

It is doubtful whether moral enterprise and bureaucratic interests can ever be sufficient explanatory variables. For example, successful entrepreneurship is likely to be dependent upon, or at least related to, other factors – primarily the social context. Similarly one cannot assume that all enforcement agencies will all be wanting or be able to expand their influence in line with the notion of bureaucratic interests. Attempted bureaucratic expansion is only going to be successful if the agencies' external environment is conducive.[22]

More fundamentally, these case studies can be criticised for failing to focus on structural factors and the importance of power in their analysis of social problems. In focusing upon significant groups and 'caretaker institutions'[23] there can be a failure to look at the underlying economic structures in which social problems emerge: 'Paradoxically for a theory which prides itself on introducing social reaction into the explanation of deviant behaviour, it is extremely limited in this respect. For the emphasis on maladministration rather than structures ignores the structural causes of reaction.'[24]

Specifically, most of the studies lack a theory of power and are thus unable to specify the criteria by which problems are recognised and defined.

The studies invariably assume a pluralistic or radical pluralist conception of power in that they recognise that not all groups have the same power nor does everyone benefit from the workings of the system.[25] But there is a failure to analyse the nature, use and distribution of power in relation to the social problem. When the concept of power is more developed they often lean heavily on a Weberian model of society. For example, Gusfield uses a Weberian conception of status and class in his multidimensional approach to social stratification and argues that 'status struggle' is implicit in the notion of status politics and symbolic action. The analysis focuses on the social categories which are thought to be in conflict and the status and role of those who are seen as crucial in establishing or modifying a social problem. Rarely is there any attempt to relate these activities to wider economic, political and ideological processes. Certainly there are dangers with studies carried out at the middle-range or case study level of analysis. The focus is likely to be on overt, political issues over which there is an observable conflict of interests – a one-dimensional view of power. As Bachrach and Baratz observe,[26] this is a narrow view of power, for the institutional procedures, rituals and practices which constitute the political system may enable dominant individuals or groups to prevent potential issues surfacing as political issues at all, through the operation of what they call 'non-decisions'. However while this two-dimensional view draws attention to issues or conflicts which are suppressed or diverted, it still requires that such conflicts and issues are in some way present for an exercise of power to be identified. As Lukes argues, power may be exercised in a mobilisation of the bias inherent in 'the socially structured and culturally patterned behaviour of groups and practices of institutions'.[27] Throughout, therefore, it will be important to locate the reaction to child abuse within the shifts in the economy and ideological forces in society.

As Clarke argues, social problems are only explicable with an adequate theory of political economy:

(a) because only this shows why particular acts have to be defined as significantly deviant (social problems) at a point in time and (b) because only the particular organisation of society at that time accounts for the particular pressures and limits set by society on individual and collective actions, which give rise to acts that are reacted to as deviant. From the point of view of ruling interests, in other words, as well as from that of deviants, an adequate account of 'how the problem arose' requires a theory of how the society is organised and operated.[28]

Abusive Families and the State

A related issue is that while many studies have recognised the need to explain the character of the rules from which the deviant deviates and the nature of social order, the conception of the State, and hence the exercise of legitimate power, has remained simple and generalised. Vague concepts such as 'the ruling elite' and 'social control' have been used. For example, in the cruder versions, it has been suggested that if there was no social control there would be no problem. The policy and practice implication of this is that all you can do is 'nothing' and this is given conceptual support with the idea of 'radical non intervention'.[29] While such an approach might be justified in 'crimes without victims'[30] it becomes very tenuous when there is actual or potential harm as in child abuse.

The changing role of the state and its relations to the economy and the family will be a crucial consideration for understanding why certain forms of parental behaviour are defined as inappropriate and abusive. Thus while I focus on the activities of certain socio-economic groups, moral entrepreneurs and enforcement agencies it is necessary to be more discriminating than many sociologists of social problems have been. What is required is a more broadly based approach which focuses on the ways in which major institutional structures, particularly of the State, systematically adopt or reject particular policies. The way child abuse is defined and policies developed is a product not only of the demands made by moral entrepreneurs who promote the issue, but also the response of different sections of the State apparatus.

If we recognise that the State may have a role to play in child abuse it is important that we critically analyse the different forms that intervention can take, and the different relationships that can be established between the family and the State.

Newberger and Bourne[31] have provided a framework which goes some way to clarifying such issues. They suggest there are two central issues in constructing policies and practices towards 'families in crisis': family autonomy versus coercive intervention; and compassion versus control. In some respects the two axis are not mutually exclusive. However, each can be taken as the ends of a continuum. They then put the two together to construct a fourfold table to illustrate the possible State reactions to and interventions in families (see Table 1.1). They suggest 'compassion' signifies responses of support, such as the provision of voluntary counselling and child care services, and 'control' signifies such responses as 'blaming the victim' for their reaction to social realities and the criminal prosecution of abusing parents. The fourth reaction can be characterised as a child 'rescue' approach. Such a schema will prove useful in trying to specify shifts in state policy and practice.

Table 1.1   *Dilemmas of social policy and professional response with chidren and families*

Response	Family Autonomy	*versus*	Coercive Intervention
Compassion (*'support'*)	**A** 1. Voluntary child development services	**B** 1.	Case reporting of family crisis and mandated family intervention
	2. Guaranteed family supports: e.g. income, housing, health services	2.	Court-ordered delivery of services
		versus	
Control (*'punishment'*)	**C** 1. *Laissez-faire:* No assured services or supports	**D** 1.	Court action to separate child from family
	2. Retributive response to family crisis	2.	Criminal prosecution of parents

SOURCE: E. H. Newberger and R. Bourne, 'The Medicalisation and Legalisation of Child Abuse' in J. M. Eekelaar and S. N. Katz (eds), *Family Violence: An International and Interdisciplinary Study* (Butterworths, 1977).

Normative Accounts of Child Abuse

I have argued that it is important to understand how the facts and assumptions concerning the problem have been constructed and the way these have structured policy and practice. In the process much of the discussion, particularly in Part Two, will be in terms of ideas and explanations. In emphasising the role of ideology I am aware that I may fail to develop the relationship between the ideological and the economic and structural. While I will attempt to specify the nature of this relationship, I am particularly keen to open up a debate about the politics and practice of child abuse in terms of the alternative conceptualisations and explanations that are available and the best way of doing something about it.

In the area of social problems explanatory theory is especially important, for if we can provide an account of how an issue identified as demanding action is caused, it is in principle possible to do something about it. However, a welter of different theories are available, and we cannot assume that those that are more readily accepted as legitimate are necessarily any more objective and scientific than those that are not acted upon. Normative judgments play a central role in differentiating alternative accounts of social problems. Often it seems that the assumptions that underpin alternative accounts are like different ways of looking at reality.

Prior to analysing the particular ways in which child abuse has been constructed it is important to outline the range of competing ideologies that are available about the nature of the problem and the most appropriate means of doing something about it. Thus 'ideology' here refers to the general assertions that are held about human behaviour, its causes and how to change it. It is being used to relate to a shared or collective set of ideas and is not being used to imply their truth or falsity. While the concept is here an ideal type referring to relatively abstract ideas and attitudes it will become apparent that certain ideologies have been crucial in policy and practice.

I will locate the dominant ideologies of abuse by analysing the research literature, official policy documents and the accepted wisdom of the 'experts'. However because ideologies do not provide methods of working which are meaningful in operational terms, working arrangements have to be derived in terms of operational philosophies, particularly for the control agencies and professionals involved. According to Smith:

> Like ideologies operational philosophies are coherent sets of ideas. They are consistent with the respective ideologies which they interpret at the situational level. An operational philosophy can therefore always be justified by referring to the ideological position which is itself seen as requiring no further justification.[32]

Operational philosophies are evident, for example, in the recommendations and guidelines for policy and practice circulated by central and local government. All areas now have arrangements and systems functioning which are usually based on DHSS circulars.[33]

Three questions are important in differentiating normative

accounts of social problems: (1) How serious is the problem seen? (2) Are the actions seen as deliberate and the actors therefore responsible for their actions? and (3) Is the problem defined as collective or individual? Clearly the three are interrelated.

The relative seriousness of a problem changes both historically and culturally. Here we are primarily concerned with shifting definitions of the value of children, appropriate parental behaviour, and of the changing social response. This will be a central focus of Chapter 2.

Secondly, and more crucially in classifying social problem ideologies, is how far there is an imputation of responsibility to the perpetrators. For, crudely, problems defined as criminal are those for which the people are held responsible because they freely chose their actions, whereas problems defined as sick refer to those for which people are not held responsible, as their behaviour or situation arose from circumstances beyond their control.[34] The classical criminal view assumes that individuals are in essence free, rational and self-seeking and freely enter into a contract with the State to preserve harmony. Thus while the State should use punishment to deter individuals from violating others' interests, such punishments should be proportional to the interests violated and should not unnecessarily interfere with the individuals' rights. The law should be minimal and limited by the notion of due process. Because individuals are responsible for their actions all are equal before the law and mitigating circumstances are not admissible.

The medical or treatment view is based on very different assumptions. Its assumptions are deterministic, so that the central concern is not whether individuals are responsible for their actions but what caused those actions in the first place. Consequently attempts are made to modify them through some treatment programme to ensure the problem does not arise in the future. The problem behaviour is seen as a symptom that draws attention to a more intractable disorder, disease or syndrome. When the problem is primarily behavioural or social, the explanation is to be found in the personality or family background of the perpetrator. Numerous writers have commented on how in modern industrial societies there has been an identifiable drift to seeing social problems in terms of this medical model and have commented on the growth of the rehabilatitive ideal.[35]

A variant of the medical model can be termed the social welfare model where, while it is assumed behaviour is determined and the emphasis should be on treatment, the explanation offered and the intervention preferred is more in terms of relationships, the family and social malfunctioning. Problems are seen as the outcome of social disadvantage acting upon people without the emotional, family or community strengths to overcome them. Again, since the object of intervention must be to ensure that needs are met, there is no conflict of interest perceived between the State and the individual. Therefore State intervention may be of an indeterminate length becaused it is difficult to predict precisely when the rehabilitation or treatment will have been achieved.

The third dimension I highlighted as important in trying to conceptualise the range of social problems ideologies was whether the problem defined was collective or individual. Clearly if an individualised conception can be accepted, any remedies implied will focus on the individual, avoiding more wide-ranging changes.Similarly, the more powerless the group seen as a problem and the less able they are to contest and articulate their definition of the problem, the more likely it is that the problem will be seen as an individual one. This is certainly likely to be the case with child abuse.

If however the problem is conceptualised in collective or social structural terms a radical account can be constructed. Unlike the individualised medical and social welfare approaches, those experiencing problems are not seen in essence as being very different from anyone else. The problem arises primarily from two sources. First, the selection process whereby some are identified as different by social workers, psychiatrists, the police and so on, is seen as biased and skewed against the marginalised and deprived. Secondly, the economic and social inequality within society puts sections of the population at greater risk of insecurity and poverty. It is not that the individuals cause and are responsible for this – the responsibility lies with society more generally, and with those who control the social, political and economic power more particularly. The recommendations implied are in terms of social change and fundamental social reorganisation.

Taking these points on board we can now set out a framework for the range of ideologies that are likely to be available for the analysis of child abuse. The critical dimensions being the sickness/criminal, individual/collective.[36] (See Table 1.2.)

Table 1.2 *Alternative child abuse ideologies*

	Penal	Medical	Social Welfare	
			Humanistic	
Framework	Legal	Scientific	(a) traditional	(b) radical
Pre-supposition	individual has free-will	behaviour is determined	child abuse	child abuse
Definition	cruelty	battered baby syndrome		
Attitude to problem	punitive; deviance is conscious defiance of rules; moralistic	results from forces beyond control of individual	compassionate; individual/ family cannot cope with situation	relative but results from social processes
Social rationale	justice; due process; individual rights	cure; treatment of needs of the child	prevention; rehabilitation by adjustment	social liberation by re-organisation
Focus of attention	act of abuse; depravation	disease process, pathology syndromes	the person; family, social situation; 'cycle of deprivation'	social processes, structural inequality
Tools	Legal code, courts	medical expertise and technology	counselling, therapeutic relationships, social experts	social change
Conception of parent	responsible	irresponsible or not responsible	psychologically, emotionally and socially inadequate	socially victimised
Stated purpose of intervention	punishment of guilt	treatment of dysfunction	personal, family rehabilitation, physical and emotional safety of child	equality and redistribution
Some practising groups	police, judiciary	doctors, some psychiatrists	social workers; some doctors e.g. paediatricians	some social workers and some sociologists

SOURCE: J. Carter, 'Problems of Professional Belief' in *The Maltreated Child* (Priory Press, 1974).

Conclusions

It is a central argument of this book that the emergence of
child abuse has helped fuel a period of uncertainty in both
child care policy and welfare practice. It has become evident
that areas of practice and decision-making that in the 1960s
and early 1970s were assumed to be the domain of professional
social workers have increasingly been subjected to scrutiny,
ideological conflict and heated debate. Not only has the media
taken a particular interest in social work with children and
families but pressure groups,[37] political representatives[38] and
Parliament have recognised that it is not a neutral, technical
activity but is riven with different values about the appropriate
role of the family, the nature of State intervention and the
rights of children and parents. Increasingly welfare practitioners, social workers in particular, have been caught in this
ideological crossfire. Child care is now a political issue. Such
concerns were made explicit in the terms of reference of the
Parliamentary Social Services Committee on Children in Care
set up in July 1982:

> The Committee will be inquiring into most aspects of policy and practice
> connected with children in the care of local authorities. They are
> particularly interested in the implementation of the relevant provisions of
> the Children Act 1975, the social and financial implications of the shift
> from residential to community care (fostering), the problems facing those
> caring for children and the way in which they are dealt with, and the role
> of the voluntary sector. They do not intend to examine in detail the
> aspects of the subject connected with juvenile delinquency, but do not at
> present exclude consideration of any aspects of the subject.[39]

It is significant that the main issue for political debate concerning social work with children and families is no longer delinquency. In the post-war period it was concern about delinquency that influenced thinking about child and family work,
but from the early 1970s this has shifted significantly and has
been fuelled by anxieties about the problem of child abuse.

In order to understand some of these wider debates it is
important to analyse the nature of the emergence, impact and
implications of child abuse. In this respect political issues are
central to developing our critical understanding. In this

chapter I have outlined a conceptual framework that informs this book, based on the sociology of social problems and social problem ideologies.

However while hoping this book can make a contribution to practice I am only too aware of the pitfalls and potential criticisms. The debate about the relationship of theory to practice is a difficult but central one to social work. Many of the grand theories seem to bear little resemblance to everyday practice[40] and rarely is it possible to take them on board without becoming disillusioned, frustrated or exhausted. There is a danger when providing a critical analysis that it does not take seriously the tensions, problems and experiences of those in practice. As Stan Cohen has written

> the most familiar reaction we encounter is encapsulated in the phrase (often quite explicitly used), 'It's all right for you to talk'. The implication is that, however interesting, amusing, correct and even morally uplifting our message might be, it is ultimately a self-indulgent intellectual exercise, a luxury which cannot be afforded to anyone tied down by the day-to-day demands of a social-work job.[41]

My hope is thus not simply to articulate the political issues involved but also to provide indicators and examples which can inform practice. In trying to indicate that social work practice is far from being insulated from political issues it is also crucial to make some suggestions about how practitioners can negotiate the constraints, appreciate the potential pitfalls and develop a creative and progressive practice with children and families. Such issues are given further force with the attempts by Thatcherism to restructure the welfare state and the role and responsibilities of families.

2

Children as Victims: Cruelty and Neglect in History

Children have been ill-treated by adults throughout history, but it is only occasionally that concern about the issue has gathered any momentum.[1] In order to assess the significance of recent developments it is important to locate the social reactions to children's problems in a wider historical context. What will become evident is that the legislative and institutional framework of policies for children has rarely given any substantive attention to children as victims. From the beginning of the nineteenth century to the 1970s concern for children has focused primarily on the protection of society from children and the control of delinquent youth. The primary concern with children has been in terms of the prevention of crime and anti-social behaviour. It is only at certain times in history, particularly towards the end of the nineteenth century and immediately after the Second World War, that there has been any explicit concern with protecting children from cruel, neglectful or abusing parents. A major focus in this chapter therefore will be to consider these two periods to see whether there might be common threads with developments in child care in the 1970s and to analyse the forms of the social reactions.

In the process we need to consider the explanations of parental behaviour that were presented to see if there is any continuity in the popular and professional accounts and images that have been evident through history. Such an approach will also reveal how the development of state welfare and social work has been centrally concerned with the family and has intervened in it in significant ways.[2]

Child Abuse in History

Throughout history children have been subjected to the kind of treatment we now call abuse and neglect. However, there is a difficulty in gathering and interpreting available historical evidence, 'indeed the intermittent nature of public concern is the most striking historical feature of the problem, and is reflected in the paucity of historical research into this aspect of family relationships'.[3] Thus, much of the literature which claims to provide a detached commentary must be treated cautiously. Several authors have provided examples of child abuse in history[4] but invariably use their 'evidence' to demonstrate the 'progress' that has been made, particularly during the twentieth century, in trying to help children. Rarely is any analysis of the historical changes provided – they are seen as essentially natural, self-evident and benevolent.

Radbill suggests that there are accounts of what might now be called child abuse in the lives of numerous famous personalities: 'Pepys beat his son until he (Pepys) was out of breath; John Wesley, Frederick the Great, Lady Jane Grey, and many others in adult life complained bitterly of their treatment in childhood.'[5]

It seems that Henry VI appealed to his Council for protection from his tutor, while Charles I substituted Mungo Murray when he was to be punished. These same authors have drawn attention to the considerable evidence of child abuse and infanticide in English literature. The relationship between illegitimacy and infanticide was the theme of the ballad 'The Cruel Mother'[6] while Shakespeare as shown by Lady Macbeth was also aware of the infanticide 'impulse'. In his novel *Sybil* Disraeli describes the early life of a child who grew up unknown and was given the name 'Devildust'. He wrote 'infanticide is practised as extensively and legally in England as it is on the banks of the Ganges'.

Margaret May[7] has suggested that the best known nineteenth-century accounts of family violence are those written by the feminists, Mary Wollstonecraft and Caroline Norton.[8] The former was terrorised by her tyrannical father. Pinchbeck and Hewitt[9] have written that:

> until the end of the eighteenth century and to a less extent even in the nineteenth century, it was common practice to expose unwanted children ... in the streets and lanes of cities or in the country. Frequently these children died before being discovered, sometimes they were discovered by beggars who would mutilate them to excite pity and hire them out to other beggars for four pence a night.

The late eighteenth and early nineteenth centuries have been viewed as at best a period of indifference and even active and cruel exploitation of children. However it is important not to use the experience, norms and perceptions of the last quarter of the twentieth century when attempting to understand the practices of other periods in history. It is not simply that concerns and norms have changed but that the diagnosis or labels attached are quite different. This is well illustrated by a case written up by Dr Samuel West in the British Medical Journal in 1888.[10] He recorded that a five-year-old child was brought by its mother with the statement that its left arm had 'dropped'. A swelling occupied the middle third of the shaft of the humerus, while similar swellings were found on the right humerus and on the left femur along with some slight bruises on the ribs. This was the fifth child in the family and he also noted that the first, third and fourth children of the family suffered from similar symptoms. Dr West's diagnosis in the 1880s was rickets – it seems very unlikely he would make a similar diagnosis in Britain in the 1980s. Many child abuse experts have commented that cases where the problem was clearly child abuse or non-accidental injury have in the past been wrongly diagnosed as rickets, brittle bones or over enthusiastic discipline.

The Emergence of 'Childhood'

There have been significant changes historically in the role and attitude towards children and the way the social category has been conceptualised. Heywood[11] has argued that in pre-Reformation England the orphaned or illegitimate child had a place in a feudal and employed community, though there were plenty of opportunities to exploit the younger members. The safeguard against this lay in the communal nature of the society and its ethical canons expressed in the teaching against usury, on the duty of alms giving and in the efficacy of the corporal works of mercy. She feels that because life was centred round the community there was an opportunity to protect unwanted, deprived and neglected children.

In pre-industrial Britain work and home were not sharply separated. While conflicting reconstructions of family life in that period have been made[12] it seems that usually husband, wife and children worked together, so that work was not separate from the other life activities, kinship shaded into community, and there was not a sharp distinction between private and public life. 'Individual family members were part of a collectivity larger than the family.'[13] There was a qualitatively different set of relationships between the family, the community and the state and a very different notion of the nature, value and conception of the little adults.

However it is important not to imagine pre-industrial society as a golden age for children. In many ways it was very harsh and restrictive. The rigidity and violence evident in parent–child relationships reflected those between adults and children in general. Donzelot[14] has pointed to the contractual form of relationship between the state and the male head of the family in feudal society, so that the family functioned in a mutually beneficial relationship with the state. He points out that in France, in return for the provision of men for military service and keeping members of the family in line, the head of the family was granted wide discretionary power over family members.

Similarly, a difference between the worlds of children and adults was not perceived. While the boundary between infancy and later life has remained fairly constant, because of the infant's inability to communicate and carry out basic tasks of living, there have been important changes in the attitudes and conceptions of childhood.

Philippe Ariès[15] has demonstrated how in the middle ages the idea of childhood did not exist, because once physical autonomy had been attained at the ages of five to seven, children went straight into the community where they shared in the work and play of adults. Analysing France he shows how the notion of childhood emerged amongst the bourgeoisie in the seventeenth and eighteenth centuries. This went through a number of stages. Initially children were seen as 'sweet' and hence 'coddled'. The second concept however sprang from a few churchmen and gentlemen of the robe during the six-teenth-century reformation and was taken up by the greater number of moralists in the seventeenth century, who were eager to ensure disciplined rational manners. They did not regard children as charming toys but as fragile creatures of God who needed to be both 'safeguarded' and 'reformed'.

These two elements were combined in the eighteenth century together with an increased concern for hygiene and physical health. This interest in health had a moral purpose as it was felt that a delicate body encouraged luxury, sloth and most of the other vices. These developments, according to Ariès, found their most explicit expression in the introduction of schooling. The child was subjected for the duration of schooling to an increasingly strict and effective discipline which separated him from the 'liberty' of adulthood.

The locus of these changes was to be found among the bourgeoisie, and during the last 150 years there has been an extension of this family form with its notion of childhood to the working class. However, while the idea of the family as primarily an affective child-rearing and socialising agency with its emphasis on the woman as the child-raiser and socialiser has become widely accepted, the process has been uneven.[16] Many of the more traditional forms of chastisement, child discipline and 'parental indifference'[17] to children and infants were still firmly implanted among all segments of the popular classes in the nineteenth century – and may still be evident today.

The main thrust of Ariès' explanation for these develop-ments rests on the changing ideas that were developing during and after the period of the Reformation based on Calvinist and Enlightenment theory. However Pat Thane[18] criticises Ariès for the lack of a systematic examination of the significance of the wider economy and social structure for conceptions of childhood. She suggests that the emergence of a capitalist economy in this period, based upon commerce and capital intensive agriculture, can be seen as underpinning these changes. Two direct effects of this economic transformation were that those with any wealth or property tried to maximise their control of it and, secondly, that work became more demanding and time consuming, particularly for those in commerce or the associated professions. The emerging bourgeoisie tried to tighten its control over the next and future generations so that acquired wealth and property were not frittered away later by undisciplined or inappropriate marriages.

In part the low status of children was conditioned by demographic factors,[19] large families and high infant mortality precluded parents from providing individual attention and emotional investment to their offspring. However the 'invention' of childhood long pre-dates the significant decline in child mortality[20] and there seems a clear correspondence between the birth of capitalism, of modern classes and of modern age groups. Changes in the economic base seem crucial.

Shorter[21] suggests that 'modernisation' meant the dissolution of the structured, changeless, compact traditional order. Ties to the community were weakened and ties binding members of the family together were reinforced. In the process the privacy of the family as a social and psychological form increased and the awareness of children as a separate category developed. The 'egoism' that was established in the market became associated with the whole domain of cultural rules that regulated family behaviour and relationships. Because the bourgeoisie profited most from these economic changes they were the first to modify their conceptions and practices towards children.

The gradual destruction of the collaborative relationships between the family and the sovereign opened up for debate the relationships between the state and the family. While the family became a central political issue it was important for the emerging liberal state that it be detached from direct political control.[22] With the development with capitalism of a more complex division of labour, and the erosion of the traditional forms of social regulation in terms of mechanistic social solidarity, the bourgeois liberal state had to tackle the problem of attempting to preserve and improve the quality of the

population, particularly children, and ensuring that they did
not pose a significant social threat. The central dilemma was
that if the State must assume responsibility for children, how
could it discharge those responsibilities while maintaining
childrearing as essentially a private responsibility?[23] If the
State was to maintain notions of individual freedom, contract
and responsibility, it could not become all-encompassing and
hence a threat to those same recently established freedoms. The
dominant solution was to allow the State to intervene into
childrearing only when families were considered to have failed.
Ostensibly this has remained the solution, though its interpretation has shifted through time, and there have been modifications in the relative boundaries and relationships between the
family, the State and the community. We see the beginnings of
this role for the liberal State in the sixteenth and seventeenth
centuries though the issue only becomes of prime significance
in the nineteenth century.

In effect the Poor Law Act of 1601 set the pattern for the
system of poor relief for the next 350 years. Those responsible
for the care of deprived children, the churchwardens and
parish overseers, took whatever measures were appropriate for
setting them to work or apprenticing them. However[24] from
the late seventeenth century onwards, the local schemes providing for such children which received the most public
support were those where children were expected to help
themselves. While such policies could be seen as a continuation
of the Elizabethan poor law principles, the emphasis on work,
not the welfare of the child, and their concern for economic
profitability rather than educational content, increasingly reflected a society which emphasised materialism, individual self-
help and the promotion of wealth, rather than the support of
national and wider community support. The philosophy based
on economic interest and individualism became pervasive.

The more intractable problems of child neglect, abandon-
ment and desertion were usually the responsibility of the Poor
Law which became increasingly punitive in its approach and
attitude to failure. Other efforts to provide alternative care for
children of an acceptable social background which were developed, usually in terms of schooling, were the response of the
bourgeoisie to the harsh methods of the Poor Law.

Child Maltreatment in the Nineteenth Century

By the early nineteenth century interest and concern for children was expressing itself in a variety of ways. Margaret May[25] has indicated that, among the upper strata at least, children's needs were becoming widely recognised, and that one expression of this could be found in the growth of literature on childrearing.

The first legislative recognition of children as having needs and rights which may be different from those of adults came with the Health and Morals of Apprentices Act of 1802 which restricted pauper cotton apprentices to 12 hours' work per day. The Factory Act of 1833 limited the working hours of children and young persons in textile mills and appointed factory inspectors with a right of entry. The 1840s included various pieces of legislation and Parliamentary reports designed to restrict and improve the conditions for children in employment.

Even so, early industrial England inherited an autocratic patriarchal social structure which was legitimated in law and which subordinated children to the power of parents, particularly fathers.

Surveying the situation of children in the late eighteenth and early nineteenth century May[26] has commented that there was a universal belief in the sanctity of parental rights including the use of moderate chastisement so that physical punishment was a part of the normal experience of most children.

Similarly James Walvin[27] has argued that 'death of the young as well as the old, was an inescapable social reality in nineteenth-century England'. In 1839–40 the death rate for children under one was 153 per 1000 live births; in 1896 it was 156 and by 1899, the worst ever recorded, it was 163. Walvin comments that:

> the new-born child's life was endangered by complex natural and social problems which nineteenth-century man seemed unable to counter. But the modern reader is struck by the fact that many of these dangers were eminently avoidable. Neglect, ill-treatment, dirt and ignorance – often interrelated – swept away large numbers of babies.[28]

Increasingly during the nineteenth century concerns were expressed about the general level of violence.[29] However the focus of attention as far as children were concerned was not the protection of the child from violence, but the protection of society from the violent or potentially violent child. With the move towards capitalist social formations, the move to the factory and the growth of urban areas, the old methods of social control were felt to be crumbling. The fear of the mob and anxiety about the growth in delinquent children and youth posed an important threat to the emerging social order of the nineteenth century:

> The presence of an unknown number of casual poor, indistinguishable to many contemporaries from criminals, apparently divorced from all forms of established religion, or ties with their social superiors, inhabiting unknown cities within the capital, constituted a disquieting alien presence in the midst of mid-Victorian plenty.[30]

The population of England and Wales stood at under 10 million in 1801, rose to 14 million in 1837 and was over 32 million in 1901. Not only had the overall population increased dramatically but the population under 14 never fell below 30 per cent and for much of the period was nearer 40 per cent. Similarly an increasing proportion lived in towns and cities – over half in 1851 and three-quarters by 1901.[31]

Many children were involved in employment, while others were dependent on begging for their existence and contributed to the pool of casual poor. The Tudor Poor Law apprenticeship system was increasingly found wanting. We find that as the nineteenth century progressed the central political concern became the control of the mob and the maintenance of order.[32] So that while there was an increasing concern for humanitarian reform and 'child-saving' the primary impetus was not to save children from abusive or cruel parents but to protect society from future delinquents.[33] Such movements received much of their support from middle-class women whose[34] social role was changing and who were able to satisfy both their symbolic and instrumental interests in such activity. Much of the ideological thrust for such responses was provided by romantic notions of the traditional society, regarding the importance of the small town, community, religion and the implicit rejection of the growing urban metropolis.

Liz Wilson[35] has argued that as the bourgeoisie expanded and became more prosperous, a part of the raised standard of living was leisure, and in particular the leisure of the wife or mother. Charitable work provided not only an opportunity to display the success of her husand but also ideologically furthered the notion of the idealised mother and wife for working class women to follow. Workers in the field thus saw their duty not only as an opportunity to rescue children, but also to articulate their new found role and bring souls to the kingdom of heaven.[36] By 1878 there were fifty philanthropic societies for children in London alone, and many important charities started at about this time, including Dr Barnado's and the National Children's Homes. The first signs of modern social work appeared during the 1850s with the introduction of paid welfare work activities.

The growth of concern about child cruelty resulted in part from the connection increasingly being made between the significance of early parental treatment and later delinquency. 'The link between parental violence and the threat of delinquency or semi-delinquency proved a potent factor in the growth of public concern with child abuse.'[37] By mid-century concern was being expressed at the violence suffered by women and children in families and the limited protection that they were offered. The concerns were expressed particularly by law encorcement agencies who were anxious about the general level of violent crime, and feminists campaigning for the emancipation of women. Judicial concern was expressed in Parliament which for the first time published a limited return of assaults on women and children by males in London. Of 6111 cases reported by ten courts between 1850 and 1854, 1059 husbands, 17 fathers and 110 other relatives, were recorded as summarily charged or convicted.[38]

This growing concern for family violence gained expression with the foundation in 1857 of the Society for the Protection of Women and Children from Aggravated Assaults. While most of the society's work was concerned with women, and it was not a well-known London charity, it pressed for legal changes and tried to publicise the problem of violence to children. Not only did it publish one of the earliest studies of cruelty to children, *Compassionate Justice*, but it was able to provide important propaganda when the issue reached a new level of recognition later in the century.[39]

Philanthropy and the Disreputable Poor

In the nineteenth century the role of the state in relation to children and families was narrow and prescribed. The system of relief enforced by the 1834 Poor Law Reform Act attempted to re-establish the traditional poor law principles of the family taking responsibility for its members, backed up where necessary by parish-based finance and discrimination between the deserving and undeserving. A binding responsibility was placed on adults for their children, for there was a fear that shared support with the State undermined individual motivation. Once individual self-reliance and obligations to kin had failed, the State insisted that familial and citizen status be withdrawn and be replaced by the overwhelming status of pauper. Thus the workhouse split up families by putting them into the institution. The central relation of the State and the family was that the State enforced family obligations but did little to assist them if families were experiencing difficulties. Poor Law Officers had no duty to go out into the slums and rescue children who might be exposed to neglect, cruelty or degradation. They usually only became involved once the family had broken down. There was considerable doubt about taking children into State Guardianship who might be ill-treated by their parents as: 'it would free the self-indulgent at the cost of the self-controlled and, worse still for the children, would put a premium on their ill-treatment'.[40]

In effect the State and the local poor law unions were the back-stop of the system of private charity.[41] The Malthusian theories, which argued that the population increase would outrun the resources available, legitimated the splitting up of families and the segregation of the sexes. Increasingly voluntary charity supported the 'deserving' poor and the poor law became associated with the 'undeserving' and feckless. Thus the impetus for the rescue of children during the century developed with the growth of voluntary philanthropic groups, particularly those which expressed evangelistic crusading influences.

Changes in the British economy and wider social structure contributed towards a shift in the organisation of charity and its relationship with the State. In the 1860s and 1870s there was neither knowledge of nor interest in poverty, for it was assumed after 25 years of economic growth and an apparently substantial rise in working-class living standards, that chronic poverty and wide-spread deprivation had disappeared – certainly for the majority. As a consequence any deprivation that did exist resulted from moral failure. This was thought to be made worse by the widespread availability of indiscriminate charity whereby 'clever paupers' could take advantage of the lack of coordination. Vigorous attempts were made to systematise charitable relief in an effort to moralise the casual poor. The Charity Organisation Society, established in 1869, is the most obvious expression of this new philanthropy – different in kind to charity:[42]

> Philanthropy in this case is not to be understood as a naively apolitical term signifying a private intervention in the sphere of so-called social problems, but must be considered as a deliberately de-politicising strategy for establishing public services and facilities at a sensitive point midway between private initiative and the state. When one examines the centres around which philanthropic activity was to organise itself in the nineteenth century, one finds that they were all characterised by the search for a calculated distance between the functions of the liberal state and the spread of techniques of welfare and admnistration of the population.[43]

The COS argued that the social mobility and separation of classes with the growth of industry and large urban areas destroyed the central reciprocal relationship so necessary to encourage discipline and morality amongst the lower orders. It was seen as essential to make contact with individuals and families on the basis of systematic visiting and provide charity only after a precise assessment of need. In this way it was hoped the life-styles of the recipient would be improved. But such attempts at moral socialisation via the use of material assistance could not intervene in families with young children if they never presented themselves for assistance.

In the 1880s however, the economic situation began to

change significantly. The depression of 1884–7 was prolonged and deep-seated, particularly in London. The optimism evident in the 1860s and 1870s dissipated. Accordingly in the 1880s attention was diverted from pauperism to chronic poverty.[44] While poverty was still associated with drink, early marriage, improvidence, irreligion and idleness, they were now seen as symptoms rather than causes. The root cause of poverty was associated with the pressures of city existence. As a consequence there is a major re-orientation of middle-class attitudes towards the casual poor in the mid-1880s. This included a movement away from the strict *laissez-faire* approach which helped support the views associated with the COS. Faced with the threat of socialism and social upheaval it was increasingly argued that a clearer distinction needed to be drawn between the 'true' respectable working class and the disreputable poor. In a period when the latter appeared increasingly as a threat it was crucial to incorporate the former more actively within the political system, and respond to their 'legitimate' grievances.[45]

However, complementary to such attempts to incorporate the respectable working class in this new welfare philosophy was the support of a more coercive and interventionist policy towards the disreputable 'residuum'. In the context of economic slump the threat of the residuum was far too great to be left to the market and the poor law, which provided no powers of compulsory detention: it was based on 'freedom of choice'. It was argued that problems of unfitness on behalf of the residuum could no longer be left to private philanthropy alone. If the problems concerned with degeneration resulted from the deleterious influences of the urban environment rather than the moral inadequacies of the individual the State would have to take a far more active role. In this respect there were increased proposals for segregating the casual poor, establishing detention centres for 'loafers' and shipping the residuum overseas. Such suggestions included the separation of pauper children from 'degenerate' parents, and gained explicit expression with the 1889 Poor Law (Children) Act which empowered the Poor Law Guardians to assume parental rights over any child in their care if they were satisfied that the parents were irresponsible. It is in this changing economic and political climate that child cruelty is recognised seriously for the first time.

The NSPCC and the Discovery of Child Cruelty

In the second half of the nineteenth century powerful sections in society were expressing concern for innocent children, and the changes introduced were consistent with the changing role for the State that was emerging. There was an increasing concern for the quality and quantity of social reproduction and the nature of the working-class family. A particular concern was baby-farming, where mothers, often unmarried, entrusted their children to women to look after for a fee. It was alleged that some of the children died and were frequently not well cared for. The cruelties of two women in particular, Margaret Waters and Sarah Ellis, took on scandal proportions and highlighted the abuses suffered by such children. There followed, in 1871, a Parliamentary Committee on the Protection of Infant Life from which came the first Infant Life Protection Act (1872) as a measure of 'social and sanitary reform'.[46] In the same year the Bastardy Laws Amendment Act was passed, strengthening a mother's claim for maintenance from the putative father, while in 1874 an Act was passed making the registration of births and deaths compulsory. Prior to this in 1868 boards of guardians had been given the power to prosecute parents who wilfully neglected their children so that their health was endangered, but it was limited to children with whom the poor law became directly involved, and its prime aim was to prevent pauperism arising from neglect.

However the last two decades of the century can be characterised as a period when the problem of child cruelty gained explicit expression, receiving much of its initial impetus from the animal welfare movement. As in the 1960s, events in Britain were influenced by similar developments in America. It was the establishment of the National Society for the Prevention of Cruelty to Children which provided the focus for recognising the problems and introducing legislation. In effect 'there was no effective method of discovering and repressing cruelty until the formation of the voluntary societies for this purpose'.[47]

The movement took shape following a visit by a Liverpool merchant banker, Thomas Agnew, to America in 1881, where he saw and heard about a number of new societies including the New York SPCC.[48] On his return in 1882 he discussed these developments with his MP, Samuel Smith, who, a few weeks later, at a meeting organised by the Society for the Prevention of Cruelty to Animals, extended an appeal for a dog's home into an appeal for the protection of children. On 19 April 1883 the Liverpool SPCC was founded and dealt with 211 cases involving 378 childen in the remainder of the year. There was considerable publicity for the issue at this time and the case of Helen Barrencon received wide coverage in the press, particularly *The Times*.

The London SPCC was founded on 8 July 1884 at a meeting at the Mansion House attended by many respected societal members.[49] The honorary secretary was Mr Ben Waugh, a Congregational minister who had previously campaigned to humanise the treatment of juvenile offenders. In 1889 the various societies, excepting Liverpool, amalgamated to form the NSPCC and Queen Victoria became the patron. Guided by Waugh the society was particularly concerned with publicising the problem and the inadequacies of existing controls, canvassing for new measures and enforcing them, and urging a wider education of the public.

The Society's first achievement was in 1885 when an amendment in the law enabled children's evidence to be received without oath where the truth of what was said was otherwise proved. However the society's campaigning made a major contribution to the passage of the Prevention of Cruelty to and Protection of Children Act in 1889.[50] Pinchbeck and Hewitt[51] have argued that the success of the 1889 Bill was a tribute to the careful preparation and patient propaganda of Waugh and the NSPCC. That it was an evangelical crusade was made explicit in the NSPCC annual report for 1895–96:

> It was nothing less than a national education which was undertaken . . . it was a crusade primarily to the intellect of the nation, preaching the existence and the magnitude of the work to be done for needlessly suffering children.[52]

The Act created an offence if anyone over 16 who had custody, control or charge of a boy under 14 or a girl under 16 wilfully ill-treated, neglected or abandoned the child in a manner likely to cause unnecessary suffering or injury to health. This was made punishable by 3 months to 2 years imprisonment and fines of £25 to £100, with increased penalties where it appeared financial benefit from child-life insurance was involved. On conviction the court could also commit the child to the charge of a relative or anyone else willing to have the care of the child. However, the parent had to have been shown to have acted wilfully and to have undergone criminal conviction. It was an essentially criminal rather than a social welfare approach.

Within five years 5792 people had been prosecuted and 5400 convicted. In the same period 47 000 complaints were investigated by the NSPCC. Mainly as a result of the work of Waugh[53] the Act was tightened up with legislation passed in 1894: committal orders were made operative to the age of 16; the age limit for boys was extended to 16; cruelty was widened to include assault; and the terms 'suffering' and 'injury' were more clearly defined. The deterrent nature of the legislation was also underlined by extending the length of the maximum imprisonment.

At the same time the 1889 Poor Law (Children) Act gave the boards of guardians in England and Wales authority to assume parental rights over a child in care until the age of 18. Such rights could be assumed only in respect of deserted children at first; but by legislation in 1899 their application was widened to include orphans and children of parents who were disabled or in prison, or unfit to have the care of them. A consolidating Act of 1904 not only made available a wider range of institutional arrangements, but also transferred the responsibility for prosecuting from the Poor Law Guardians to the Local Authority. Thus Local Authorities were given coercive powers of child removal for the first time. Rather than the Poor Law or the NSPCC, from the early twentieth century it is the local state which becomes the focal agency.

Following the 1889 Act the justification for state intervention was that the parent's conduct offended against the moral conception of society held by the Act's supporters.[54] While the aim of legislation was to protect children, the method adopted was the moral reform of the parents. The

> Power to assume parental rights by the state was an expression of the
> public interest in the welfare of children and was intended to lay down a
> definite standard of parental care; failure to reach this standard by
> individual parents gave to the state authority to intervene and assume
> responsibility till the child became eighteen and to require the parents to
> contribute to the cost of the child.[55]

The NSPCC attempted to develop a system of warnings, with
parents reinforced by supervision, and in the process hoped
directly and indirectly to stimulate a sense of responsibility. In
1901 the Society made a list of the types of persons most guilty
of active cruelty to their children and these included:[56] 'the
drunkard'; 'the devil-may-care and idle'; 'the married and
estranged'; 'the married and unfaithful'; 'the unmarried'; 'the
tramp'; 'the better and gambler'; 'the speculator in child-life
insurance'; 'the avaricious and greedy'. May has suggested that:

> Many observers propagated an image of family violence as a lower class
> phenomenon, the culturally-transmitted product of a cramped environ-
> ment which limited opportunities for the distillation of aggression, and of
> a social life centred on pub and street which legitimised physical force.[57]

Children of the State

The interest in child cruelty and neglect in the late nineteenth
century was predicated on an approach of 'rescue' from the
environment rather than rehabilitation and prevention. Families were expected to take full responsibility for their members
and if this was not possible the state would intervene in a harsh,
controlling way – in effect 'rescuing' the child and punishing
the parents. The bulk of the work was carried by the voluntary
societies, particularly the NSPCC, and the state played a
minimal, residual, but authoritative role.

At the turn of the century, however, and during the Edwar-
dian period, this interest in children, the family and social
reproduction began to develop in new directions. A variety of
concerns and anxieties combined to legitimate a more central
and broad-based role for the state. The rise of international
economic competition, the emergence of an indigenous socialist
movement in this country and evidence of the general unfitness

of the working class for both manual labour and military service all contributed to a feeling of national decline. By the beginning of the twentieth century 'national efficiency' became a popular slogan.[58]

Concern about the relative decline of Britain's position in the league of military and industrial nations had been growing throughout the late nineteenth century. Industrialisation had occurred early in Britain but as the rapid economic growth of the mid-Victorian era began to slow down and other countries' own industrial revolutions began to 'take off', Britain's industrial supremacy was challenged and, in some areas, overtaken by the USA, Germany and Japan.[59] Such anxieties were crystallised by the Boer War, for, apart from the revelation of military incompetence and administrative blunders, there was considerable evidence of unfitness among the recruits which led to a crisis in national confidence.[60]

Britain[61] was also lagging behind in terms of population for although the birth rate had been declining throughout the last quarter of the nineteenth century it was not until the end of the century and the beginning of the twentieth century that alarm was expressed. While most Western European nations had experienced a decline in their birth rates during this period (with the exception of France) this trend was most marked in Britain. The population of the USA was rapidly expanding while that of Germany exceeded Britain's population by over ten million.

As a result increasing attention was paid to providing support to respectable working-class families in the guise of old age pensions, health insurance, school meals, more education, labour exchanges and so on. However, it was also recognised that it was important to reinforce the state's power for prosecuting cruel parents, rescuing children and taking over parental rights – particularly from the disreputable. Thus, by the early twentieth century the state no longer leaves responsibility for child care problems to the narrowly defined poor law or the philanthropic societies. It is beginning to take on a broader-based preventative welfare approach along with the residual coercive powers as illustrated by the Prevention of Cruelty to Children Act of 1904 which for the first time gave the state in the form of the local authority powers to remove children.

Thus while there are new found freedoms for most families there is much greater surveillance and coercive intervention by the state for others.

The former relationship between families and the state Donzelot[62] refers to as 'contract', the latter as 'tutelage'. The contractual relationship 'corresponds to an accelerated liberalization of relations, both within and outside the family, there, norms are joined – harmoniously in principle – to a liberal law that fluidifies the family'. While the system of tutelage 'is for social categories that combine a difficulty in supplying their own needs with resistances to the new medical and educative norms'.

For the first time the state attempted to anticipate deviance by developing a more explicitly preventative, social welfare role, while always holding in readiness the coercive intervention if surveillance was resisted or there was an obvious lack of compliance to the new moral standards of family or parental behaviour. This changing role for the state was most evident in the area of juvenile delinquency. Increasingly ideas were stressed of a more explicit welfare orientation which attempted to reform rather than simply punish, and it was argued that children should be dealt with in a qualitatively different way to adults.

While the 1908 Children Act introduced no radically new principles in this area, it was a major piece of consolidating legislation which was welcomed by some as a 'Children's Charter'. The framework provided by that Act remained essentially unchanged until 1933. While the Act was concerned with cases of cruelty and neglect and did attempt to strengthen the powers of the courts over the welfare of the child at risk, it was primarily concerned with delinquency. The Act established juvenile courts and was based on the principle that young offenders under 14 should be treated separately from adults. In effect cruelty and neglect were not conceptualised or legislated for as independent from delinquency.

Perhaps more significantly the Act symbolises the many changes that had been taking place, for by the beginning of the twentieth century it is possible to identify a quite distinct conception of childhood and a separate social, legal and institutional space for children. Within this however, specific concerns about child cruelty and the neglectful behaviour of certain parents towards their offspring occupied the centre of stage for only a brief period from the early 1880s to the early twentieth century. While this concern remained and was legislated for, increasingly other issues concerning families, child care and youth became of primary importance. It was only from the 1870s onwards that the state seriously began to recognise that children were not simple appendages of their parents (particularly father) but had needs and rights of their own. However, at no time, including the 1889 Act, were children given an independent voice: interventions were carried out by adults who 'acted in the child's best interests'.

The Post-War Settlement in Child Care

During the inter-war period two themes can be identified, both of which were central issues and priorities of the nineteenth century. The first is simply that concerns in child care policy, practice and legislation were still primarily prompted by preventative penology – trying to protect society from potentially troublesome children. And secondly, when attempts were made to intervene in 'cruel' or 'neglectful' families the primary method was the physical removal of the child from the family.

Both themes are evident in the main piece of child care legislation of the period, the 1933 Children and Young Persons Act, which was the product of the 1927 Departmental Committee on Young Offenders. The task of the 1927 Committee was 'to enquire into the treatment of young offenders and young people who, owing to bad associations or surroundings require protection and training'. It was a secondary remit to include 'young people who are the victims of cruelty or other offences committed by adults and whost natural guardianship having proved insufficient or unworthy of trust must be replaced'. Under the 1933 Act provisions were strengthened for protecting children in the latter category as local education authorities were now placed under a duty to enquire into such cases and bring them before a court which was empowered to commit them to the care of the local authority. However, the definition of neglect which informed the legislation was more concerned with the parents' behaviour and control than with the welfare of the child. As a consequence children at risk of cruelty or neglect became subsumed in a more general concern about preventing and controlling delinquency. Cruelty and neglect was no longer of prime concern in its own right.

MacLeod[63] has argued that the 1933 Act, in stressing the responsibility of the court to have regard 'to the welfare of the child or young person and in a proper case take steps for removing him from undesirable surroundings and for securing that proper provision is made for his education and training' reflected wider priorities in policy and practice at the time. She argues that attempts to keep families under stress together and rehabilitate children were rare and regarded as likely to be unsuccessful. More generally, children from poor families were seen to need rescue and a change of environment. Certainly the increased committal powers available under the Act with a duty to board out in a foster home increased the likelihood of the child's final break with the family. As Heywood has written:

> Although the emphasis on rehabilitation of the child is forward looking, the concept of care is still nineteenth century, based on removal from the degrading environmental conditions of squalor and poverty, and provides a substitute family for the home which has failed.[64]

The emphasis was on rescue not prevention or trying to ensure families could be supported together in the community. It is perhaps not surprising, in the context of the social and economic problems of the inter-war period, that this was the prime response to families in difficulty. The high unemployment, wide ranging poverty, the break-up of families in the search for work or via the means test, the rising numbers of separations recorded in the matrimonial courts, all indicated that the strength of family life was breaking down. The alternative to the more authoritative rescue approach would have been the development of greater economic support for the family, a more reformist approach to welfare, with the emphasis on wider responsibilities for the state and the introduction of Keynesian type policies. But the emphasis was instead upon tight monetary control, a residual role for the state and therefore a prescribed view of the appropriate interventions in family life.

As with the Boer War, the mobilisation for war after 1939 changed the ideological climate of the country, the role of the state and views of the family. At the start of the war the family was seen as an institution which, in the interests of the war effort and the preservation of young lives, could adapt to separation, with children being able to adapt in very different surroundings away from their natural parents. Titmuss has documented how the experience of war, particularly the evacuation of children, made a significant impact on views of the family.[65]

It seems that the war severely dislocated families and it was feared that this might have important implications for the security, physical and mental health of children. Similarly the evacuation of children to the country demonstrated to sections of society, who had previously no contact with life in the inner city, the wide scale neglect and deprivation that many children experienced. It was argued that such problems, because they were so prevalent, could not be overcome by the traditional removal and rescue methods. A far more positive and supportive approach to the family was required so that the family and the state should work in partnership to ensure children were provided with appropriate conditions in which to develop. 'It was aserted that the evacuation experience demonstrated that families (including presumably pauper families) needed to be together. This somewhat evident fact became a firm key-stone of policy and for the next three decades – until 1975 – the importance of the natural family was affirmed.'[66]

Such an approach had an implicit view of the natural family form and the role of women. During the war a variety of services were developed to encourage women to take an active role in the war effort and encouraging families to be separated. However at the end of the war such policies and arguments were reversed to accommodate men back into the labour force and into firm family groups. Social planning assumed that the family consisted of a male breadwinner and a female whose sole or prime responsibility was caring for children.[67] What becomes evident in the post-war period is that the relationship between the state and the family was based on the ideal of the small nuclear family unit. More particularly we can identify a close link between the growth of state sponsored social work as a profession and the rise of the family as an object of positive social policy in the post-war period. Such views of the family became naturalised in social work practice so that social workers can be seen as its practical missionaries.

The 1948 Children Act, which was the specific piece of legislation which gave expression to this new approach, was introduced during the post-war economic and social reconstruction.[68] Heywood has argued that the legislation was passed in 'a fresh and hopeful atmosphere' and that by the 1948 Act 'the old paternalistic pattern of the poor law was brought to an end, and services which the individual could claim as a right were substituted'.[69] The post-war reconstruction, based on the Beveridge plan, aimed to ensure that the state would take responsibility for individual and family needs in the general areas of health, education and income maintenance. It was also assumed that Keynesian policies would be maintained to provide full employment. In the process the role of the newly created child care service would be residual but based on a far more positive and optimistic view of the family. The Act was of significance in giving state recognition to the professionalised model of social work which replaced the administratively-patterned approach that had been the hallmark of the Poor Law and Public Assistance.

The aim of the 1948 Act was not to punish bad parents but to act in the interests of the children. As the emphasis was on the strength and formative power of the natural family this meant trying to maintain children in the family. It heralded an era where most families were encouraged and helped to care for their own children in their own homes, and underlined the importance of both the natural home and the child's own parents to his or her development.

The Act was primarily concerned with abandoned, orphaned and destitute children. Not only did it embody the principle that the natural family should be helped to care for its own, but there was an obligation for the first time, to try to restore children to their parents. There was a duty under Section One, to restore those received into care to the natural home on the request of the parents. As Heywood has said, the duty:

to receive deprived children into care, as a voluntary arrangement with the child's guardians, replaced the old poor law provisions, and is complementary to the duty of undertaking compulsorily the care of a child committed for care or protection by the courts under the Children and Young Persons Act 1933.[70]

There was also a duty to inform parents of their entitlement to appeal against parental rights resolutions. The aim not to punish bad parents was made explicit by the fact that it was no longer a punishable offence to abandon a child chargeable to the local authority.

While the establishment of Children's Departments was essentially a rationalisation and centralisation of existing services they were imbued with a very different philosophy. The emphasis throughout was to encourage voluntary arrangements between the new child care departments and families, based on mutual agreement and partnership. For those received into care there should be good compensatory care. As Bill Jordan and I have argued:

> As part of the attempt to provide more comprehensive protection against pre-war social problems and to do so without loss of citizenship, the political decision was made to establish a new form of local authority social work. Although these new services were (like the National Assistance Board) residual, in the sense that they were seen as 'safety nets' whose clientele would diminish with the growth of national prosperity, they were nonetheless part of an integrated social policy plan. Furthermore, at least one of them (the Children's Department) embodied the revolutionary principle that it should require officials to seek the *best* development of children deprived of normal home life.[71]

The beginnings of the new child care service took place amidst these more overreaching attempts to establish the welfare state. It was certainly assumed that such reforms together with high employment meant that the problems and widespread deprivation of the inter-war years would be overcome. The 1950s and most of the 1960s were periods of optimism, gradual economic expansion and rising living standards.

This optimism seems to have been central to attitudes in child care in the 1950s and 1960s. State social workers moved away from the bureaucratic rationality of the poor law philosophy towards a more obviously professional social welfare approach. There was a confidence in children's officers, who it was thought could effect major changes in families through their casework and counselling skills. As a consequence greater emphasis was put on prevention than on the protective rescue aspects of the work:

> The child care service was ceasing to be a protective service alone and was beginning to see itself as a service which would enable families to function more effectively, and provide for children those services which no other group of persons or institutions could provide so well. The family began to be seen not only as the natural organisation for child care, but also as the extension of the state's caring function; an organisation which deserved to have state support.[72]

In the economic and political context of the time, when it was assumed that poverty had disappeared, there was always a danger that explanations of problems would be found where they lay: within the families themselves. Increasingly the ideology of social work reflected a medical model with perceptible psychoanalytic influences. As Handler has suggested,[73] the assumption was that:

> the various forms of deviant behaviour engaged in by clients were only symptoms of more basic, deep-seated pathologies and that treating the symptoms was either too late, or haphazard, or worked at 'cross-purposes'. If the problems of the family were to be 'solved' then early intervention would have to be made at the 'source' of the problems rather than waiting for the appearance of the symptoms.

More particularly, the link was increasingly made between neglect or deprivation, particularly in early life, and delinquency. This association sprang from the premise that delinquent children were no different from deprived children who had not been in trouble with the law. They were seen as victims of both family and environmental circumstances and suffered from neglectful, unhappy and often broken homes. As a consequence it was quite arbitrary whether one committed an offence while the other did not. Their needs were the same and they should thus be treated the same.[74] Therefore, while there was an increasing attempt to become involved with family problems at an early stage and to try to do preventative work, the overriding concern and rationale was to do something about delinquency. This was evident in reports and legislation during the 1950s and 1960s.

While the remit of the Ingleby Committee[75] was to make recommendations on the workings of the law in relation to juveniles in trouble, it was also asked to consider 'the prevention of cruelty to, and exposure to moral and physical danger of juveniles', but this was secondary and became consumed by the other concerns so that it virtually disappeared:

> In dealing with the general issue of the circumstances in which the state may properly intervene in proceedings against parents for child neglect, the committee states that 'difficulty has not arisen for several years over the reasonable requirements for nutrition, housing, clothing and schooling ...' by 1960, then, our society had become blind to potential conflicts between family autonomy and child protection.[76]

In effect the newly emerging social welfare model, with its prime concern on the relationship between neglect and delinquency saw no clash of interests between the wider society, the state and different family members. Everything could be tackled by humane regulation and non-coercive welfare intervention techniques. The Ingleby Committee's stress on prevention gained legislative expression in the 1963 Children and Young Persons Act. This emphasis is even more evident in the 1960s when child care discussions were taken over with the reports on how to control and reduce the seemingly growing problem of delinquency. The Labour Party document 'Crime, a Challenge to us all'[77] and the White Papers 'The Child, the Family and the Young Offender'[78] and 'Children in Trouble'[79] were clear on this and formed the basis of the 1969 Children and Young Persons Act.

Under the 1969 Children and Young Persons Act, children in trouble with the law were treated in virtually the same way as children who were not offenders. In the process of conceptualising and treating all problems to do with children as being essentially the same, any reference to children as victims was lost. It is almost as if it was assumed that a conflict of interest between child, parents and the state had disappeared and the nineteenth-century problems of cruelty and neglect had been virtually abolished.

Conclusions

I have argued that the problem of children as victims conceptualised in any independent form, has only appeared very
fleetingly on the political agenda. Its initial appearance in the
1880s and early 1890s was dependent upon the emergence of
the idea of childhood as being a separate category, with
children having needs different to little adults. Such a development was interrelated with wider socio-economic changes in
society. The response to the problem at that time however was
influenced by the poor law philosophy, with heavy overtones of
rescue, control and parental irresponsibility.

During the twentieth century the problem effectively disappeared. Certainly in the post-war period the establishment of
the child care service in the context of welfare reconstruction
put much greater emphasis on supporting parents, trying to
maintain families and establishing a mutually agreed voluntary relationship between families, professionals and the state.
It was a period of optimism for state welfare, particularly
social work.

As a consequence the notions of cruelty to children and child
abuse were not defined in any independent way. When cruelty
was discussed as a separate phenomenon this was usually done
in one of two ways. First, cases were still brought to court for
prosecution by the Police, NSPCC or children departments
and were discussed in the context of a criminal offence. There
were occasions when it was suggested that the penalties should
be increased for such offences in order to act as a deterrent.[80]
Secondly, and more commonly, cruelty was conceptualised as a
symptom of the wider problem of neglect. It is interesting to see
how the work of the NSPCC itself was reflecting this shift. The
1956 NSPCC Annual Report, published on 31 May 1956, said
that 'cases of physical ill-treatment are less severe than they
were' and recorded that 64 291 of 98 277 children helped by
the society in the previous year were suffering from neglect.
The report suggested that this change with only a few cases of
cruelty being known may have been due to the welfare reforms
in the post-war period.

Clearly I am not arguing that the British legal tradition
failed to recognise cruelty to children, for there are numerous

cases resulting in the legal punishment of parents recorded in the official statistics and in the press. However the socio-legal reactions were sporadic and did not constitute a sustained reaction against a firmly labelled deviant category.

It is in this context of an apparent reduction in physical cruelty and a greater concern with neglect, deprivation and delinquency that we must try and locate and explain the discovery of what we now call child abuse and non-accidental injury.

3

The Discovery of the 'Battered Baby'

It is now important to establish where, when, and to whom the problem we now call child abuse was initially discovered. I will attempt to locate the discovery historically and answer a series of interrelated questions: who took the initiative and when? Was there a distinguishable group of moral entrepreneurs? How important were organisational interests? How was the problem defined, conceptualised and explained? What were the recommendations for policy and practice? What was specific to the issue and how was it seen to differ from other children's problems? If the issue was to be more generally regarded as a problem and the state to take a more active role in doing something about it, the initial concern and discovery *had* to be shared and made more widespread. Therefore others had to be convinced that the situation was dangerous and important enough to require public attention. What tactics were involved and how did these relate to wider changes in the socio-political environment? I will thus be looking at wider social processes and, more particularly, the role of the media and the state in promoting the problem.

The period covered in this chapter is from the Second World War to the death of Maria Colwell in early 1973. As I will argue, the issue had barely been established as a social problem promoting wide concern by early 1973 – this awaited the subsequent scandal concerning Maria Colwell. However, considerable groundwork in terms of publicity, research and campaigning had been carried out during the period which significantly informed and structured subsequent events.

The Discovery in the USA

Many of the early articles related to the problem which were written in Britain registered their debt to the work of certain US researchers; it is my contention that the discovery in Britain was not only influenced by, but was dependent upon these developments. Thus to understand the process of discovery in Britain it is important to appreciate earlier developments in the USA.

The discovery in the USA began in the mid 1940s with the work of Dr John Caffey, a distinguished specialist in paediatric radiology.[1] He discussed the fact that many infants whose principal disease was chronic subdural haematoma (a collection of blood immediately underneath the skull) upon X-ray were found to have fresh, healing and healed multiple fractures in the long bones (arms and legs). In none of the cases he came across was there a history of injury to which the skeletal lesions could reasonably be attributed and in no case was there evidence of any disease which would predispose to fractures. He suggested therefore that not only was there a relationship between the two conditions but also that they were traumatic in origin. However, he did not attempt to define the source of the trauma nor provide a firm label.

Support for Caffey's observations of bone lesions and subdural haematoma quickly followed, and some began to refer to the role of parents as possible sources of the trauma.[2] This link was made explicit in 1955 by Woolley and Evans[3] who went much further by actually suggesting explanations in terms of parental behaviour. They reviewed material seen over a period of eight years with radiographic findings suggesting injury, with or without a history of trauma, and concluded that in both cases the skeletal lesions 'are due to undesirable vectors of force'. The article then made reference to 'parental indifference', 'alcoholism', 'irresponsibility', and 'immaturity manifested by uncontrollable aggressions', as the causes of the injuries. Not only are such ideas far from value-free but the nature of the research could not begin to offer such wide-ranging explanations on strictly scientific criteria.

By the end of the decade in the USA there were a number of articles in professional medical journals which focused attention directly on child abuse, and in each the emphasis was placed on the importance of roentgenological (X-ray) examination of children suffering from multiple injuries, and the importance of careful and adroit history-taking to confirm suspected abuse.[4] Also in this period other sections of the medical profession reported their findings[5] and recommendations and Elizabeth Elmer[6] published the first article on the subject by a social worker.

It is apparent that the radiological interest in child abuse in the late 1940s and early 1950s provided the initial location for the discovery in the USA and provided the basis from which the social, legal and psychiatric interest in the problem developed. However, during the 1950s there were some important developments which provided an opportunity for these more discrete professional interests to publicise and propagate the problem.[7]

In the autumn of 1954 the American Humane Association's[8] Children's Division under the leadership of its new director, Dr Vincent De Francis began the first nationwide survey on neglected, abused and exploited children. The results[9] were distributed to child welfare departments and other interested professions and the findings were presented to a meeting of child welfare experts coordinated by the AHA, at which the Children's Bureau[10] was represented.

Such meetings helped demonstrate to the Children's Bureau that child abuse was a national problem. Similarly, the AHA's report emphasised that child-protective services were congruent with the social work perspective of the CB. The suggested method of intervention, casework, was also the CB's preferred response to most child care problems and encouraged the CB to consider policy options.[11] Steiner has argued that the Children's Bureau was never a particularly well-respected organisation and was never overworked. However, while it had slack organisational resources it retained a fairly defined narrow view of its role. Thus when the issue of child abuse, which was so congruent to its mission, was brought to its attention, not only was there a consensus and resources available with which to respond, but also a real opportunity to raise its credibility, status and legitimacy as a worthwhile organisation. The issue of child abuse was important for a range of reasons to the CB.

The CB's early support for child abuse research developed a small group whose entrepreneurial activities were to prove crucial in publicising the problem and precipitating action in both the USA and Britain. In the late 1950s the CB gave support to Dr C. Henry Kempe to explore with his colleages in Denver the physical abuse of children.[12] He first reported his findings at a meeting of the American Academy of Paediatrics in November 1961. Because he was a member of the programme committee he could organise a seminar on the area of his choice. According to Nelson,[13] his colleagues on the programme committee suggested that a title such as 'Physical Abuse' might make some members wary of attending as it emphasised the legally liable and socially deviant aspects of the problem. As a result the seminar was renamed the 'Battered Child Syndrome'.

The label was to prove crucial in helping to gain the attention of the wider medical profession to the problem, helping to publicise it and encouraging the state to take action. While the label was emotive it played down the legal and socially deviant aspects and defined it as an illness – a syndrome. The label proved a powerful factor in mobilising wider concern, and in the process conceptualised it centrally as a medical problem.

The research was published in the following year under this label[14] in the prestigious journal of the American Medical Association. The article claimed that the syndrome characterised a clinical condition in young children usually under three who had received serious physical abuse, usually from a parent, and that it was a significant cause of childhood disability and death. It argued that the syndrome was often misdiagnosed and that it should be considered in any child showing evidence of possible trauma or neglect, or where there was a marked discrepancy between the clinical findings and the story presented by the parents. The use of X-rays to aid diagnosis was stressed, and it was argued that the prime concern of the physician was to make the correct diagnosis and to make certain that a similar event did not occur again. The authors recommended that doctors report all incidents to law enforcement or child protective agencies.

It was also said that the problem was not simply concerned

with poverty and that the characteristics of the parents were that: 'they are immature, impulsive, self-centred, hypersensitive and quick to react with poorly controlled aggression'.[15]

The problem of battered children was quickly adopted by the press and television, so that when Vincent de Francis reported in 1963 on a year-long study undertaken by the AHA, he documented 662 cases reported nationally in the press in 1962 alone. The information provided about the families pointed to the same gamut of problems that in Britain at the time were associated with the problem family: marital difficulty, drinking, adult crime and delinquency.[16] The work of Kempe and his colleagues in Denver has continued to be of central importance in the whole area of child abuse and neglect.[17] At that time policies and practices developed very rapidly following closely the recommendations of the medical profession, particularly those working in the area of paediatrics. By the end of 1963, thirteen states had enacted statutory reporting laws whereby professionals who suspected abuse or neglect were legally required to report this to a designated police or child care agency. Ten more were added in 1964, twenty six in 1965, and by 1967 every state had passed some form of reporting law.[18] Certainly by the mid 1960s in the USA there was a recognition of a new and distinctive problem called 'the battered child syndrome' which, while it begins with a pattern of injuries to the child, is really descriptive of a pattern of conduct on the part of the parents or others who care for children.

Clearly the way the problem was articulated and presented was hardly passive, for the radiologists and paediatricians involved were orientated towards seeking out and establishing a new illness. The problem was defined as a syndrome and certain doctors were seen as having the central role to play in its diagnosis, treatment, and reporting. As a consequence the way it was conceptualised focused attention on a disease model of physical abuse from parents, thus emphasising the injuries to the child and deflecting attention from wider social, cultural and economic factors that might impinge – particularly as it was argued that the problem did not only strike at the poor. While the entrepreneurial efforts of Henry Kempe and his colleagues were clearly crucial in this process it is also important to consider the implications of wider organisational and professional interests that might have encouraged such developments.

Stephen Antler[19] has suggested that by the middle of the twentieth century in the USA most major causes of infant mortality had been overcome and child abuse presented itself as a new frontier for medical involvement in problems traditionally associated with social service agencies. Certainly it is one of the greatest ambitions of most doctors to discover and describe a new disease or syndrome, and to be immortalised by having their name used to identify it.[20] Pfohl[21] has tried to analyse more specifically why paediatric radiology played such a crucial role in the discovery of child abuse in America. He argues that at the time of the discovery paediatric radiology was a marginal specialism within organised medicine. It was a research orientated sub-field in a profession that emphasised face-to-face clinical interaction, and was a secure pursuit within a profession that placed a premium on 'risky pragmatic enterprise'. As a consequence paediatric radiologists traditionally ranked lower than other medical specialities.

Pfohl argues that the discovery of child abuse offered paediatric radiologists an alternative to their marginal medical status. By linking themselves to the problem, they could become involved in the crucial clinical task of patient diagnosis. In addition, they became a direct source of input concerning the possible life or death consequences of child abuse. This could represent an advance in status and a new basis for recognition within the medical profession. This was symbolised by the appearance of articles in the prestigious journal of the American Medical Association. The discovery also offered an opportunity to form a coalition with other more prestigious disciplines, particularly paediatrics and psycho-dynamically orientated psychiatry. The interests of all three groups could be advanced by such a coalition, and served to reinforce paediatric radiology in its enterprise.

However while the initial discovery was by paediatric radiologists, the application of the successful label and the recognition of a new social problem is associated with the work of Henry Kempe and his colleagues in Denver. As we have seen, a number of agencies and interests are important in this, though the critical impetus is very much with certain sections of the medical profession.[22]

The Discovery in Britain

Recognition of the problem in Britain developed much more slowly and in part had to await the changes across the Atlantic. Concerns about cruelty were well established but were seen as primarily a criminal problem and the responsibility of the crime control and child care agencies. While there is evidence of medical concern about physical injuries to children the clinical diagnosis was often in terms of some bone weakness and the behaviour of parents was not seen as crucial.[23] Even a leader article in September 1963 in the *British Medical Journal*, reflecting the support of the British Medical Association[24] to the principles behind and introduction of the 1963 Children and Young Persons Act, made hardly any mention of cruelty to children and none of the issue of battered babies.

The issue was first recognised by two orthopaedic surgeons, Griffiths and Moynihan, in an article published in the *British Medical Journal* in December 1963, and was labelled the 'Battered Baby Syndrome'.[25] They presented four cases of such children all aged under one, and argued that they wanted to give publicity to a 'syndrome' which they were convinced was being 'misdiagnosed'. They argued that doctors should always consider that babies may have been injured by 'brutal violence' with 'the culprit' almost always the parent. They quoted Kempe and his colleagues and asserted that 'for every child who is abused and enters a hospital there must be another 100 treated by unsuspecting doctors. . . . it may be a more frequent cause of death than . . . leukaemia, cystic fibrosis and muscular dystrophy'.[26] They concluded by arguing that doctors needed not only to recognise the 'syndrome' but that they should also report such cases to the police.

The article was well received by the *British Medical Journal* and a leader in the same issue[27] said that Griffiths and Moynihan 'deserved the thanks of the medical profession for drawing attention to the problem'. It said that while it may seem that such cases are rare, it is a mistake to think they are uncommon, as the work 'of that spendid institution the NSPCC suggests'. It felt that 'clearly this tragic matter deserves more attention than it has received' and that the syndrome was important for two reasons: first, if the diagnosis was missed, the child might be subject to further injury; and secondly, it was one of the few conditions in which clinical and radiological investigations could produce irrefutable proof that the affected child had been cruelly treated.[28]

The article certainly created some interest in the letters column of the *British Medical Journal* in the ensuing few weeks. One letter in particular[29] is of interest in that it reflects not only the way the medical profession was to view the problem in the next few years but some of the tensions involved in the way it was defined, explained and responded to. Dr Eric Turner wrote that he was 'relieved' to see the article, as he felt many GPs were aware of the problem. However he felt that doctors should not act as lawyers or judges but should 'prevent disease', and that there were two approaches required. First, it was important that doctors publicise it to create an atmosphere in the community which did not overlook violence, and he argued that 'what is really needed is a *cause célèbre* with front page treatment in the press'. Secondly, it was important to make conviction virtually certain and then give an exemplary sentence of many years in prison. He concluded by arguing that 'we can start by moving the great palpitating British conscience'. The question of whether the problem is a crime or a disease is not clear, for while the problem is defined at one level as a medical syndrome with the role of medicine as crucial in identification and diagnosis, the nature of the response is punitive, though it is justified partly in terms of treating the child and the family. There are clearly elements of both the medical and legal ideology here. What tended to happen therefore was that while it was assumed that the perpetrators did not freely choose to batter their children and therefore were not truly criminal, nor were they sick in the physical sense of the term. Their lack of control was seen in moral terms and they were seen as in some way feckless or depraved and warranted pity, benign intervention and perhaps discipline from those who know and behave differently. This would also act to set as an example to others.

While the initial discovery in Britain was by two orthopaedic surgeons, the main branches of the medical profession that were most active during this period were paediatricians and forensic pathologists. There were a number of articles published in *Medicine, Science and the Law*, the official journal of the Association of Forensic Pathologists.[30]

In early 1965 an eminent forensic pathologist firmly placed his support for the problem. Professor Keith Simpson had been Professor of Forensic Medicine at the University of London since 1962 and was a member of the Home Office Scientific Advisory Council. He published a short but evocative article in the *British Medical Journal* under the heading of 'medico-legal' problems,[31] in which he referred to the case of a father who had recently been convicted of the murder of two of his children. He argued that both infants were typical of the 'battered baby syndrome' which had only recently been recognised as a 'widespread crime that can only too easily escape detection'. He suggested that GPs were the 'guardians' of such infants and should adopt the role of investigator in such cases.

The campaign was furthered by the efforts of Dr Camps and his colleagues in the Department of Forensic Medicine at the London Hospital Medical College[32] who argued that the incidence of this 'widespread crime', was 'startling' and of 'increasing importance' and called for the full co-operation of the medical, legal and social authorities. The doctor was seen as the 'first line of defence in the fight to combat the problem' and he should remember 'that his moral obligation is to the child and he should be aware that at least 60 per cent of these children are liable to suffer further injuries or death'. Doctors should thus have a 'low threshhold of suspicion'. Dr Camps made clear his intentions to continue the campaign when he asked in the *British Medical Journal* the following year for cases of 'battered children' to aid his research on the 'psychopathology' of the parents.

Thus in the middle of the 1960s it appears that a number of eminent forensic pathologists saw themselves as not simply involved in a crusade but a war against abusive parents. The war analogy was continually drawn upon in references to campaigns, combat, fight, attack and so on.

The British Paediatric Association entered the fray when

they published a memorandum in the *British Medical Journal*
which discussed the recognition and management of the problem.[33] After outlining the clinical symptoms of the 'syndrome'
and the importance of hospital casualty officers in its recognition, it argued that the doctor must look for evidence of
previous or other injuries and should learn something of the
background of the family in its social setting and its interrela-
tionships. It recommended that when the diagnosis is suspected
all children should be admitted to hospital while the history is
investigated and the possibility of physical disease is excluded.
If the 'battered baby syndrome' is still suspected 'the proper
person to consult at this stage is the children's officer of the
Local Authority'. This is something of a new departure as the
previous articles, particularly those by forensic pathologists,
had all assumed the police should be involved at this stage. In
fact the memo stresses that a 'purely punitive attitude' to the
person inflicting the injury is ill-advised, and that it is not the
doctor's role to make the parent admit liability. The memo
clearly felt that the 'management' of the problem was the
responsibility of the 'medical' and 'social welfare' agencies.
This led to some discussion in the correspondence columns as to
how far the interests of the child and the rehabilitation of the
whole family were consistent and realistic aims.[34]

The discovery of the battered baby syndrome, can thus be
located in Britain with certain sections of the medical profession.[35] However, unlike the USA, the impetus came from
forensic pathologists and paediatricians. This is perhaps not
surprising, bearing in mind that the initial discovery had
already been made, and simply needed people to take up the
cause in this country. Nor is it surprising that members of the
legal and social welfare agencies were not centrally involved at
this stage, for both would rarely see such cases, and the latter at
this time laid emphasis on the need to work with whole families
and prevent delinquency.

It has also been suggested that there were numerous reasons
why most doctors did not recognise the problem. First, doctors
in casualty departments were simply unaware of the
possibility,[36] secondly, they were psychologically unwilling to
believe that parents could do such things,[37] thirdly they were
unhappy at violating the principle of client confidentiality, and

fourthly, doctors are usually reluctant to become involved in the criminal justice process that might forfeit both their time and ability to control the outcome.[38]

In contrast forensic pathologists were closely allied to the courts and the criminal justice process and the issue provided an excellent opportunity to demonstrate their distinctive role in being able to bridge the gap between medicine and the law. It is also likely that they would be confronted with the most extreme cases which could make a real impact. While paedia-trics *raison d'être* is children, as Pfohl has argued,[39] the increased use of preventative drugs and treatments for previously dangerous children's diseases meant that it was no longer such a crucial specialism and might have been sliding to the margins of the medical profession. Such a slide may have been further reinforced by the falling birth rate from the middle 1960s onwards. The discovery of the battered baby could be seen to reinforce paediatrics in a crucial life-saving area of work which might help it to attract resources and re-establish its previous status.

The NSPCC Battered Child Research Unit

Before 1968 any awareness of the problem outside the medical profession was minimal.[40] However, in the period from 1968 to 1972 considerable work was done which laid the groundwork for the events that were to follow. During this period the NSPCC Battered Child Research Unit was established and became crucial in sustaining and disseminating publicity to other professional groups. The Unit was the primary influence on the way the problem was taken up by the media and civil servants, so that its definition of the problem, its explanation, management and resolutions became dominant. In order to understand the crucial role of the Unit it is necessary to explore the moral, professional and organisational interests that were at stake.

It seems that in the post-war period the nature of the NSPCC's work began to change from its traditional nine-teenth-century role. Allen and Morton claim that the cruder physical sufferings became less frequent so that 'most of the work of the Society is in dealing with neglect not cruelty'.[41] Not only did the nature of the work change so that in 1964 of the 120 000 children helped only 9632 were said to be assaulted,[42] but increasingly the Society attempted to move from its more legalistic, police, inspectorial role to a more professional child care agency. Before 1900 up to 21 per cent of the cases dealt with led to a prosecution while in 1964 it was below 2 per cent[43] and in 1968 0.5 per cent.[44]

During the post-war period there were a number of significant moves by the NSPCC to become a modern social work agency. On the recommendations of the Ingleby Committee it appointed a training officer in 1961, and in 1964 it instituted a one-year training course for new inspectors, which gave more attention to casework. The traditional uniform was withdrawn from service in 1965 and withdrawn altogether in June 1969, which symbolised the shift from the legal-punishment model and the greater emphasis on the 'prevention' in the title rather than 'cruelty'. The NSPCC agreed with the Ingleby Committee when it argued that the imprisonment of parents was of no help if the objective was the rehabilitation of the family. However, in trying to become a more professional social work organisation as opposed to a pioneering child-saving movement, the Society increasingly competed with and duplicated the work of the state-sponsored and fast expanding Children's Departments.[45]

Even before the 1963 Children and Young Persons Act many Children's Departments were already carrying out preventative casework[46] and the 1952 Amendment to the 1948 Children Act had given them the duty of investigating cruelty and neglect. In fact the Ingleby Committee, with one dissenter, proposed that the power to bring before a Juvenile Court a child 'in need of care and protection' should be taken from the NSPCC, and while this recommendation was not put into effect, the NSPCC was expected to work closely with Children's Departments. Such developments prompted Ann Lapping in 1965 to comment: 'if the Society continues to provide a parallel service to the Children's Departments it is bound to find itself out of work eventually. Forward looking officers of the Society are aware of this predicament.'[47] The annual report of the NSPCC for 1964–5 said that it dealt with 5 per cent

fewer cases than the previous year and that this was probably
due to an increase in 'local authority caseworkers' reducing the
NSPCC workload. The report also indicated that it was facing
a financial crisis. Expenditure exceeded income by £261 961
during the year, and would have been worse if inspectors'
houses had been included; on 1 March 1965 the NSPCC
launched a three-year appeal to raise £250 000. It was in this
context of crisis that the society discovered the 'battered child'
and decided to establish a research unit.

In late 1964 the Revd Arthur Morton,[48] the NSPCC Director,
after seeing some articles on the 'syndrome' went to the USA
where he spent some time with Henry Kempe and Brandt
Steele looking at the Denver Project. When he returned early
in the following year he recommended to the Society's executive committee that a research unit modelled on the Denver
project should be set up. The NSPCC's support was reinforced
after Professor Keith Simpson gave an address on the 'Battered
Child' to the 1965 annual conference in July, but any decisions
to set up a unit had to await the election of the next executive
committee.

Following a further visit by the Revd Morton to the USA in
the summer of 1967 the decision was made to set up the
Battered Child Research Unit. A scientific advisory committee
was established to supervise the project and included a range of
eminent medical, legal and social work experts who had an
interest in the problem. The committee, which was presented
as a 'scientific' enterprise, enabled a number of individuals who
had previously been working in relative isolation to come
together. According to the 1969 NSPCC annual report the
objectives of the unit were 'to carry through a comprehensive
programme of study and treatment of families where a child
has been battered, and to help build up an informed body of
opinion on the "Battered Child Syndrome"'. But its most
important function was to publicise the problem and educate
the professionals concerned.

In October 1968 Miss Joan Court, a psychiatric social
worker trained at the psycho-dynamically orientated Smith
College of Social Work in the USA, was appointed to head the
unit along with Ray Castle, Angela Skinner and Caroline
Okell. Both Joan Court and Ray Castle were immediately
seconded to study in Denver and elsewhere in the US. From

the beginning, the unit was modelled on the Denver project, the unit building was called Denver House, and in 1969–70 Henry Kempe spent a sabbatical year based at the unit.

Not only was the research unit to prove important in disseminating recognition of the problem of battered children, but its work was central to the future of the NSPCC. It reflected some of the changes attempted by the society in the previous years and was perhaps the first time a 'professional social work group' existed within it which could act as a catalyst for further change. Its importance was evidenced by the fact that it was immediately responsible to the director Certainly these developments provided an opportunity for the NSPCC to overcome its problems. In effect it could return to its innovatory beginnings, forging new ideas and schemes as it did in the late nineteenth century. It could provide a specialist role which was qualititatively different from that provided by local authority social work departments. However, the approach had shifted from a legalistic, police role to one consistent with, if not the epitome of, professional social work, where scientific expertise and relationship skills were central.[49]

Between January 1969 and February 1973 members of the unit had seventeen articles published in a variety of professional journals, of which Joan Court wrote ten,[50] and the unit was quickly recognised as the main agency concerned with the problem. The approach followed very closely that of the Denver project. The primary focus was prevention and treatment. It was argued that 60 per cent of children were re-battered[51] so that bruises and injuries that might seem of minor importance may signify the beginning of the 'syndrome'.

The problem and its control was conceptualised as a 'medico-social problem'[52] where the stress was upon early identification and 'non-punitive' treatment. As Okell argued:

Increased knowledge of the dynamics of the battered child syndrome is already leading to the development of predictive techniques aimed at identifying parents who are very deficient in mothering ability and at risk of injuring their children. These techniques have exciting implications for the ultimate goal, of primary prevention.[53]

The crucial factor for the social worker was not to establish whether the law had been broken and whether the parents were guilty or innocent, the main objective was to form a 'consistent, trusting, professional relationship'.[54]

Child battering was seen as a symptom of family breakdown, and all the articles argue that the one problem battering parents all have in common is that their own childhood was grossly deprived and unhappy, so that there is a breakdown in the 'ability to mother'. Intervention should therefore be based on a careful psycho-social diagnosis and should provide a 'transfusion of mothering ... in the hope they will identify with us and eventually interject a less punitive self image'.[55]

It is apparent that the unit conceptualised and approached the problem in terms of an ego-psychological, psycho-dynamic theory of human behaviour that was consistent with the established professional model of family casework, with its allegiances to a medical model of social problems. So the legal system and the courts were only seen as significant when they were part of a more general rehabilititive or treatment programme.

The two most significant documents to be published by the unit were the research reports of 1969 and 1972,[56] for it was these reports in particular which brought the problem to the attention of the media and central government for the first time.

The first report was based on a retrospective study of 78 battered children known to the NSPCC during the twelve months following 1 July 1967. Apart from arguing for 'the need for earlier protection of the battered child' and for the 'development of therapeutic services for the battering parents' the report made some specific recommendations which directly parallelled developments in the USA earlier in the decade. It recommended that new legislation be considered to ensure that doctors notified a child protection agency of any suspicions. It also recommended that 'early identification of battered children should be assisted by the wider distribution of present knowledge' and more particularly that 'the education of all members of the medical, legal, social work and nursing professions who are required to treat or assist the families of battered children, should embrace a more understanding approach to problems and crisis in people with character disorders'. At no stage were the police included in the recommendations.

The second report was based on cases reported to the Battered Child Research Unit by NSPCC social workers in England, Wales and Northern Ireland during 1970. The report referred to the increased professional recognition of the syndrome in the three years since the first report. The sample comprised 292 children under the age of four who were suspected, at the time of referral, to have been injured by a parent or guardian. Although three times as many cases were referred, there were twice as many 'seriously' injured and eight times as many 'moderately' injured children compared with the first study. The authors suggested that the increase in publicity and education of the syndrome had lead to a growth in awareness of the need for intervention in less serious cases of 'child abuse'.

The report also stressed the importance of the 'multi-disciplinary approach' and recommended that consideration should be given to the establishment of central registers of cases of suspected abuse at local level where their primary function would be the identification of repeated abuse within a family and treatment planning. The medical conceptualisation of the problem was made explicit in the foreword to the report when the Revd Arthur Morton likened it to a 'contagious disease', where the parents 'are so grievously inadequate in coping with the demands of the parental situation'.

The Role of the Media 1968–72

If the problem was to gain more widespread recognition outside professional circles it was important that the media take it up, but while there is some evidence that the media begins to publicise the problem in the late 1960s and early 1970s[57] it was given a low profile. Far from campaigning in its own right, in essence the media reflected the views and publications of the NSPCC Battered Child Research Unit. It is also evident that the professional journals, including those of the medical profession, increasingly saw the unit as the focal agency. The journals present an explicitly ego-psychological, psycho-dynamic definition and explanation reminiscent of the unit and gave priority to its recommendations for policy and practice.

An analysis of entries in *The Times* supports the view that the NSPCC and specifically the research unit, was the crucial agency during the period. Prior to 1968 there were just four entries, and only one, a report of a lecture by Professor Simpson to the Royal Society when he said that London pathologists were using X-rays to identify such cases, is not a report of moves by the NSPCC to publicise the problem and establish the unit.

Thereafter until the end of 1972 nearly all the reporting is related to the work of the unit and its approach to the problem. For example, a feature article on the Woman's Page on 8 January 1969 outlined the work of the unit and stressed the close links with Denver, and Joan Court was quoted as seeing the problem as a 'cry for help' and saying that 'there won't be an inquisition on what occurred – we want to find out the underlying disturbance'.

A report announcing the publication of the first report on 12 September 1969 and its recommendations led to an interesting debate in the correspondence column which reflected some of the arguments that were to become so crucial a few years later. A Dr Alexander Spiers wrote saying that, while he was pleased the problem was receiving publicity, he felt the practice of trying to keep the abused child at home a bad one. He also felt that new legislation was required to combat what was 'certainly the most evil of social evils today'. In reply Revd Morton argued that Dr Spiers' attack was too broad and emotional, and re-asserted that the removal of the child should only be used as a last resort.

However the coverage of the problem virtually disappeared[58] between publication of the 1969 and 1972 NSPCC research unit reports, indicating the significance of the unit during this period in maintaining any interest in the problem in the media.

Similarly an anlaysis of the professional medical journals from 1968 onwards suggests that coverage, while maintained, was not as fervent as earlier in the decade and was more concerned with refining the clinical picture and, again, reporting the work of the NSPCC unit. In fact between July 1967 and September 1969 the only reference to the problem in the *British Medical Journal* was in two letters, and the first substantive piece was a leading article on 20 September 1969 favourably commenting on the first NSPCC report and arguing that doctors had a crucial role to play in both diagnosing and preventing the problem. From then to May 1971 the only entries were two letters. But from May 1971 onwards the 'Battered Baby Syndrome' was given its own section in the journals index and a number of articles appeared which were primarily concerned with the clinical aspects of the problem – each focusing on new dimensions which tended to broaden the medical definition.[59]

An article by an eminent child psychiatrist, Dr Susan Isaacs,[60] on the emotional and psychiatric aspects explicitly demonstrates the application to the problem of the medical/social welfare model that was increasingly being developed during this period. As with the NSPCC unit the problem is seen in psycho-dynamic terms and the role of intervention is conceptualised in strict professional terms where it is assumed that the expert is able benevolently to discover the real underlying cause in the interests of all. She is particularly condemnatory of strict legalistic intervention, for 'punishment plays no part in curing the problem or preventing recurrences, so investigation by the police . . . can be dangerously inappropriate. On the other hand, a juvenile court may be of great help, concerned as it is for the welfare of the child in its family as a whole'. It is not that the law is inappropriate but that its role is conceptualised in the context of a welfare model. Due process is subsumed within the needs of the family. Child abuse is a symptom of an underlying family dysfunction of some sort and the court takes on the guise of a treatment agency.

It would thus seem that between 1968 and 1972 the dominant ideology adopted by the *British Medical Journal* becomes more consistent, and the more legalistic approach previously propounded by forensic pathologists was less in evidence. While increasing reference was made to attempts to 'manage' the problem, this reflected the more psycho-dynamic social welfare model propounded by the NSPCC Battered Child Research Unit.

During the period other professional groups were being sensitised to the issue[61] and some local initiatives to coordinate efforts and to identify and manage the problem arose.[62] It was

suggested that the problem was on the increase.[63] The work of
the NSPCC Battered Child Research Unit and the Denver
approach were paramount.[64] An interesting comparison of the
problems of cruelty, which had been recognised for some time,
and the battered baby, was provided by Gibbens. He compared the findings of his research published in 1956[65] with that
published in 1972[66] and found that the majority of cases of
'cruelty' known to the NSPCC in the earlier research were aged
3–13 but in the latter research, when the prime focus was
'battered babies', more attention was directed to those aged
0–3.

Increasingly, because of the influence of the NSPCC unit, it
was being argued that while the problem was a clinical
condition there was a need for a social work psycho-social
assessment and the need for a full coordinated team approach:
social work agencies should play a central role. However, it
seems that social work generally was very slow, compared to
other professional groups, to respond to the problem. A review
of the social work journals for the period demonstrates that
apart from the articles produced by the NSPCC unit there
were no articles on the problem written by social workers. In
particular *Social Work Today*, the professional social work
journal, from its inception in 1970 to January 1974, included
no articles directly on the subject.[67]

The Beginnings of State Intervention

I have already mentioned that there was evidence that by the
end of 1972 a number of local statutory agencies were beginning to set up 'early warning systems', or 'coordinating committees' in an attempt to monitor, identify and possibly prevent
the problem.[68] These may well have been related to low level
initiatives taken by central government, for in 1970 and 1972
the DHSS published two circulars for Medical Officers of
Health and Children's Officers (in 1972 Directors of Social
Services) which attempted to encourage action at the local
level. [69] The central role of the NSPCC unit however, again
becomes critical, for both circulars very much reflect the views,
explanations and recommendations of the unit and Henry

Kempe. The first circular is essentially a formal response to the first NSPCC Report in 1969, *78 Battered Children.*[70]

The 1970 circular supported the inter-professional team approach. It asked Children's Officers and Medical Officers of Health to consult together and with 'representatives of the Local Medical Committee, paediatricians, consultants responsible for accident and emergency services, and other local agences'. The recommendations of the 1969 NSPCC report were followed almost to the letter and the final paragraph of the circular said:

> The importance of the continuing risk must be stressed and the NSPCC report in particular, points to the unsatisfactory aftercare arrangements which have been made by many hospitals despite the evidence of repeated, unexplained injury in childhood. A coordinated local organisation should remedy this. Awareness of the syndrome, its background and implications, and the effective management of the case by a cooperative effort from all agencies who have a part to play, may pay dividends in preventing childhood distress and death.[71]

The circular also said 'there is value in the setting up of a registry of injuries to children which are not satisfactorily explained'.

The influence of the NSPCC unit approach was reinforced when Joan Court, following her departure from the unit in 1971, was appointed to the Social Work Service at the DHSS.[72] Such an approach was certainly evident in the 1972 DHSS circular which argued that 'the best chance for progress lies in the increasing emphasis and resources being put into preventative work'. While the 'protection of the child' was seen as crucial, it was felt that this could generally be done in terms of rehabilitation for the whole family.

According to the 1972 circular it seems that the recommendation of the 1970 circular that area review committees and case committees be set up was responded to in many areas. There was an overriding majority of medical personnel on such committees, with a consensus that a consultant paediatrician normally be regarded as the convenor of the case committees. The medical conceptualisation and management of the problem thus seems pre-eminent. While all concerned felt that inter-professional communication was at the 'crux' of the problem, it is interesting that very few police officers were included on such committees.

Conclusions

In this chapter I have argued that while the initial discovery can be located with paediatric radiologists working in the USA in the late 1940s and 1950s, the introduction of the label 'battered child syndrome' by Henry Kempe was crucial in establishing it as a major social problem. These developments prompted a similar discovery in this country from 1963 onwards particularly by paediatricians and forensic pathologists.

Increasingly the work of the NSPCC Battered Child Research Unit played an important role in publicising the problem and bringing it to the attention of various professional groups and central government. However it seems that the problem was not seen as a major priority, and was given a fairly low profile in many professional groups, the media, and central and local government. For example the 1972 DHSS circular had stressed 'the utmost care should be taken to avoid labelling parents and children as "battering" or "battered"'. In the House of Commons on 22 December 1972 Mr Michael Alison, an under-secretary at the DHSS, in reply to Dr Trafford's (Conservative: the Wrekin) criticisms of the local authority's handling of the death of Graham Bagnall in May 1972 made what could be interpreted as a statement of official policy regarding the problem. He stressed that the preventative approach was both the 'logical and strategic' point at which forces should be brought to bear on the problem, and that greater and greater dividends could be looked for in tackling the 'syndrome' from a concentration on prevention via the 'team' approach. However this had only been 'gently pressed' on to the local authorities. It is in the context of this fairly low key approach that we must try and explain the developments surrounding the Maria Colwell case in 1973 and 1974.

4

The Social React[...] Maria Colwell

The case of Maria Colwell proved crucial in establishing the issue as a major social problem and in introducing fundamental changes in policy and practice. Not only was the death of Maria Colwell constructed as a national scandal in its own right but the reaction to it reflected a more pervasive social anxiety about inadequate families and the role and activities of social workers.[1] The case ensured that from then on the issue would no longer be experienced by the professionals concerned as marginal to their everyday practice but would take on the highest priority and would generate considerable concern and 'fear'.[2]

Maria Colwell died on 7 January 1973 at the age of seven (born 25 March 1965) being one of nine children that her mother had borne by that time. She spent over 5 years in the foster care of her aunt, but was returned to her mother and step-father (Mr Kepple) at the age of 6 years and 8 months, being placed on a supervision order to the local authority from that date. The family was visited by a variety of social workers, and concern about Maria was expressed by her school teacher and by neighbours. However, she was 'battered' to death by her step-father on the night of 6/7 January 1973, and was found to weigh only about three-quarters of what would have been expected for her age and height. Mr Kepple was convicted of manslaughter and sentenced to eight years imprisonment. He had a poor physical health record and had been convicted of relatively minor offences of violence on two occasions. The DHSS report was published in September 1974.

... action to the case and the events that followed signified a ...matic event such that it took on the proportions of a moral ...nic. According to Cohen:

> Societies appear to be subject, every now and then, to periods of moral panic. A condition, episode, person or group of persons emerges to become defined as a threat to societal values and interests . . . sometimes the object of the panic is quite novel and at other times it is something which has been in existence long enough but suddenly appears in the limelight.[3]

The parents and guardians who perpetrate such evil behaviour, the parents (Kepples) and social workers in the case of Maria Colwell, take on the guise of an 'alter ego for virtue' or 'folk devil' on to whom our most intense feelings about things going wrong and our insecurities are projected. The construction of a moral panic is not dependent on the existence of qualitatively different information or events but is related to changes and shifts in wider social processes and social anxieties. At the time of the Colwell panic Bob Holman drew attention to a similar case in Scotland when a child had died at the hands of its private foster parents, which had been the subject of a public inquiry in 1969 but which never gave rise to a sustained moral panic on the issue.[4]

Stuart Hall and his colleagues have developed a marxist interpretation of the concept of moral panic[5] which they argue is 'one of the forms of appearance of a more deep seated historical crisis'. They argue that it is one of the key ideological forms by which the 'silent majority' is won over to support increased coercive state intervention. They identify a number of 'signification spirals' which generate and sustain a moral panic where a 'signification spiral' intrinsically escalates the supposed threat of the event which makes it appear far more dramatic. The mechanisms of 'convergence' and 'thresholds' are seen as crucial in the spiral.

Convergence occurs when two or more activities are linked so as to draw parallels between them – often implicitly. Another form of convergence is by simply listing a series of problems and speaking of them as part of a much bigger underlying problem. The problem can thus be presented as 'the tip of the iceberg'.[6] The net effect is an amplification of the 'threat-potential' to society. The process can exaggerate the degree of convergence or produce altogether spurious identities which can grossly over-simplify otherwise complex issues. It invariably singles out from a complex of different strands the most worrying element – usually the violent one. As I will suggest, the media invariably plays a central role in this process.

In the public signification of troubling events Hall *et al.* suggest there are 'thresholds' which symbolically mark out the limits of societal tolerance. The higher an event can be placed in the hierarchy of thresholds, the greater is the perceived threat to the social order, and the tougher and more automatic the response is likely to be. They identify three thresholds in the hierarchy: (1) permissiveness, (2) legality and (3) violence. As issues and groups are projected across thresholds, the easier it becomes to legitimate state intervention, often of a coercive nature. Thus if a new social problem is identified, child abuse, in which the children are seen to be in actual or potential danger from physical violence it is easier to construct a successful campaign to ensure formal state intervention and surveillance than if they are seen as primarily 'neglectful' or 'inadequate' problem families. This might be represented as follows:

Figure 4.1 *Thresholds of societal tolerance*

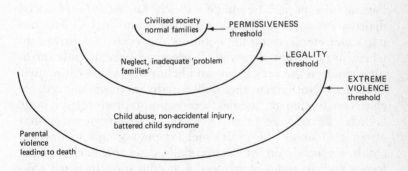

Hall *et al.* argue further that there has taken place a change in the nature of moral panics in the post-war period whereby there has been an increased 'mapping together' of previously discrete moral panics into a more general panic about the social order and the increasing level of violence throughout society, culminating in 1972–3 with a 'law and order' campaign. It thus is important to see how far the panic about child abuse was related to a more general moral panic at the time, and how far it symbolised a 'more widespread social morass' in British society in the early 1970s.[7]

Sir Keith Joseph and the Role of the DHSS

As I have argued previously[8] the issue takes on the proportions of a moral panic signifying a major social problem during the public inquiry into the death of Maria Colwell. The actual death of Maria Colwell and subsequent trial of her step-father received little publicity except in and around Brighton where she had lived.[9] It was not the death of Maria as a dramatic event in itself but the public inquiry following the decision of the Secretary of State, Sir Keith Joseph, that sensitised the public and the media to the issue of child abuse. Again however, this is only part of the story for, as Bob Holman argued, the establishment of a public inquiry does not ensure there will necessarily be such a level of social reaction and outrage.[10]

Sir Keith was the Conservative Minister of State for Social Services in the government of Edward Heath from 1970–4. During this period he made explicit his analysis of social deprivation and suggested solutions accordingly.[11] He put particular emphasis on the notion of the 'cycle of deprivation' which argued that deprived, inadequate parents pass on to their children the very habits and behaviour which cause their condition. Not given the skills, motivation or strength of character to change, the next generation reproduces the same failings. Thereby emphasis is given to welfare services that attempt to break the cycle, such as play-groups to develop children's social and intellectual skills, casework to change the habits and attitudes of parents, and education to teach children and adults the skills and role of good parenting. The priority is thus placed on developing selective welfare services to teach those in 'real' need, particularly 'problem families', rather than providing universal services that aim to improve the lot of all children and families.

The thesis seems to have had an increasingly pervasive influence at the DHSS at the time, both in the way problems were conceptualised and the way priorities were set. As Adrian Webb noted

> the concept of a 'cycle of deprivation' has come to the fore because it is a way of ordering some of the information accruing within the Department of Health and Social Security. But while the concept is partly a response to current problems it also influences the way these are perceived. Because of the Minister's interest, all kinds of issues may be fitted into this framework and it will encourage civil servants to notice problems which they may otherwise have ignored, and vice versa . . . at the very least a theme like the 'cycle of deprivation' will affect the regulation of demands and thus have an indirect impact on policy.[12]

The emphasis in social policy shifted at this time and as a result a number of new measures such as the Family Income Supplement were introduced, which consolidated the move towards more selective state welfare. The 'cycle of deprivation' thesis implied that certain families and groups required intervention because of their potential deviance rather than simply because they lacked resources, and could not actively maintain their citizenship rights. In exchange for limited material assistance such groups would have their family relationships scrutinised, primarily by social workers, in a detailed way. As a consequence there was a much greater emphasis on the surveillance and direct control of family relationships, parental attitudes and social behaviour.

Essentially the thesis and its implications for policy and practice, particularly for social workers, was paternalistic. It implied that the social control of certain groups should be central to the process of material assistance but in a precise and structured way. It tended to assume that such control was necessarily in the interests of the families and groups who received it and that there was a concensus of interests between the recipient and the state. Social workers with their skills in relationships and coordinating and negotiating the services of the welfare state should play a critical role.[13]

What I am suggesting is that the conceptualisation and

explanation of the problem of child abuse dominant in the early 1970s can be seen to closely reflect the definition of social deprivation that was articulated by the cycle of deprivation thesis. Not only was it argued that abusing families could be characterised as suffering from an underlying pathology which was passed on from generation to generation[14] but it constructed a role for social workers which was very consistent with the thesis. Benign paternalistic social work intervention was seen as crucial with such cases.

At the organisational level it is likely that the civil servants in the DHSS would have played an active role in bringing the issue of child abuse and the work of the NSPCC Battered Child Research Unit to the attention of the Minister, particularly after Joan Court, the first director of the NSPCC unit was relieved of her duties in 1971, and was subsequently appointed to the Social Work Service at the DHSS. However, the intervention of the Tunbridge Wells Study Group on Child Abuse was crucial in re-affirming Sir Keith's interest in the issue and crystallising DHSS policy.

The Tunbridge Wells Study Group on Child Abuse

The Tunbridge Wells Study Group was a 'self-appointed *ad hoc* group' who saw themselves 'not as pioneers, but as providing a link between the medical profession, the social services, the legal profession and the police'. They 'wanted to share and to discuss with other professionals the newer views which stem from Dr Henry Kempe and his team in Denver and the ideas which inspire the casework of the NSPCC'.[15] The group consisted of leading paediatricians, psychiatrists, social workers, health visitors and the police, and was chaired by Dr Alfred White Franklin, an eminent paediatrician who was instrumental in establishing the group.[16]

The British Paediatric Association had been aware of the problem of battered children for some time[17] and it seems that Dr Franklin[18] felt that while many professionals, particularly doctors, were aware of Henry Kempe's work in the USA and accepted it in principle, many did not apply the thinking and diagnosis to their particular cases. In 1971 he was asked to give advice for the defence of parents charged with neglect under Section 1 of the Children and Young Persons Act 1933. Three of the five children had died in the space of four years under extraordinary circumstances. Dr Franklin felt the indictment revealed the 'complicated but recognisable story of child abuse'. While counsel for the prosecution gave what seemed a clear account of what had happened, the judge ordered the prosecuting counsel to re-draft the indictment in accordance with the law in terms of the particular incidents which related to the case, so that there was a danger that the watered-down indictment might fail. In fact both parents were found guilty and the father was sent to prison and the mother was put on probation. However, the case made an impact on Dr Franklin as he felt it demonstrated that knowledge of child abuse was still limited and was not informing decision-making in the child care field.

He articulated his concerns in a short article in the *British Medical Journal*[19] when he argued that two changes were urgently needed: (1) a free discussion between doctors and lawyers about 'the nature of the problem'; and (2) a change in public opinion so that child abuse would be regarded as 'the result of mental illness in parents who were themselves emotionally deprived if not abused in their own childhood'. Such a conceptualisation and explanation of the problem defined it clearly in medical/social welfare terms and demonstrated how it was consistent with the 'cycle of deprivation' thesis.

It seems that Dr Franklin then liaised with Dr Christine Cooper, a consultant paediatrician in Newcastle, who had been doing some work on the problem, and both agreed it was important to try and link the medical and legal concepts and approaches. He then wrote to the DHSS and the British Paediatric Association and established that nothing was being done actively to encourage inter-professional co-operation and communication. After further consultations a small *ad hoc* working party was established, consisting of Dr Franklin, Dr Cooper, Mr E. S. Higgins (Director of Wandsworth Social Services Department), Mr Leo Goodman (Chief Clerk to the Bow Street Magistrates Court and then editor of *Clark-Hall and Morrison on Children*)[20] and Dr Michael Power (Medical Research Council Sociology Research Unit). The two central questions they were concerned with were: (1) under present law is it possible to improve the management of these families, perhaps with some change in court procedure?; and (2) if not, should the present law be changed and if so in what way and by what means?

In order to focus attention on the issue both professionally and politically, it was decided to organise a conference. This was sponsored by the Medical Education and Information Unit of the Spastics Society, though the DHSS was informed and provided some organisational and financial assistance. The conference was held at Tunbridge Wells (after which the group is called) from 15 to 18 May 1973 and was attended by Sir Keith Joseph and senior civil servants from the DHSS.[21]

Apart from focusing on the aspects which stressed the psychopathological and generational aspects of the problem, the conference also had a contribution which said there was a high association between low social class and child abuse and that there was a strong likelihood of re-battering with such families, so that 'strong consideration should be given to permanent removal of children from parental care'.[22] Another from a detective chief superintendent of the Lancashire police drew the attention of the conference to, and made the association between, child abuse and the general growth of 'violence' during the 1960s.[23] Such associations would be important if the problem of child abuse was to be seen as symptomatic of much more fundamental problems in British society. Similarly the conceptualisation of the problem had shifted away from the narrowly defined 'battered baby syndrome' to the more all-inclusive notion of 'child abuse'.

The timing of the conference is interesting for the announcement of the inquiry into the death of Maria Colwell was made on the 24 May 1973, only a few days after the conference, even though Maria had died on the 7 January 1973. It is apparent that the Tunbridge Wells Study Group played an important campaigning role in influencing events in early 1973. They had close links with the DHSS and rarely acted without informing it. It was a group of distinguished experts who gave the problem legitimacy and were able to use their links with the state agencies to ensure the minister and those with authority were made aware of the issue. It certainly seems that the work of the Tunbridge Wells Study Group on Child Abuse was crucial in re-affirming Sir Keith's interest in the problem, crystallising DHSS policy and informing the decision to set up a public inquiry 'into the care and supervision provided by local authorities and other agencies in relation to Maria Colwell and the coordination between them'.

Sir Keith clearly took an active interest and a speech made the same day as the opening of the inquiry[24] set the tone of what was to follow and demonstrated how influential had been the work of the NSPCC unit, the TWSG and Henry Kempe in the USA. He urged that more aid was needed to help battered babies and did not want the recent publicity related to battered wives to take the focus of this 'more horrible phenomenon'. 'Probably scores of children died annually after being battered and thousands more were battered who did not die'. He suggested that social workers were often reluctant to take a case to court because of insufficient evidence. He argued that bruises and minor injuries, particularly to a young child, often signified the beginning of more serious violence and warned magistrates who were asked to place a battered child in care, not to refuse to make such an order without first obtaining a social work report, as medical evidence alone was insufficient to complete the diagnosis of the battered child syndrome.

The report and resolutions of the TWSG conference were circulated to local authorities and Health Service Executive Councils in October 1973 at the same time as the opening of the inquiry, indicating the close tie up between experts and the central state. 'While the timing of Maria Colwell and Tunbridge Wells was coincidental the combination was explosive.'[25]

'The Violent Society'

It would be wrong, however, to see the panic arising from the inquiry into the death of Maria Colwell as simply arising from the more specific concerns about injury to children. It should not be seen in isolation for it connected with much wider social anxiety about the decline of the family, the growth of violence and permissiveness, and concerns about the relationship between inadequate families and welfare professionals, particularly social workers. Concerns about child abuse have been inextricably interrelated with debates about the nature and direction of social work and the accountability of social workers. These surfaced very clearly at the time of the Maria Colwell inquiry.[26]

Changes in the economic base and cultural climate of post-war Britain combined to produce a sense of 'social anxiety' amongst significant sections of the population during the late 1960s and early 1970s. The welfare-consensus established after 1945 restored the strength of finance capital in the state, and increasingly reflected the needs and interests of multi-national corporations. There was also an explicit recognition through the 1950s and 1960s of the need to involve organised labour in the running of the state and the economy. New government priorities were accepted which included the financing of social services out of general taxation, a larger public sector, and government intervention in the economy to maintain full employment. However, the real concessions were not made by finance capital and the large industrial corporations but by the small businesses.[27] Increasingly small capital found its interests being bypassed by successive governments as it was squeezed by the trade unions on the one side and large industrial corporations on the other. There was an increasing despair amongst traditional middle class groups at the failure of their former political allies to represent their interests and recognise their fears. Tied in with this was a growing disenchantment with the obvious commercialism and affluence of the period which was seen as undermining further the traditional virtues. Such disenchantment was particularly evident in the general reaction to the feeling that there had been a growth in 'permissiveness' in the 1960s. Such feelings had a tangible basis in reality as far as many were concerned.

Apart from a number of legislative innovations which were regarded as shifting legal definitions of morality in a permissive direction,[28] there was a steady increase in the rates of divorce, delinquency and violent crime all of which suggested that there was a reduced commitment in society to the traditional virtues. Institutions and values which were thought to be fundamental to the 'English way of life'[29] were considered to be under attack, particularly from misguided liberals who were increasingly leading the country astray. The rise of the women's movement at this time tended to reinforce such fears and provided both an economic and ideological threat to the more traditional values and forms of personal life. The central institution which was felt to be 'at risk' in such circumstances, and which required defending, was the family. It is this central concern for the family which helps us to understand the growth of a number of moral campaigns in the late 1960s[30] and which is at the root of the growing social anxiety amongst traditionalist middle class groups at the time. The production of 'social anxiety' amongst these groups resulted in a predisposition to the use of scapegoats on to whom disturbing experiences could be condensed. Such scapegoats have attributed to them the role of causing the various elements of disorganisation and dislocation which produced the social anxiety in the first place. In particular the traditional values such as hard work, individual initiative, respectability, responsibility, honesty, delayed gratification and social discipline were felt to be under attack. Such values are inextricably connected with an over-riding concern about the family, where it is thought that moral and social compulsions are generated and primary socialisation is carried out. Thus fears about the breakdown of the social order invariably focus on the family, and those who have a responsibility for ensuring its 'proper' functioning.

If the family is seen to be under assault then it is the child who suffers most, for children are especially vulnerable from exposure to permissiveness and are seen as the 'innocent victims' of social indiscipline. Thus the problems of violence, delinquency, mental illness, and so on increase as a direct result of broken or inadequate homes. The changes in legislation and societal attitudes during the 1960s were seen to encourage promiscuity and undermine the family.

Such feelings could also be located in sections of the traditional working class, for many of the post-war changes seemed to erode the patterns of life and community supports of traditional working class culture.[31] There was a particular concern that the removal of well-established kinship and neighbourhood ties might isolate families, particularly if they were housed on a new estate or in a tower block. It was thus feared that the family in such circumstances had been under-mined by the withering of its traditional supports.

Increasingly such concerns became influential in changing the direction of political debate in the mid to late 1960s and found their most explicit expression in the growth of the New Right. While this had a direct impact upon the Conservative Party there was a populist dimension which expressed many of the fears of many traditional working class supporters of the Labour Party, particularly about immigration.[32] The New Right stood for a new form of social organisation very similar to nineteenth-century liberalism, and was based on a belief in the market as the fairest and most efficient means of resource allocation, and a commitment to individual freedom. How-ever, while it called for a reduced role for the state it demanded a strong state, particularly where it was considered that 'permissiveness' had increased social disorder.

Increasingly during the 1960s we see the policies and value premises of the liberal New Right becoming evident within the Conservative Party. The dominating and escalating issue of British politics since the early 1960s has been the deteriorating performance of the economy as shown particularly by growing inflation, the falling rate of profit and the poor balance of payments.[33] As the policies established under the welfare consensus (and accepted by large elements of the Conservative Party in the late 1950s and early 1960s) were found wanting, the party moved increasingly to the right, spurred on by the New Right and their supporters in the constituencies. The failure of the welfare consensus in the economic sphere was also thought to be reflected in failures in the social and cultural spheres, where permissiveness was seen to be becoming increasingly pervasive. Decline in both the economic and social institutions was felt to require stern measures.

Violence was the aspect of permissiveness most feared, for it was assumed that an increase in violence was inevitable if traditional values and discipline were relaxed. As a conse-quence there was a growing pre-occupation in the rank and file of the Conservative Party with violent crime, law and order and the decline of the family.[34] The Heath government came to office in June 1970 after a long 'law and order' campaign during which Lord Hailsham commented 'the theme is the safety of the citizen as he lives in his own home with his wife and children, as he goes about the streets, as he attends his places of amusement.[35] It is perhaps not surprising that the social reaction to child abuse in the early 1970s should be so forceful, as it coalesced fears relating to both violence and the decline of the family.

The Heath government initially tried to be qualitatively different from Wilsonian 'voluntary restraint', and was more in line with the sentiments of the liberal New Right than traditional conservatism, placing an increased reliance on discipline and the law in the social, cultural and economic spheres, to re-establish the traditional virtues as a springboard for growth.

By 1972 the sense of 'crisis' no longer seemed fanciful or marginal, for Britain seemed to be entering a period of major economic, political and social upheaval.[36] Increasingly anxieties were being centred on violence – the final threshold in Hall *et al.*'s signification spiral. Once society becomes obsessed by violence as Britain seems to have done by 1972/73 it becomes the common denominator which converts all threats into 'the threat', all panics into 'the panic'.

Chibnall[37] has traced the emergence of 'The Violent Society' as a pre-eminent theme in newspaper coverage on law and order and wider political debate. Paralleling the analysis of Stuart Hall and his colleagues he argues that this results from the convergence of a criminal violence theme, originating in the mid-sixties, and a political violence theme which developed a few years later. He identifies the late 1960s and early 1970s as a period of law and order crisis coming to a head in 1972/73 (see Figure 4.2).

The category of 'violence' is both potentially all-encompassing and ideologically very powerful, so that it is very difficult to argue against. This is particularly so when the victim is seen as 'innocent', as in the case of children. The case of Maria Colwell provided a focus for the expression of a range of social anxieties concerned with the collapse of the 'English way of life', the growth in violence, the decline in individual and social discipline and morality, and the need to re-establish the traditional family.

Figure 4.2   *The Violent Society: convergence of themes*[38].

Criminal violence theme   Political violence theme

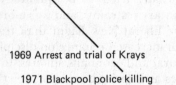

1965 Growth of organised crime
     Moors Murders

1966 Shepherds Bush killings
1967 Richardsons 'Torture Trial'

                                    1968–9 Student demonstrations
                                           Escalation of conflict
                                           in Northern Ireland

     1969 Arrest and trial of Krays   1970 Political bombings/IRA
       1971 Blackpool police killing   1971 Angry Brigade
                    1972 Violent picketing

            The violent society theme established

                    1972–3 Mugging

            1973 – IRA bombing campaign in England

Social Work, Social Democracy and the Family

The newly created Social Services Departments had been in
existence for about two years and there was increasing disquiet
about their role and level of operation and the activities of
social workers. It was increasingly being suggested that the
quality of social work had deteriorated, especially in the area
of child care and social work with families. The inquiry into
the death of Maria Colwell provided an opportunity to explore
such issues and give social workers a jolt.[39]

While the practice of social work has a long history, it was
the reorganisation of Social Services Departments following
Seebohm that consolidated and established it as a central part
of the state's activity. It took place very much within the
parameters of Keynesian social democracy and can be seen as
part of the re-assessment that was taking place at that time of
the deficiencies of the welfare state established after 1945.[40] It
was argued that while the welfare state was largely successful

and that the majority of the population had benefited there were still identifiable gaps, particularly amongst the elderly and children, and that this arose from two interdependent sources.[41] It was argued that there was a growing bureaucratic inefficiency between the various state welfare services such that co-ordination was difficult. This was reinforced by the often complex procedures required for receiving benefits. Secondly, there was a section of the population who were so deprived and inadequate that they could not utilise the welfare benefits and at the same time generated a disproportionate number of individual, and social problems such as delinquency, child neglect, mental illness, financial debts etc.[42] These explanations were fore-runners of the 'cycle of deprivation' thesis.

The role outlined for the new service was one of co-ordinating aspects of other welfare services and trying to improve the functioning of certain families by using social work skills such as casework. It was established as the 'fifth social service'[43] with the family and the community as its *raison d'etre*. It would provide the personalised, humanistic dimension to the welfare state, the primary tool being the worker's personality and use of relationships. Thus the new service, and the profession which would be its hallmark, was to be flexible, liberal and perhaps permissive in philosophy and approach.

The construction of the new service and the establishment of a new group of welfare 'experts' took place with little public support or understanding. It was symptomatic of the attempts at the time to find personalised and technical solutions to social problems and was established via the pressure group activities of social workers themselves and the alliances forged between certain senior civil servants, politicians, professionals and social science academics.[44] While it may have been intended otherwise the 'fifth social service' was constructed in such a way, in most areas, that it provided few opportunities for active control or participation by consumers or the wider community and quickly became bureaucratic, impervious and controlled by experts.

The establishment of social work and social service departments could thus be seen as the most recent and obvious manifestations of the post-war social democratic welfare state and its adjunct the 'rehabilitative ideal', just at the time when such developments were being subjected to growing social and critical scrutiny which were focused in the rise of the New Right.

While not coherently argued at the time the critique of social work was expressed along two dimensions. It was increasingly argued that the social services, as with any state activity, generated higher taxes, increased budget deficits, acted as a disincentive to work and encouraged a bloated class of unproductive workers. An influential account of this argument was presented by Bacon and Eltis in 1975.[45] Local authorities and central government had expanded their activities by 53 per cent and 14 per cent respectively in the decade up to 1972. 'Armies of teachers, social workers and civil servants' were putting pressure on the productive sector, causing exports to fall and investment to be diverted. The opportunities of the 'technological revolution' of the 1960s had been wasted, according to Bacon and Eltis, by the enormous political commitment to the public services. This had established a cycle of increased government action, higher taxes, rising unemployment and falling investment and profitability.

Secondly, and perhaps more forceably, it was argued that social work encourages soft, 'namby pamby' attitudes to deviance, fecklessness and the undeserving. It does not simply drain resources but undermines national and individual responsibility and morality. The activities of social workers were potentially dangerous.[46]

Such arguments were appealing because they connected with much working class and traditional middle class experience of the social democratic welfare services. It recognised certain social anxieties and experiences and drew them into a critique of social work and social services departments. The inquiry into the death of Maria Colwell provided the opportunity whereby such arguments could be articulated and in which the media had a crucial role to play. The highly publicised 'mistakes' and 'errors' of welfare professionals, particularly social workers, in relation to cases of child abuse provided powerful ammunition for the 'traditionalist' assault on the 'soft liberalism' of the welfare agencies.

The Media and Social Problems

Before providing a more detailed analysis of the role of the media at the time of the Maria Colwell inquiry I want to make some general observations about the media and social problems. In modern industrial society the media has a central role in mediating information and forming public opinion. The media tells people about what they do not directly experience and renders otherwise remote happenings observable and meaningful.[47] Certainly if an issue is to be established in modern industrial society as a social problem requiring state intervention, the role of the media is crucial. Since the early 1970s social workers, and the personal social services more generally, have shown a considerable amount of interest in the media and many have felt it has played a significant role in changing the way they experience their practice and relate to the wider society. Essentially many social workers feel that they and the work they are involved in receive very rough handling, particularly by the popular press.[48] The association of social workers with the problem of child abuse and the case of Maria Colwell in particular has been central to this development. For example, in 1974 Chris Andrews, the then General Secretary of the British Association of Social Workers reacted to press coverage of the Maria Colwell inquiry in the following terms:

> It has at times seemingly become a witchhunt seeking out those who could be blamed. If individuals or authorities have been negligent it is of course right that their negligence is exposed. But if society is seeking a scapegoat, the vulnerable position of the social worker has been all too apparent. . .
> Apart from the individuals who have been pilloried, social work itself has at times appeared to be on trial. Basic assumptions have been questioned, as has the legal and judicial framework in which much social work is practised.[49]

However, there is very little research available on the way social work[50] and child abuse are presented in the media. More generally, the role and the influence of the mass media on particular issues and social[51] problems is a relatively unexplored territory.

In their analysis of the mugging problem in Britain in 1972–73 researchers at the Centre for Contemporary Cultural

Studies at Birmingham University have developed three models for analysing the relationship between what they call the societal control culture and the news media.[52]

The first type of relationship is where the control culture is the primary definer of the problem and the media simply reproduces these definitions. Thus news items are based on the reproductions of primary definitions and explanations presented by the control culture, for instance the police, the judiciary, the Home Office. In the case of child abuse prior to 1973, as we have seen, any mention of the problem in the media essentially reproduced the definitions of the experts in the field, particularly the NSPCC Research Unit, Henry Kempe and his colleagues in Denver, and certain paediatricians and forensic pathologists. In many respects we can see that during this period these moral entrepreneurs and agencies were making particular efforts to publicise the problem via the media. The media took a relatively passive role and never campaigned on the issue in any independent way. On occasions after a specific deviant event the media might go to the 'experts' for their comment, data, definition and explanation but this hardly happened in the period before Maria Colwell:

$$deviant\ event \rightarrow \genfrac{}{}{0pt}{}{control\ culture\ as}{primary\ definers} \rightarrow media\ reproducers$$

However, once the primary definitions are in play, the media is able to transform them into its own language, based on its assumption about its audience, and place it in the existing public imagery: 'This transformation into a public idiom thus gives the item an *external public reference*, and validity in images and connotations already sedimented in the stock of knowledge which the paper and its public share.'[53] In the process of transforming the issue into popular imagery the issue becomes objectified so that it appears far more as a real social problem which is quite independent of the experts as primary definers. In the process the media can take on the guise of not only representing 'public opinion' but being 'public opinion' and can campaign on issues on that basis. Certainly editorials can claim to speak and campaign on behalf of the people – perhaps the silent majority. In this relationship the media can be seen not just to reproduce the definitions of primary definers but to produce independently the news, and in the process transform and objectify the issue into a real social problem that the general public is concerned about and demands action. The events and developments around the Maria Colwell inquiry can be seen to reflect such a role for the media which has been maintained ever since. The media actively helps set the agenda:

$$deviant\ event \rightarrow \frac{control\ culture\ as}{primary\ definers} \rightarrow media\ as\ producers \binom{assumed}{audience}$$

Finally, it is suggested that it is possible for the circle to be closed.

> Once the media have spoken in their voice, on behalf of the inaudible public, the primary definers can use the media's statements and claims as legitimations (magically, without any visible connection) for their actions and statements, by claiming press – and via the press, public – support. In turn, the ever attentive media reproduce the Control Culture statements, thus completing the magical circle, with such effect that it is no longer possible to tell who first began the process; each legitimates the other in turn.[54]

$$\frac{deviant}{event} \rightarrow \frac{control\ culture\ as}{primary\ definers} \rightarrow \frac{media\ as}{producers} \rightarrow \frac{control\ culture}{as\ reproducers} \rightarrow \frac{media\ as}{reproducers}$$

It is not being suggested that newspapers, and the media generally, distort reality in random ways, rather that they create the news in a systematic fashion which exhibits patterned regularities governed by a consistent set of interests, practices and professional relationships. According to Chibnall there are two basic components in the system by which the press identifies and interprets the news.[55] First there is a framework of concepts and values which classifies events into story types, such as political, crime, welfare, human interest, and shapes the meaning of the event, implicitly defining it in a number of ways. Perhaps the central background assumption is the consensual nature of society whereby it is assumed that there is essentially only one perspective on events, which is informed by the central value system: everyone knows what these events look like and what constitutes them, so that there is no real dispute or disagreement. However, because the media is presenting events which are outside most people's everyday experience it not only defines what are significant events but, implicity, how these might be interpreted.

The second component is more distinctly professional and is supplied primarily by the professional imperatives of journalism. These professional imperatives constitute what is seen as newsworthy events and is structured by an orientation which defines events as abnormal. Chibnall identifies eight professional imperatives which implicitly guide the construction of news stories: immediacy; dramatisation; personalisation; simplification; titillation; conventionalism; structured access; novelty.

Immediacy underlines that news is about what has just happened so that 'it is centrally concerned with the present rather than the past, change rather than inertia, and events rather than long-term processes'. As a consequence large elements of events are left out and are taken out of an historical or social context which might give them meaning to the participants. This event orientation is reinforced by the emphasis on the dramatic which attempts to make an impact on the reader. Concrete events and actions are related at the cost of any broader discussion. In the process many events are personalised, with a concentration on a few significant individuals rather than on any wider social processes. The presentation of events simplifies reality so that subtleties of interpretation and shades of grey are glossed over so that social situations are presented in terms of absolutes – good versus bad, moral versus immoral. This can be furthered by offering stories in a titillating, alluring, but forbidden way.

However, to make sense of seemingly new events they are situated in commonly accepted meaning and language so that stories appear as objective and understood. In order to legitimate this attempt at producing objectivity, events are often 'grounded in the authoritative pronouncement of experts in the fields covered by the stories', as we have seen. In the process there is a systematic tendency to structure the access of the definitions and explanations of events in terms of those in privileged institutional positions. Invariably the medical profession, the police, the judiciary, civil service, ministers, have such privileged access.

Finally, Chibnall argues, there is one imperative which introduces an element of randomness into newspaper accounts, for it is always important that where possible novelty be created by demonstrating the differentness or newness in the item which demands attention from its audience. This can foster speculation which is barely substantiated by the evidence.

The consequence of such professional imperatives and the concepts and values that inform them is that:

> They promote a peculiarly restricted mode of understanding by signifying the definitional characteristics of a phenomenon and its causation by reference to highly selective aspects of the phenomenon. This process 'works', it is suggested, because the aspects selected are ones to which most readers can easily relate.[56]

While each newspaper's professional sense of what is newsworthy will vary according to its organisation, history and view of what its audience[57] is like, the nature of news production and the processes involved whereby an event is defined as newsworthy severely limit the range of views expressed:

> The 'consensus of values' which is so deeply embedded in all the forms of public language is more limited than the variety of the forms of public 'language in use' would suggest. Their publics, however distinct, are assumed to fall within that very broad spectrum of 'reasonable men' and readers are addressed broadly in those terms.[58]

It is important to see how the media's role and relationship to the issue of child abuse shifted at the time of Maria Colwell and the impact and implications this had.

The Media and Maria Colwell

For some time the press had been concerned to try and improve the rights of foster parents and the law relating to adoptions.[59] There had been a campaign to support the claims of foster parents, particularly where it appeared that natural parents did not have the interests of the child at heart. It was argued that both foster parents and often the children were unjustly treated by the emphasis on the 'blood-tie'.

In the late 1960s a number of cases received publicity where the parents had demanded the return of their children when the foster parents had looked after them for many years. There was a case reported in Lancashire of Christine, aged 6, taken from her 'mother' and the foster mother was reported as saying, 'we've done everything possible for her – I can't describe my feelings' (*Daily Mail* 25 August 1967). Christine left with her mother whom she had not seen since she was 5 months old. Similar cases in Buckinghamshire and Monmouthshire (see for example *Western Mail* 10 March 1967 and *Daily Mail* 17 August 1967) received publicity, and in all cases the press supported the foster parents in their claims. Similar sympathy for foster parents was also aroused in 1971 (*Daily Express* 15 March 1971) when a child aged 8 was allowed to choose between her parents and the foster mother with whom she had lived since she was 6 months old. The child eventually went to her mother. The death of Maria Colwell demonstrated just what might happen to a child removed from loving foster parents to be placed back with uncaring natural or step-parents.

In 1972 the Houghton Committee (Departmental Committee on the Adoption of Children) had reported and made recommendations, which if implemented would have considerably changed the law, policy and practice on adoption and fostering. It would have improved the rights of foster parents, attempted to ensure continuity for the child and, the longer the child was in care, limited the control exercised by the natural parents. However, the report had not been discussed in Parliament and it seemed unlikely that new legislation would be introduced in the near future. The inquiry into the death of Maria Colwell provided an opportunity to campaign on such issues.

Early in 1973 the inquiry into the death of Graham Bagnall sensitised the press to the issue.[60] *The Times* reported the inquiries on the death by Shropshire County Council and Shrewsbury Group Hospital Management Committee (see *The*

Times, 5 February and 29 April 1973). It expressed dissatisfaction as it feared the internal enquiries might have led to some kind of 'whitewash'. The press reflected the major conclusion of the inquiries that there was a lack of communication between the agencies concerned and inadequate management of the case, particularly by the Social Services Department.

However it was the inquiry into the death of Maria Colwell that really prompted press interest in the problem and encouraged the press to campaign on the issue in a far more independent way, rather than simply reproducing the efforts of the primary definers.

Apart from reporting that the inquiry was being set up (on 25 May 1973), *The Times* took little interest in the case of Maria Colwell until the inquiry opened. Between 10 October, when the inquiry opened, and 7 December, when it closed, the issue attracted over 320 paragraphs of space, most of which was concerned with reporting a blow by blow account of the inquiry. There was reporting or comment of the case on forty three days during this period. The first entry announced that the inquiry was opening in a twenty-one paragraph report with the headline 'Thirty Complaints Of Ill Treatment Before Girl Died' and included a photograph of the dead girl. The publication of the final report also attracted considerable newspaper space (see *The Times*, 5 September 1974) including 112 paragraphs of leader comment, summary of the report and related issues.

While the press now began to reconstruct the issue in a more independent way the primary definers, or experts, were still central characters. Because the inquiry was reported on every day of its sitting in some detail it meant that the reports and evidence from the professionals directly concerned and the expert witnesses gained considerable coverage. In some respects the inquiry, together with the heightened sensitivity of the media – the press in particular – provided the platform whereby the issues, definitions and explanations which had been available for some time received massive exposure. As will be evident, however, the nature of the case and the way it was presented provided a more severe reaction which demanded a more authoritative role with families than was originally suggested in the NSPCC Battered Child Research Unit approach. The media tended to over-simplify, sensationalise and personalise the problem.

Even in *The Times* it was the dramatic, immediate impact aspects which grabbed the headlines: 'Girl Was Like A Skeleton, Neighbour Tells Inquiry' (11 October 1973); 'Girl's Bones "Sticking Out"' (12 October 1973); 'Children Screaming From Girl's Window, PC says' (13 October 1973). Increasingly however, the headlines become personalised around the role and activities of the social worker in the case, so that the presentation in the media became increasingly associated with an inquiry into social work. The more the inquiry developed the more the headlines implied that the social worker was responsible for what happened. *The Times* headlines include: 'Social Worker Made Error Of Judgement' (3 November); 'Social Worker Booed At Brighton Enquiry' (6 November); 'Social Workers Wrong, QC Tells Inquiry Into The Death Of Maria Colwell' (8 November); 'Social Worker Accepted Bruises' (13 November); 'Social Worker's Job "Not At Risk" After Took Little Interest In the Child's Death' (14 November). A number of themes are articulated and related to each other: that the problem of battered babies is an identifiable syndrome; that social workers and social service departments are the central responsible agency; that there needs to be a less sentimental attitude towards natural parents and the 'blood-tie', and that there needs to be a change in the law relating to fostering and adoption. An example appeared in *The Times* on 19 October under the headline, 'Battered Baby Expert Tells Of Child's Injury'.

Dr James Cameron 'an authority on the battered baby syndrome' told the inquiry that sending the child back to a resentful mother and a violent drunken step-father was an 'open invitation to a case of child abuse'. When asked if the GP who visited the child a month before she died would have been expected to take some action, Dr Cameron said it depended whether the GP had been given all the background information available to social workers: 'It is easy to be wise in retrospect but these were classic features one would find in a case of child abuse. But a GP, who might only see one case of child abuse a year, might not have such a low threshold of suspicion as I have.' This report headlines the problem 'battered babies' (to describe a 7 year old child), which is far more likely to catch the public imagination than is 'child abuse', suggests it is a specific medical condition, and at the same time directs the responsibility for its prevention to social workers not doctors. The report thus manages to publicise the problem of 'battered babies', criticise social workers and suggest certain people should not be parents, all in one go.

These themes were reinforced on many occasions during the reporting of the inquiry. On 15 November under the headline 'Decision To Return Child To Her Mother Was A Very Dangerous Thing To Do'. *The Times* reported that Dr A. White Franklin (Chairman, Tunbridge Wells Study Group) said of the social worker's decision to return Maria to her mother, that all the signs were negative and likened the process of returning the child to her mother to an 'organ transplant in a human body', with all the same risks. This again stresses the medical conceptualisation of the problem and lays the responsibility for its prevention with social workers.

Throughout the inquiry the paper introjected articles of comment. In a 22 paragraph article entitled 'A Better Safety Net For Battered Babies' (9 November), David Leigh stressed the weakness of social work practice and policies towards child care based on the 'blood-tie' and felt that a debate on the Houghton Report was urgently needed. He also felt that there should be a greater coordination. In a leader article on 12 November the paper argued that even though they have the powers, social workers do not remove children from their home and try to obtain 'care orders', because their thinking sees such action very much as a last resort. It argued that the case of Maria Colwell highlighted many of the problems in this area and 'spurs' action on the Houghton Report. Then on 16 November in the 'Science Report! Psychiatry', under the title 'Battered Babies', the research by Dr Selwyn Smith from Birmingham University is referred to.[61] In particular the article emphasised that 'in many cases of the "battered baby syndrome" further serious injury can only be prevented by permanent removal from parental care'.

These themes were pursued in numerous letters and were brought together again in an article by David Leigh, on 8 December ('Many Reforms likely after Colwell') that marked the end of the inquiry. The article concluded that the inquiry had given enormous publicity to the problem of 'baby battering' in the country and given new impetus to David Owen's private member's 'Children's Bill' which was based on the recommendations of the Houghton Report.

While it is evident that *The Times* gave the inquiry prodigious exposure other newspapers seem to have campaigned even more actively. The role of *The Sunday Times* is particularly interesting. On 11 November 1973 the paper launched a crusade entitled 'The Battered Babies Scandal'. This edition was dominated by the issue and included a lengthy front page article, and two further articles that virtually covered the centre pages, 128 paragraphs in all. It also printed photographs of Maria, two other children who suffered similar fates, Maria's mother, step-father, the family home, a neighbour, the social worker and the foster-parents mourning at the graveside.

The front page report is head-lined 'Two Babies Are Battered To Death Each Day' (a figure presented by Dr Hall at the Tunbridge Wells Conference, based on research at Preston Infirmary and extrapolated to the whole country).[62] It outlined four other cases where children had died in similar circumstances to Maria Colwell and said: 'And even these five cases are only the tip of a major national scandal that is slowly emerging from the files of professional workers concerned with the problems of battered babies and child abuse.' It goes on to state that:

> the scale of the tragedy has not yet emerged ... Urging greater public awareness, Sir Keith Joseph told *The Sunday Times* last week that although much was being done it was a delicate and difficult problem which could not be solved by relying on punitive action against parents – greater stress is also likely to be given to the importance of battered children not being returned to their parents until home conditions are subjected to penetrating social study.

It is also said that Sir Keith handed *The Sunday Times* a study of 29 men imprisoned at Brixton for killing their children.[63] 'One of the most disturbing findings ... is the lack of guaranteed security for abused children once their plight has come to light ... eight men in the Brixton cases were being visited by social agencies because of child abuse when they killed their children.' The article concluded that:

> In the light of the Maria Colwell inquiry, calls for a more determined drive to save the battered child are expected to build up. John Cronnin, Labour MP for Loughborough, who raised the question in the commons last week, said yesterday: 'All the time we seem to be afraid to hurt the feelings of parents and doctors. The situation is now too serious for that.'

This forthright campaign by *The Sunday Times* was further reflected in the other two articles. One provided a detailed account of the events leading up to Maria's death, while the other levelled the charge that society was failing to protect such children which, it was argued, was a 'National Scandal'. Under the headline 'Let Us End The Killings' the work of the NSPCC and Dr Henry Kempe was quoted to argue that it was possible to 'prevent' child abuse, and a 'Five-Point Plan Of Action To Save Lives' was recommended: This included: (1) enforcement by the DHSS and the Home Office of swifter and more coordinated action to prevent child battery; (2) Statutory notification of all child abuse cases; (3) a new legal deal for children, giving them independent representation before the courts and full rights to police protection; (4) more money for voluntary agencies – and more social support for families in stress; (5) greater willingness to terminate parental rights where love and care are impossible. And concluded: 'If the graves of Maria, Graham, Peter and Samantha show the way to a new deal for Britain's other battered children, their cruelly shortened lives will have served some purpose.'

This dramatic presentation was continued in the next three editions under the banner of 'The Battered Baby Scandal' which used a smiling picture of Maria Colwell as its emblem. On 18 November under the headline of 'Children's Rights Law Urged', the paper reported that 'following *The Sunday Times* disclosure that 700 children are being battered to death in their own homes every year ... a new bill of Children's Rights is likely to be presented to Parliament early next year.' This was David Owen's private members bill based on the Houghton Report. The article also reported the findings of Selweyn Smith's research based on 214 battered babies[64] which urged that there should be strong consideration of the permanent removal of children from parents who appeared unlikely to respond to treatment. The same edition included 22 paragraphs of correspondence under the title 'Problem Parents Should Lose Adult Rights'. The letters were continued the following week (26 paragraphs) under the heading of 'Victim's View of Cruel Parents'. There were further reader's letters on 2 December 1973, 10 February 1974 and 17 February 1974. However, on 27 January 1974 the paper reported an advance interview with Sir Keith Joseph entitled 'Battered Babies: New Guidelines': 'The new advice will stress that the aim should be to rehabilitate the family where practicable . . . but cases where this is not possible need to be identified. In those cases . . . the child, and not the child in the family, is to be the over-riding focus of attention.' It is thus quite apparent that *The Sunday Times* maintained a determined campaign both during and immediately following the public inquiry into the death of Maria Colwell.

A more general review indicates that similar campaigns were being carried out in other sections of the media during 1973 and early 1974.[65] There were also important articles in the popular press (see particularly *Daily Mirror* 16 November 1973), and a continual radio and television coverage (see particularly the Panorama programme of 22 April 1974 on 'Battered Babies').

While the level of the campaign dropped somewhat in the spring and early summer of 1974, it was resurrected again just before and after the publication of the Report of the Colwell Inquiry. On 5 September 1974 *The Times* gave enormous coverage to the publication of the Report, which said that Maria Colwell's death had not been prevented primarily because of the lack of coordination amongst the agencies concerned. Even so, the front page headline pointed out that 'Children's Advocate Is Proposed After Report On Maria Colwell Case', and the report quotes Mrs Castle (Secretary of State) as saying she wanted social workers to place less stress on the 'blood-tie'. Altogether the edition included over 120 paragraphs related to the Report.

The main headline in *The Sunday Times* of 1 September 1974 was also devoted to a pre-publication summary of the Report ('Colwell Verdict Too Many Deaf Ears'). The article, said that while 'critics of the changes in social service training following the Seebholm report in 1968 will find support for their view that social workers should be less generalist and more able to specialise the report proposes only small legal changes' and for that reason seems an 'anti-climax'.

Conclusions

In this chapter I have argued that it was the inquiry into the death of Maria Colwell late in 1973 that was the crucial event in establishing the issue as a major social problem and for providing the catalyst for the rapid emergence of a 'moral panic'. The efforts of the Tunbridge Wells Study Group, Sir Keith Joseph and the DHSS, while central to this process, were also dependent upon and fed into significant changes in the socio-political climate at the time. There was evident a growing social anxiety about the issues of violence and the family as expressed by attempts to re-establish a return to more traditional values and modes of family and social life. Central to the panic about child abuse was a growing disquiet about the growth, role and activities of social workers who were held centrally responsible, particularly by the media, for the death of Maria Colwell. The case symbolised many of the fears of the time and provided an opportunity to do something about them.

In the process however, the nature of the problem and the best way of controlling it seems to have been modified. I have suggested that prior to 1968 there was still a significant element of the control culture that located the problem on the 'borderline between medicine and the law'. But, increasingly after 1968, under the influence of the NSPCC Battered Child Research Unit the problem was conceptualised squarely in terms of a medical and social welfare problem. As a consequence the act of abuse was given far less importance than the fact that it was a 'symptom of family breakdown' and that the family needed treatment and rehabilitation. It was increasingly suggested that the parents themselves had been the subject of similar deprivations in their own childhood and that they required a transfusion of mothering. It was thus argued that in most circumstances treatment should take place with the whole family and with the child at home. Even when recourse was taken to the powers of the juvenile court this was seen as part of the rehabilitative, treatment process. After 1972, while the debate still took place within the medical social welfare model, increasing emphasis was placed on removing the child from home and putting less stress on the 'blood-tie'. Social work intervention should be 'authoritative, intrusive and insistent'.[66]

I have argued that the media played a crucial role and increasingly campaigned in an independent way. While I have concentrated on presenting material from *The Times* and *Sunday Times* it is evident that press coverage generally increased rapidly between 1972 and 1973. It is now apparent that the press has given far more coverage to public inquiries than they ever do to the criminal court proceedings that may have preceded them. In the process the central focus had been on the culpability of the professionals involved, and a dramatic, simplified and personalised image of child abuse has been presented.

It has been suggested[67] that the moral panic in the press in Britain was at its most intense between 1973 and 1976 but that this had subsided considerably by the end of the decade. However the issue was by then so well established that the main themes of the panic have continued to reappear at very regular intervals since.

The case of Maria Colwell has continued to provide the bench-mark for the way such cases are presented in the media. Golding and Middleton[68] have commented on some recent examples of the way the popular press has presented the issues, pointing up the way they provide the opportunity for social work to be attacked. In 1980 alone they note the following headlines: 'Malcolm Died As He Lived. Freezing Cold, Starving And Surrounded By Social Workers' (*Daily Mirror*, 16 January); 'Social Shirkers' (leader, *Daily Mail*, 21 February); 'Early Victim Of Do-Nothing Welfare Team' (*Daily Mail*, 21 February); 'Welfare Woman in Row over a Dead Baby' (*Daily Mail*, 4 November).

More recently press headlines of the inquiry into the death of two year old Lucie Gates reported on 13 November 1982 included: 'Clear Signs Of Ill Treatment Ignored, says report: Failures That Let Lucie Gates Die' (*Daily Telegraph*); 'Lucie: The Tiny Victim Of A Sorry Saga Of Blunders' (*Daily Express*); 'Doomed Girl "Failed" By Welfare Worker' (*Daily Mail*); 'Council Slammed Over Lucie' (*Sun*); 'Why "Little Angel" Lucie Need Not Have Died' (*Daily Mirror*). Incapsulating the comments Auberon Waugh wrote:

> The final lesson of Lucie Gates must be that since the welfare services are unable, with the best will in the world, to do anything about the various imperfections in human nature which led to the tragedy, they should not try to assume such responsibilities. Their role should be reduced rather than increased.[69]

As Golding and Middleton argue:

> That such children suffer from ineffectual intervention by incompetent social workers is a common theme in these cases ... social workers represent in human form the excessive intervention of the state in people's lives, and also the naivety of the bureacratic mind ... thus social workers are too numerous, do not act when they should, and are largely unnecessary.[70]

5

Policy Developments and Practice Issues

In the last chapter I analysed how the social reaction to the case of Maria Colwell acted to rapidly publicise the problem throughout British society so that it took on the proportions of a moral panic and major social problem requiring state intervention. I now want to outline how this process has been consolidated, reinforced and formalised in a variety of interrelated policy developments.

Perhaps more critically it will be important to analyse the impact of the moral panic on the experience and everyday practice of welfare workers – particularly social workers. For it is now clear that the problem has had important implications for the direction and practice of social work with families and children and the priorities of departments. Investigations into the workload and tasks of the fieldworker demonstrate that work with children and families is now taken for granted as the top priority.[1] The balance of caseloads and the priority allocated to 'statutory' work reflects this. Not only are child care cases, 'NAI' in particular, seen as being more demanding, but there is a pervasive fear of 'a Maria Colwell happening here'. It is not simply a professional anxiety for the well-being of certain children that is evident, but a fear of being found wanting and called to account for any 'mistakes' or 'wrong' decisions.

Public Inquiries

While the public inquiry into the death of Maria Colwell must be seen as the critical event which spurred rapid recognition of and consolidation of the problem of child abuse, a series of subsequent inquiries by DHSS, or the Local Authorities and Area Health Authorities concerned have served to underline many of the issues already highlighted.[2] Such reports, now over twenty in total, are symptomatic of the great sensitivity that has surrounded the problem and have demonstrated that Colwell was not an isolated scandal but simply the tip of a much bigger iceberg. These inquiries have played a crucial role in the development of public and political concern, and have provided the impetus for stimulating administrative and management procedures for identifying and handling cases of child abuse. Their impact in helping to usher in changes in policy and practice in this area have probably been more significant than if substantive pieces of legislation had been put on the statute book as happened in numerous other countries.

The inquiries themselves have almost without exception, taken a limited approach to the issues. They have tended to focus on three main tasks: to set out the central 'facts' of the case as they saw them; to critically outline the role and functions of the agencies concerned and the nature and quality of their relationships; and to produce a set of recommendations for future professional action. Little discussion has taken place about the causes or nature of the problem, as this has been assumed to be either self-evident or of little significance. As a consequence the work of certain experts has been taken on board somewhat uncritically. The prime concern throughout has been to institute a range of practices and policies which would advance the 'management' of the problem in an individualised way. The principal policy conclusions have been the prime need for better 'identification' of children at risk from abuse and improved methods of inter-agency and inter-professional coordination.

The argument presented is usually in terms that sufficient 'signs' or worrying factors were in evidence prior to the major abuse, and that the social workers, as they were the primary statutory agency involved, could/should have acted upon such knowledge in order to protect the child. Often the retrospective case histories present a scenario whereby it appears that there were sufficient potential abuse factors in evidence for the eventual fatality to have been avoided. Olive Stevenson in her minority report to the Maria Colwell Inquiry Report, suggests however that the identification and interpretation of such 'facts' is not nearly so straightforward or clear-cut.[3] Perhaps the major exception to the majority of inquiry reports was that on Wayne Brewer, which was unable to find any major faults in the administration, communication, record-keeping or adherence to laid-down policies or procedures.[4]

The Central Government Response

While the series of inquiries into child abuse cases had the effect of further sensitising public opinion and the state to the problem, it would be too simple to see this as a straightforward reflexive response which had the cumulative effect of reinforcing the issue and legitimising certain policies and practices. The process is more complex, for to some degree we must see central government as initiating or at least pre-empting the process. I have already argued that the DHSS and the Tunbridge Wells Study Group played significant roles in establishing the crucial Maria Colwell Inquiry, and that the DHSS published and circulated the proceedings and resolutions of the TWSG conference just as the inquiry began. Similarly, an analysis of the circulars that have followed suggests that many of the policies formulated since 1974 have depended significantly upon the work of the TWSG, the NSPCC, and more recently the British Association for the Study and Prevention of Child Abuse and Neglect.

The report and resolutions of the Tunbridge Wells Study Group on Non-Accidental Injury to children is an important document, since it provided the groundwork for much of the policy formulation that has followed. It was circulated by the DHSS in both October 1973 and January 1974 'for the information of Local Authorities and Executive Councils'. The report was primarily concerned with the 'management of families from the time that suspicion on non-accidental injury to a child arose'. In this respect it emphasised the importance of the 'case conference' which would formulate a future plan for each case and provide an arena to discuss the appropriate roles and tasks for all the professionals concerned. It recommended that every suspected case of abuse should automatically be admitted to hospital for observation. The report reinforced a recommendation identified earlier by the DHSS[5] of the importance of establishing area review committees in each area to formulate policies, procedures and training initiatives. It is thus evident that the report considered that the best way of overcoming and controlling the problem lay in improved team work and coordination between the agencies and professionals concerned. In this respect a major cause of the problem was seen to be failure in these areas of teamwork and coordination such that knowledge of potential or 'at risk' situations was being dissipated. It was also suggested that the social services department should take on the central role in this, and that the establishment of a 'child abuse register' was an important aid to prevention and treatment.

The present system of child abuse management was effectively inaugurated with the issue of the DHSS circular LASSL(74)(13) on 22 April 1974.[6] The problem, following the title of the Tunbridge Wells report, was officially labelled 'Non-Accidental Injury to Children' and thus established the term by which it was and still is referred to by the primary professionals involved i.e. NAI. It is evident that the circular followed the resolutions of Tunbridge Wells very closely indeed.[7]

Paragraph 2 of the circular attempts to sensitise professionals about the 'first signs' which may indicate they are dealing with a case of NAI. As we might expect, it follows closely the recent 'research' both in the USA, particularly Henry Kempe, and in Britain, particularly the NSPCC. The circular reads:

It is vital that all concerned with infants and young children should be alert for the first signs of non-accidental injury. Older children are not immune. The first signs may be very slight – for example: (a) Minor injuries such as facial bruises, damage in the mouth region or small burns, (b) bruising which could indicate that the child has been gripped tightly and possibly shaken; or (c) an unexplained failure to thrive.

Other signs may be given by the behaviour of parents, including delays in seeking advice, a plausible explanation of an injury which does not quite fit the case, very severe distress or over-frequent attendances at clinics or surgeries without convincing reasons. Once suspicion is aroused the behaviour of the parents is always a factor to consider, and where possible attention should be paid to the condition of any other children and to the general situation in the home. Older children and relatives sometimes support dubious statements made by parents or guardians or may themselves invent false explanations.

Apart from this initial section on diagnosis and how to recognise the problem, the remainder of the circular is primarily concerned with the management of individual cases and the local organisation of agencies, professionals and resources to meet the problem. It thus emphasised the value of teamwork and 'strongly recommended' the establishment of case conferences and area review committees, as it was felt important that the professionals concerned should share the responsibility. It is of interest to note that the police were not seen as crucial to the workings of case conferences at this stage, as they were listed under 'others who may be invited'. However, it was stressed that children should always be admitted to hospital if 'non-accidental injury' is suspected, and that upon discharge the case conference should consider four alternatives for the child: '(a) return home with planned help to the family; (b) reception into care; (c) supervision in the home under court order; (d) committal to care by court order'.

If a child has to be removed from its home for a period, this should always be on a statutory care order, rather than voluntary, under Section One of the 1948 Children Act (Section Two of the 1980 Act). Once in the care of the local authority the child should then only be returned home on the advice of the case conference. However, whenever there is evidence of NAI it argues that case decisions should only be made on the basis of 'social, material and psychiatric assessments' of the family and whether they can or will respond to the support and advice offered to them. Further, paragraph 9 states:

There will be occasions when the child should not be returned to his parents. On occasions the child's needs both short and long term may require a clear separation from the family. This is often a most difficult *professional judgement* to make. It is important that the judgement should be based on comprehensive knowledge of the family situation as well as the principles of good child care practice and taken in the light of the case conference.

It is clear that the arena for making decisions is seen as the case conference based on the professional judgement of a range of health and welfare experts and their practice knowledge of the family concerned, and the needs of the child. In the process it is argued that it is important to establish a set of administrative procedures to ensure this develops in the most technically efficient way. The circular argued that it was 'essential' to establish a 'register' to aid 'good communication' as 'the outcome of any case will depend on the communicating skill of the professionals involved as much as their expertise'. In the long term, however, the circular considered the prospects of reducing the problem rested on 'training' and 'preventative' work.

Circular LASSL(74)(13) provided the crucial stimulus that prompted local authorities and area health authorities, usually via the social service department, to establish their local management systems for monitoring the problem and led directly to the establishment of area review committees and case conferences. It provided the political catalyst in a period of considerable social, professional and organisational anxiety.

Area review committees had been established for each area in England and Wales by the end of 1974.[8] They were set up to provide a forum for consultation between representatives of all the agencies involved in the treatment of non-accidental injury and were responsible for the formulation of local practice, procedures, training, inquiries and general advice. At the end of 1974 of one hundred English area review committees, sixty-seven were chaired by directors of social services (or their representatives), seventeen by community physicians or medical officers of health, fifteen by paediatricians, two by psychiatrists, one by a GP, and five by others.[9] Representatives on the committees included social service departments, housing departments, education, health authorities, the probation service, the police and NSPCC.

Also by the mid 1970s the convening of case conferences was 'recognised in all areas as a vital process in the handling of cases of children injured or at risk, the responsibility for which rested with a senior member of the social services staff.[10] It is also evident that by this period considerable progress had been made in institutionalising the third element that was seen as crucial in improving the operational management of the problem, that is, NAI registers, for 'by the end of 1975 nearly all areas review committees had set up a central register of information on non-accidental injury in their area. They were under consideration in the remaining areas'.[11] Again, these have usually been the responsibility of the social services department or sometimes if there is one in the area, a specialist NSPCC Unit.[12]

After the DHSS circular of April 1974, which provided the organisational framework for coping with the problem, there followed a series of circulars which both indicated the concern of central government and demonstrated that, while the problem may not have been legislated for, it continued to be taken very seriously.

In October there followed a circular forwarding a copy of the report of the Committee of Inquiry into the case of Maria Colwell and of the Secretary of State's press statement at the time of publication, noting the main points which concerned the authorities. In November 1974 a circular was forwarded enclosing a questionnaire asking directors of social services both for detailed information on the handling of NAI in their area and comments on the problems encountered. This provided the information that was then circulated in February 1976 (LASSL(76)(2)). This proved a very hectic period, and numerous circulars were forthcoming in the aftermath of the Colwell scandal. A circular recommending a set of model instructions for accident and emergency departments of hospitals was forwarded by the DHSS in February 1975. This also included guidance on the recognition of NAI and on the action to be taken by staff when it was suspected. A reprint of articles by Dr M. H. Hall and John Furness[13] from *The Police Journal* (October 1974) was enclosed in a circular in October 1975 (LASSL(75)(2a)).[14] The circular also listed five books on NAI which were recommended reading. These included the most recent publications from Denver, the NSPCC and Tunbridge Wells and all reflected the individualised medical model of the problem which dominated professional debates.[15]

A circular of November 1975 drew attention to a recent court ruling that evidence that a person in charge of a child who had been convicted of ill-treating or neglecting a child in another household may be cited in support of an application for a care order. In the same month copies of the report of the Committee of Inquiry into the Aukland case[16] were forwarded to authorities with a covering circular that drew attention to the report's main recommendations, and in December of that year copies of the proceedings of a conference held by the DHSS in June 1974 were forwarded.[17]

The conference, organised and financed by the DHSS, is indicative of the importance attached to the problem at this time. It was attended by over 150 senior representatives of all the health and welfare professions concerned, and the seniority and status of the participants was significant. Over forty people from the DHSS attended including the Secretary of State, Barbara Castle, and the Under Secretary of State (Health), Dr David Owen. The conference was concerned with attempting to publicise the problem, suggest how it could be identified in the community and outline the way this should be managed. There was an interesting contribution by Leo Goodman when discussing 'Aspects of Law in relation to NAI'. Interesting in that it suggests how the authority of the law could/should be used in such cases in the future. In fact, he suggests social workers were falling down on their duty in this area and were failing to act as the good parent:

> The low number of cases brought relative to the supposed incidence of non-accidental injury makes one wonder how the local authorities are fulfilling their statutory duties ... one may sometimes detect a certain reluctance to accept that abuse has occurred, one may also see a reluctance to use the court as an instrument of therapy.[18]

The circular of February 1976 (LASSL(76)(2)) provided an overview of the progress made by local authorities in establishing their arrangements regarding area review committees, case conferences, registers, training and so on. It also provided guidelines for such arrangements in an attempt to establish 'minimum standards or safeguards that are acceptable'. To illustrate these a number of appendices were enclosed which included the instructions distributed to staff in Rochdale and Durham as good practice examples. In these the guidelines established by the TWSG and the DHSS April 1974 circular were very evident. Both examples of good practice stressed: 'always remember that symptoms that are difficult to explain may be the result of inflicted injuries'.

By 1976 it would certainly seem that the guidelines recommended by the DHSS and the management arrangements developed round the country closely reflected a medical/social welfare conceptualisation which underlined the need for both medical and social work expertise in order to identify and diagnose the problem. The roles of paediatrician, GP, social worker and health visitor were seen as crucial, and the social services department was established as being central to the coordination of all concerned. It can be seen that while certain sections of the medical profession and the NSPCC vied for 'ownership' of the problem it was social workers in social service departments who were given prime 'political responsibility' for it. Throughout, the explanation of the problem and the best way of doing something about it was seen in terms of difficulties or pathologies with certain individual parents or families.

However, there is evidence that the police were increasingly becoming dissatisfied with the developments. For example, at the annual conference of the Police Superintendents Association of England and Wales at Eastbourne[19] a series of speakers criticised social services departments (and indirectly paediatricians) for keeping cases of 'battered children' from the attention of the police. Chief Superintendent Willis Vickers of Essex Police said that in practically every case the attitude of the social services was to keep the family together at all costs and that 'it is my experience that the cost is usually to the detriment of the child'. Superintendent Swanbridge of Dorset said that the most efficient social worker working at present was a police officer.

In response to such criticisms the DHSS released a circular on 18 November 1976: 'Non-Accidental Injury to Children: The Police and case conferences[20] which was aimed primarily at promoting understanding between the police and other agencies involved in the problem. While it recognised the 'difference of approach' of the professions concerned, it stressed the importance of close co-operation. The circular made it clear that from now on a senior police officer should be included on all area review committees and case conferences. The circular [21] also recommended that the police should release to case conferences and other agencies any relevant information about a family when they were 'assessing the suitability of a person to have care of children' including 'any relevant previous convictions' regardless of whether they were 'spent' or not.

At the same time however, the police were expected, if possible, to be flexible and comply with the recommendations of the case conference. In my own experience and from discussions with others it would appear that these recommendations regarding the role and function of the police in case conferences have been taken on board and they are now included as active participants in the management of the problem. This is not to say that frictions and disagreements do not ensue as a result.[22]

Thus while the overall conceptualisation and response to the problem has remained squarely within the individualised social welfare model there has been an increasing emphasis on the need for using the full authority of the law if children are to be protected. The police and the courts have been fully included in attempts to improve the operational effectiveness of the child abuse management system.

The Select Committee on Violence in the Family

The interest and concern of central government was given perhaps its most explicit expression with the deliberations and reports from the House of Commons Select Committee on Violence in the Family. In 1975 the House of Commons set up a select committee to consider 'violence in marriage'. When the select committee was reconstituted in 1976 it had the wider brief of covering 'violence in the family'. This meant it had to consider the extent, nature and causes of violence between partners and where children suffer non-accidental injury.

The report *Violence to Children*[23] plus a volume of evidence and a volume of appendices was published in mid 1977, and was followed 12 months later by a government White Paper[24] which was the official government response to the select committee report. While the central focus was 'violence to children' the committee also felt that 'violence against children is only part of the much larger problem of child abuse and neglect and how children should be brought up'. The report therefore made recommendations that it felt would benefit families and children generally and not just those that might prevent the most severe cases.

The report also included findings which suggested that up to 40 000 children in England and Wales may suffer from moderate or mild abuse. It is apparent that this was considered to be a major social problem, the causes of which were 'diverse', though the importance of the 'cycle of violence', stress, isolation, 'bonding' and unwanted pregnancies were emphasised. The report supported the DHSS efforts and agreed that the principle of 'coordination' was vital in identifying and helping the families concerned. However, it argued that the main thrust must be 'prevention'. In this it made a number of fairly wide-ranging but quite specific suggestions, and argued that priority should be given to services for the 'under fives'. The development of child-minders, day-nurseries and pre-school playgroups were seen as vital, as were increased publicity telling people where to go for help. Medicals for all under fives were suggested as a method of reaching all the 'unreachables'. A number of recommendations were made to increase the 'preparation for parenthood', particularly at the ante-natal stage.

In many ways the broad approach conceptualises the problem more as one of 'social pathology' rather than 'individual' or 'family pathology'. In this respect the report argues that the major thrust for prevention must come from the 'community' to reduce isolation and increase 'neighbourliness'. 'Substitute grannies' were thought to have an important role to play in helping young mothers.

The committee did not feel any legislative changes were needed to cope with the problem, but was pleased that the 1975 Children's Act introduced the possibility that supervision orders could have powers included which would allow the officer concerned to gain 'access' to, and have a full medical examination of, the child. The report also stressed the import-ance of 'treatment' with such cases and felt the general principles suggested by the NSPCC were good, but argued there would always be 'a fifth' of the cases that were beyond treatment. It also agreed that police involvement was import-ant, particularly as there would always be the cases 'of cold, calculated cruelty or extreme neglect' (paragraph 114). In this respect the report suggested that while the majority of cases want and respond to help and treatment, there would always be a hard core that needed more traditional (punitive) inter-vention.

The White Paper was rather more cautious in response and made a particular note of the difficulties in making resources available in a period of 'constraints on public spending'. In its conclusion however, it stated that: 'It is encouraging that the results of research and developments in services are identifying ways of predicting – and preventing – cases before they arise.'[25] How far this is the case I will assess in the next chapter.

The 1980 Circular

More recent central government initiatives suggest that de-bates in the literature and research have continued to make an impact on the way central government conceptualises and attempts to deal with the problem. It is important to note the shift in DHSS circulars with reference to the problem. In 1970 it was 'battered babies', in 1974 'non-accidental injury to children', and since 1978 'child abuse'.[26]

DHSS concerns towards the end of the decade were focused on attempts to rationalise the management and role of regis-ters, and in particular there was an attempt to broaden the criteria for including cases. These arose primarily because of debates in the literature which increasingly argued that the physical trauma dimensions of abuse did not take into account the often more damaging effects that resulted from more general neglect, sexual abuse, emotional abuse and the fact that older as well as younger children were 'at risk'. As a result of this and recommendations from the White Paper on Violence to Children,[27] the DHSS circulated a draft circular in December 1978[28] requesting comments by 1 April 1979. Following this process the most recent circular has been published 'Child Abuse: Central Register Systems'[29] in August 1980.

The circular aimed to consolidate and extend guidance from the DHSS on register systems for recording cases of non-accidental injury to children. It recommended (1) an extension of arrangements to cover mental and emotional abuse as well as physical injury and neglect and maintenance of a register in each area; (2) the criteria for including names on a register and the information required; (3) the procedures for monitoring cases and for removing names from a register and other aspects of its management and operations; (4) more general advice, including the need to inform parents 'in most circumstances' of the inclusion of their child's name on a register, arrangements for recording enquiries regarding a child whose name is not on a register, and the transfer of information when a child moves to another area.

The attempt to broaden the definition of the problem was made quite explicit:

> Previous guidance stressed the importance of multi-disciplinary management of cases of non-accidental injury, that is, physical injury and the extremes of deprivation and neglect. However, it is increasingly being recognised that the same requirements should also apply to children who suffer severe mental or emotional abuse. This memorandum, therefore, refers throughout to 'child abuse' and it is recommended that existing arrangements for proven or suspected non-accidental injury should be extended to such cases.[30]

As a consequence the criteria for including names on registers were broadened and applied to all children under 17 years. The criteria include: (1) Physical injury, 'where the nature of the injury is not consistent with the account of how it occurred or where there is definite knowledge, or a reasonable suspicion, that the injury was inflicted (or knowingly not prevented) by any person having custody, charge, or care of the child. This includes children to whom it is suspected poisonous substances have been administered.' (2) Physical neglect where children 'who have been persistently or severely neglected physically, for example, by exposure to dangers of different kinds, including cold and starvation'. (3) Failure to thrive and emotional abuse where children have either 'been medically diagnosed as suffering from severe non-organic failure to thrive; or whose behaviour and emotional development have been severely affected; where medical and social assessments find evidence of either persistent or severe neglect or rejection'. (4) Children living in a household with or which is regularly visited by a parent or another person who has abused a child and are considered at risk of abuse.[31]

Such criteria clearly extend the need for professional involvement, for a psycho-social assessment of the parents and family background becomes even more crucial. Even so, this is more restricted than the suggestions in the original draft circular of 1978. Here the criteria also included 'babies at risk of abuse'[32] where 'babies whose perinatal and family histories, supported by multi-professional observation and assessment of the parent/infant relationships, suggest a high degree of risk of abuse'.[33] Such a criteria was based on the assumption that abuse can be predicted and therefore prevented in a scientific manner. The draft circular also included a final catch-all 'other forms of abuse' which, while it included the emotional and failure to thrive category, was far more wide-ranging.

Returning to the 1980 circular itself we find some important implications for policy and practice in the way the recommendations were prioritised. The circular was split into four sections: introduction, minimum requirements, optional recommendations and general advice. It is interesting that all the recommendations on broadening criteria were in the 'minimum requirements' section. The optional recommendations were concerned with the management and monitoring of registers. Essentially this suggests that the 'custodian of the register' should be a senior officer with considerable experience in the field of child abuse, that they should have adequate administrative support and that there should be regular updating and reassessments (every 6 months) of cases on the register. The final section, general advice, includes issues which have direct implications for the civil liberties aspects of registers – how cases can be taken off a register, informing parents and confidentiality.

A primary reason why the recommendations were prioritised in this way was cost, for the criteria for including cases on registers could be broadened at little or no cost, while employing senior staff to control them and ensuring that the administration was improved would cost money. The covering letter enclosing the circular made this quite explicit: the second section included 'those features which are likely to cost little or nothing, and which all authorities are asked to adopt', while the third section included 'arrangements which while strongly recommended as good practice, may have unacceptable resource implications for some authorities' and were therefore '*optional*'.[34]

This attempt to broaden the criteria for inclusion of cases, while failing to provide the resources whereby expertise could be developed and not tightening up the procedures whereby registers are managed has very unfortunate implications for the rights and civil liberties of children, parents and families who might be included. Ironically even though the letter sent out with the 1980 circular made specific reference to the BASW report[35] on registers published in 1978, and claims that 'much of the advice contained in the attached memorandum has been constructed on those findings', the BASW report specifically argued that its recommendations should not be prioritised or introduced partially – the recommendations provided a complete and interdependent package. If they were not introduced as a package, unintended, unfortunate and unforeseen implications for civil liberties, rights and the way social work interventions were experienced might follow.

The 1975 Children Act and 'the Blood-Tie'

These developments in the area of child abuse have both reflected and contributed to important shifts in child care policy and practice. The inquiries and circulars during the 1970s all stressed the need for accurate information, clear decision-making, informed medical and legal advice and intervention that is 'authoritative, intrusive and insistent'.[36] The principles and procedures introduced attempted to move social work practice away from a woolly paternalism towards a sharper decisiveness and emphasised the importance of good inter-professional communication and coordination.

As we have seen however, it is important to locate these shifts in a broader analysis of changes in the social and political climate and the emergence of certain debates about the relationship between the State, the market and the family and a more general disillusionment with the social democratic welfare consensus. Certainly developments in the more specific area of child abuse connect with debates about fostering and adoption, the nature and direction of decision-making in child care practice, the importance of the blood-tie and the most apropriate use of statutory interventions.

As we have seen, during the late 1960s there had been a growing concern, particularly in the press, about 'the rights of foster-parents', 'changing attitudes to the blood-tie' and the law relating to adoptions. It was increasingly suggested that to increase the consistency for the child and to improve the rights of foster parents the law needed changing. A Departmental Committee on the Adoption of Children (the Houghton Committee) was appointed on 21 July 1969 to 'consider law, policy and procedures on the adoption of children and what changes are desirable' and reported in 1972.[37] It seemed unlikely that action would be forthcoming, as on 9 November 1973 the government announced that it was not proposing to introduce legislation in that session of Parliament, but the death of Maria Colwell at the hands of her step-father, after she had been returned from her foster parents to her natural mother at her mother's request, provided an ideal opportunity for furthering the issue. It was argued very forcibly that too much emphasis in child care had been placed on rehabilitation and preserving family ties, and parental rights had been guarded too fiercely at the expense of substitute parents and of the children themselves.

On 28 November 1973 Dr David Owen (then Labour MP for Plymouth Sutton) introduced a private member's Bill to implement all the Houghton recommendations, with additional clauses relating to the protection of ill-treated children, but it was far from certain that the Bill would reach the statute book. However, following Labour's return to power in February 1974 and Dr Owen's appointment as Minister of State for Health, the government introduced its own Bill in

December of that year. Virtually all the Houghton recommendations were included, together with some important clauses relating to the separate representation of children in court. It received support from a number of MPs who were themselves adopted or adoptees and some significant sections of the media who were very sympathetic to the issue.[38] However, there was no one in or out of parliament who provided a voice for the natural parent of children in care – though the Bill was fiercely debated.

The 1975 Children Act can thus be seen to result in part from the social reaction to child abuse in 1973/4 and represents an attempt to institute wider changes in child care policy and practice. The Act emphasised the needs of the child over and against those of parents, and reflected a less optimistic view about the solution of family problems than prevailed in 1948 or 1963. The welfare and rights of the child were not seen as necessarily complementary to the welfare and rights of the parents and provision was made in the Act for the separate representation of children in court hearings. It was the welfare of the child which was seen as paramount.

The Act attempted to give far greater control to local authorities over the lives of children in their care, to allow for an easier severance of parental ties and give greater security to children in their substitute homes. Local authorities were given greater power in relation to the parents of children in care so that parental rights could be more easily assumed, and parents must give twenty-eight days notice of their intention to remove a child once he/she has been in care for six months. In effect the longer a child is in voluntary care the more power accrues to the local authority. The Act also extended the grounds on which the consent of parents to adoption could be dispensed with to include cases where 'the parent has seriously ill-treated the child and the rehabilitation of the child within the household of the parent is unlikely'.

This legislation can be seen to symbolise a more general shift in favour of a school of thought in relation to child care which Lorraine Fox terms the 'society-as-parent protagonists'. According to Fox the 'society-as-parent protagonists' place great faith in the possibility of beneficent state intervention to protect children's well-being.[39]

Indeed, the responsibility and necessity for such action to defend children against parental mistreatment is strongly emphasised. When parental care is inadequate, children should be placed with those who are best able to care for them. Because of the emphasis on good care rather than biological bonds, this school of thought tends to hold a fairly favourable view of good substitute careers and to wish to strengthen their position *vis-à-vis* the natural parents. A high value tends to be placed on certainty and permanence, so that when a child is removed from his natural parents and rapid rehabilitation seems unlikely, he should not be confused by multiple parent figures or uncertain plans for his future.[40]

The emphasis is on the child as a unit distinct from his family, and on the responsibility of society to care for him in the best way possible. The notions of 'parental and the blood-tie rights' as being pre-eminent are subjected to considerable criticism.

Perhaps the clearest exposition of the assumptions and concerns of this school has been articulated by John Howells, who argued that the death of Maria Colwell could be attributed to misconceptions about the appropriate care for children by social workers and used the scandal as an opportunity to argue for changes in thinking and practice:[41]

The major and overwhelmingly decisive factor that led to the removal of Maria from the foster parents was the supposed 'special feeling' about the natural parents (although one was dead) and thus the need to be with her mother. Here the child care authorities leant on established opinion – the supposed ever-present strong bond between child and mother. It is one of the main objects of this book to show that this bond is not ever present.[42]

He goes on to argue that 'these misconceptions killed Maria Colwell – and they will kill many other children'. He attempts to construct a new form of social work practice with families in which the parent–child bond 'is not mystical, nor is it ever-present', for the quality of parenting is more important than parents and the principle of keeping to the blood-tie. He argues that a tradition has been established which regards that separation from parents should be avoided at all costs and a child's own home should be preferred to any other home whatever the circumstances:

Once we disprove this misconception we open the door to procedures of enormous benefit to both parents and children . . . the commonest causes of lack of loving care are present in the child's home. The number of unhappy homes and unhappy children at home far out number the number of unhappy institutions and unhappy children in institutions.[43]

Essentially social workers should be less sentimental when working with deprived families and not afraid to remove children and place them with loving foster or prospective adoptive parents. The essential message is that social workers should be more decisive, authoritative and interventive in their practice.

The most significant publication which has had wide implications for developing such thinking was *Beyond the Best Interests of the Child*, by Goldstein, Freud and Solnit.[44] This argued that the ability and sense of responsibility required for parenthood is not necessarily a consequence of biological parenthood. The stress is on psychological parenthood. It was argued that the role of psychological parent can be fulfilled by any caring adult whatever the biological or legal relationship to the child. The critical requirement for the child is continuity and certainty in parenting figures. If this cannot be provided by the natural parents then care should be transferred to those who can – preferably adoptive parents. Fostering, particularly long-term fostering, is seen as a dangerous compromise as it fails to provide the child with the security and permanency provided by either natural or adoptive parents. Children require one set of psychological parents.

BAAF and Planning for Permanency

Perhaps the most articulate pressure group within social work that has supported such arguments can be associated with the research, publications and practice guidelines issued by the British Agencies for Adoption and Fostering (BAAF) formerly the Association of British Adoption and Fostering Agencies (ABAFA). Underpinning much of their literature is the view tha when children come into care they tend to be allowed 'to drift'[45] and to become isolated from their families, and are not found any alternative permanent and secure places in substitute families. As a consequence it is argued that large numbers of children remain in inappropriate institutional care which does not meet their longer term needs. The study by Rowe and Lambert, *Children Who Wait*, originally commissioned by the Houghton committee, was particularly important in helping to publicise and develop these ideas just at the time of Maria Colwell.[46] The study argued that every child in care has a right to their own family and that adoption as well as fostering should be considered as a real alternative for many of these children. Rowe and Lambert investigated children in care where social workers considered a substitute family would be suitable. The study found that for a sizeable minority of such children decisions about alternative permanent placements were being delayed for long periods while efforts were being made to solve the problems of the natural family, yet for many of the children there was little parental contact, and rehabilitation with the family was realistically considered with only about a quarter of the chidren in the study.

From this Rowe and Lambert argue that for many children in long-term care rehabilitation with their family is very unlikely, and so social workers should be more committed to providing children in care with alternative permanent placements with other families. Thus if a child cannot be speedily returned home, or this does not seem likely, he or she should be placed in a permanent substitute family and adoption should be given serious consideration.

A central theme in this literature is the need for certainty, continuity and consistency (the three 'C's) particularly for the child and foster or prospective adoptive parents. It is suggested that in seeing the blood-tie and parental care of the natural parent as the ideal, any other alternatives are seen as a very poor second best. Social workers work in the romantic hope that the child will be reunited with their parents, but decisions are delayed and the professionals involved become inhibited by the prospect of removing parental rights. Many of the publications aim to help clarify the psychological needs of children and the legal instruments available in an attempt to help social workers terminate parental rights in favour of long-term fostering and adoption. They also emphasise the need for a thorough assessment of a parent's ability to give good enough care as early as possible so that these long-term plans can be made if parents are unable to meet their children's needs.[47] The literature also suggests that unplanned voluntary receptions into care should be avoided.

The main message is that if children do come into care they should be rehabilitated with their natural parents through intensive work within the first six months of the care period. If this is not achieved then strenuous efforts must be made to plan decisively for their long-term future, which includes serious consideration of adoption by a new family. It is clear this message has had an important impact on the way departments approach this area of work, and the way thinking in child care has shifted during the 1970s. However, as Bill Jordan has suggested, the message may not always have been heard in quite the way it was intended, for:

> the trouble is that the way social workers have understood this message has largely been in terms of *controlling*, children's futures, rather than *planning*. The emphasis has been on arming the department with the necessary legal powers to make unilateral decisions (care orders, parental rights etc.) rather than on actually making plans and getting them implemented.[48]

There is no doubt that following the 1975 Children Act, which placed a duty on local authorities to develop plans for establishing their own adoption agencies, adoption has been seen as a real alternative to long-term foster or institutional care. Such developments have been given added attraction in the context of cuts and tight financial controls since the mid 1970s, so that not only are permanent placements with substitute families seen as better but also cheaper than children's homes. Often local authorities have developed their schemes for adoption and professional fostering on the explicit understanding that other resources such as children's homes and day nurseries will be reduced or closed down. Similarly, while BAAF may argue for the need for an intensive policy of preventative work in the community, such work often takes a low priority in a period of financial retrenchment. In a period of recession when family poverty and deprivation is increasing, it is just the sort of preventative measures in the community which can support families that are the first to be cut back. Increasingly the priority for work with children and families is seen by social service departments in terms of maintaining responsibilities to statutory child care work. As a consequence the principles of practice espoused by BAAF seem to be increasingly taken on board by social workers and social service departments, but there is a danger of them becoming far more controlling than may have been intended.

The way such developments have been put into operation in many social service departments can be illustrated by reference to Lambeth.[49] For many departments have or are in the process of introducing child care policies which in their central principles are very similar. The debt to the work of BAAF is clear and explicit.[50] The objectives of the Lambeth scheme are (1) that no child should spend the major part of his childhood in care (as a target, no child who comes into care under the age of ten shall remain in care for more than two years); (2) priorities in making plans for children are: (a) rehabilitation; (b) permanent substitute family. It is stressed that 'it is therefore as much to do with good quality imaginative preventative and rehabilitation work as with permanent separation'.

In practice the scheme means planning within the time scale of the child being clear about their needs and putting their interests first. Being open with parents, presenting choices, and writing down agreements in contracts or letters which may mean trying rehabilitation when there are doubts that it will work. Developing proper monitoring and support systems for the professional and not being afraid to use the courts and the law. The keystone to good child care is seen in terms of 'permanence'. Thus it is argued that 'young children must have an expectation of permanence and this can only be provided within a child's own home or in a substitute home that is intended to last and is protected legally'.

As a consequence local authority care is viewed as a 'channel', towards securing a permanent home either with parents or substitute families, which should not be done without a plan that will lead to discharge within a clearly defined period. When decisions about termination of parental contact have to be taken this should be at an early stage, so that when a child remains in care for more than one year 'this is an occurrence which should attract the same kind of high level concern and should be subject to the same monitoring procedures as when a child is battered'. Following Goldstein, Freud and Solnit[51] it is argued that the personal growth and development of a child is dependent on the presence of parents fulfilling the tasks of parenthood as psychological parents within a private and exclusive nuclear family. As a consequence parental visiting alone does not meet the needs of the child. Similarly 'no placement in care whether in residential or foster home is ever sufficient for the needs of a child even though it may provide consistency, continuity and parental contact, if it does not carry with it an expectation of a permanent parental relationship'.

It is interesting to note that these developments 'have the effect of bringing child care planning into line with child abuse procedures'. It is evident that the panic and subsequent procedures and practices developed to 'manage' the problem of child abuse, have had far more wide ranging implications than simply work with children in physical danger. The more alert, anxious and decisive approach has been applied to children of all ages and very different circumstances. The whole field of child care is now far more infused with a resolute approach to families which relies on 'positive planning' and a greater reliance on the law and lawyers.

Shifts in Policy and Practice

An analysis of child care statistics certainly suggests that social service departments during the 1970s have increasingly relied upon the use of statutory powers (usually care orders) and are now far more unhappy with care arrangements based on voluntary arrangements and where the parents are influential participants in deciding when, where and how they use care facilities in a mutually negotiated way. It now seems that in many areas place of safety orders or care proceedings may be used even when parents may have requested their child's reception into care or where the child may have asked to come into care. There has been a dramatic rise in the number of place or safety orders taken out (Table 5.1). Since 1976 the figures have been collated on a different basis. Rather than the number of place of safety orders in force on 31 March the

Table 5.1 *Place of safety orders 1972–6*

Date	No. of Place of Safety Orders*
March 1972	204
March 1973	214
Maria Colwell Enquiry Sitting	
March 1974	353
Publication of Maria Colwell Report	
March 1975	596
March 1976	759

* In force to local authorities at 31 March 1972–76.
SOURCE: Hallett, C. T. and Stevenson, O., *Child Abuse Aspects of Interprofessional Co-operation* (Allen & Unwin, 1980).

figures now cover the number of children removed to a place of safety during the year. However, while direct comparison is therefore difficult it would seem that this increase has been maintained (Table 5.2). Jean Packman[52] in her research in a social services department, found that such orders were considered in half of all decisions about any child coming into care, and that they were actually used in a third of those actually received into care. As the above figures suggest, these were not necessarily small children, the majority being older children and teenagers. There is also evidence of an increase in the numbers of statutory removals of newborn babies from

Table 5.2 *Number of children removed to a place of safety during the year 1 April to 31 March for England, 1977–80*

Year	Aged under 5	5–16	16+	Total
1977–78	2101	3117	253	5471
1978–79 (excludes Wandsworth, no figures available)	2335	3109	261	5705
1979–80	2556	3788	269	6613

SOURCE: DHSS Personal Social Service Statistics. Fostering and Place of Safety, Financial Statistics (A/F/15).

their parents. Research by Tredinnick and Fairburn[53] from a 61 per cent return to a questionnaire to the 132 social services departments identified 160 babies taken into care since 1967. Again, such action has increased dramatically from one case per year in 1967, 1968 and 1970 to 42 such cases in 1978. Not surprisingly there has been an increase in the numbers of children coming into care because of concerns about abuse and neglect. While the numbers of children committed to care because they had committed offences showed little variation between 1972 and 1976, the number committed under other sections of the 1969 Children and Young Persons Act increased from 4000 in 1972 to 6400 in 1976. Similarly there has been an increase in the numbers committed to care under section 1(2)(a) of the Act, the section usually used for children thought to have been abused or neglected, from 1200 for the year ending 31 March 1977 to 2347 for the year ending 31 March 1980.

More generally, while the number of children coming into care has remained fairly constant and even declined, overall numbers in care at any one time have increased from 90 000 in 1972 to 100 700 in 1978 and gone down slightly to 100 200 in 1980. This rise can be accounted for by the fact that once children are admitted to care they are more likely to remain in care longer. For example, the number of children leaving care to become self-supporting or to return to a parent, guardian, relative or friend has declined from 38 900 in 1972 to 25 700 in 1980, while the numbers leaving care at the maximum age of eighteen or nineteen has increased from 6300 in 1972 to 9100 in 1980.[54] 'Departments appear to be taking long-term responsibility for a greater proportion of the children in their care and to be risking "rehabilitation" rather less frequently.'[55]

Similarly a growing proportion of children have been admitted to care on court orders or have had their voluntary admissions converted by local authority parental rights resolutions. As a consequence there has been a significant increase in the proportion of children in care where the parental rights are vested in the local authority. Voluntary admissions into care have declined from 43 500 in 1972 to 32 200 in 1980. Of the 48 100 in care under Section One of the Children Act 1948 in 1972 only 12 200 (25 per cent) were under parental rights resolutions. In 1975 there were 50 600 in care under Section One, of which 13 200 (26 per cent) were under a parental rights resolutions, while in 1980 of 44 300 in care under Section One 18 400 (41 per cent) were under parental rights resolutions. The net result is a big shift away from children being voluntarily in local authority care. At the beginning of the decade over two-thirds were in care voluntarily and one-third on some sort of statutory order or parental rights resolution. By 1980 only a quarter of children in care were not on some sort of statutory order.

The increased demands for the curtailment of parental rights, so that children can be better protected from parental rejection and plans can be made for their long-term welfare, has also played an important part in the growth of wardship litigation involving local authorities.[56] While there have been numerous contributing factors to this it is no coincidence that the growth in the use of wardship has taken place during the 1970s. This growth is shown in Table 5.3 which reveals the steady increase since 1951 and the enormous growth since

Table 5.3 *Wardship: number of originating summons 1951–81*

Year	No. of originating summons
1951	74
1961	258
1971	622
1974	959
1975	1203
1976	1369
1977	1491
1978	1595
1979	1685
1980	1962
1981	1903

SOURCE: See N. V. Lowe and R. A. H. White, *Wards of Court* (Butterworths, 1979); S. Maidment, 'Wardship and Local Authorities – The Current Limits', *New Law Journal*, vol. 132, no. 6060, July 8, 1982, pp. 667–70; A. Bainham, 'Wardship, Care and the Welfare Principle', *Family Law*, vol. 11, no. 8, 1981. For the figures prior to 1978 see Lowe and White, p. 9. The figures for 1978 onwards can be found in the annual Judicial Statistics.

1971. The recent increase in references to the Official Solicitor is also indicative of the growth (Table 5.4).

Many local authorities have recognised that the existing child care legislation does not always provide the appropriate solution, particularly as specific grounds have to be proven before they can gain powers against the parent's wishes.

Table 5.4   *Wardship: new references and total number of references to the Official Solicitor*

Year	New references	Total number of references
1974	106	437
1975	161	521
1976	218	688
1977	203	779
1978	270	946
1979	309	1090
1980	346	1250
1981	296	1291

SOURCE: See N. V. Lowe and R. A. H. White, *Wards of Court* (Butterworths, 1979); S. Maidment, 'Wardship and Local Authorities – The Current Limits', *New Law Journal*, vol. 132, no. 6060, July 8, 1982, pp. 667–70; A. Bainham, 'Wardship, Care and the Welfare Principle', *Family Law*, vol. 11, no. 8, 1981. For the figures prior to 1978 see Lowe and White, p. 9. The figures for 1978 onwards can be found in the annual Judicial Statistics.

Conscious of their responsibilities and fuelled with the panic in the 1970s, they have increasingly sought powers outside the statutory scheme. They have turned for assistance to wardship jurisdiction, which combines a much greater degree of flexibility with a relative lack of formality and ease of access to the court. It is the court that exercises the supervisory parental function throughout wardship from the moment the application is made until the wardship is terminated. In effect a circle of care is drawn up around the child even before an order is made, so that as soon as the child is warded no significant steps in the child's life can be taken without the court's consent.

Conclusions

It would thus appear that social work practice with children and families has become far more authoritative and decisive and has increasingly come to intervene in ways which can be experienced by families as threats or punishments. Social workers seem to be developing a practice which says to deprived families that they should be able to care for their children without welfare support and that firm, speedy action will follow if they are not able to provide such care adequately. If local authority care is to be always a brief interlude when decisions have to be made between rehabilitation or permanent substitute families, preferably adoption, it is not surprising if parents and families become suspicious of social workers. Jean Packman[57] found that some families refer to the social services as the 'SS' and to social workers as 'Nazis', and the 'Gestapo'.

These develoments can be seen to reflect and feed into wider changes that have been taking place in the relationship between the state, the family and the economy. In the process social work practice in child care is being restructured in significant ways. In emphasising the need for official control over decision-making and the increased use of statutory powers as well as presenting a stark choice between full parental responsibility or full state responsibility for children, social work can be seen to be coming into line with the social market economy doctrine in this area of practice.[58] Essentially this doctrine stresses the importance of individual responsibility, choice and freedom, supports the disciplines of the market against the interference of the state urging reductions in taxation and public expenditure. However, while it calls for a much reduced state it also calls for a strong state to establish certain modes of family life and social discipline. It rests on a vision of the conjugal two-parent family unit in which the woman, with the economic support of her husband, performs the major childrearing tasks. It is the family, primarily women, who are seen as responsible for rearing children in an appropriate way, while the state takes on a surveillance role, intervening only when 'things go wrong'. Social work is assigned a residual role working in an authoritative, controlling and prescribed way and the principles of rationing, punishment and statutory interventions are explicit and pre-eminent.

The recent developments in child care practice suggest that individuals are deemed responsible for their actions and little weight is given to structural, environmental and material factors. Problems are seen to reside with and have their genesis in the individuals concerned, so that social workers should be centrally concerned with upholding and demonstrating the need for greater social–morality, discipline and standards. It is the concept of individual responsibility that is now crucial, for the success of good child care is seen to depend ultimately on the extent to which individuals and families are prepared and able to implement the desired changes in their life-style. While it may have been intended otherwise it does seem consistent with the social market economy strategy of shrinking state support for families, a reduced state with fewer resources and active assistance, but more demands to be made on families, and if they are unable to meet these demands a style of social work intervention which is more controlling, authoritative and decisive. The issue of child abuse has been focal for such developments.

PART TWO

A CRITIQUE

6

Child Abuse as Disease

In Part One I have analysed the way in which the problem of child abuse emerged in Britain and the implications this has had for policy and practice. Throughout a number of assumptions about how the problem can be explained have had considerable influence on the nature of the societal response. More particularly, it has been assumed that the use of registers, case conferences, area review committees and improved inter-professional coordination will enhance the central aims of prevention, prediction and early identification. However, because of the pervading anxiety and the speed at which these changes were introduced, little attempt has been made to evaluate either the new policies and practices or the research and explanations on which they were based.

The perspective that has dominated the literature and research during this period can be characterised as a disease model of child abuse. The first and still very influential proponents of this perspective were Henry Kempe and his colleagues in Denver who coined the medical term of 'the battered baby syndrome' in the early 1960s. It was widely accepted by the main interested parties in this country, so it is not surprising that, for example, the Revd Arthur Morton, then Director of the NSPCC, in his foreword to the 1972 NSPCC report referred to the problem as 'a contagious disease which must be notified'.[1] The central aim of this chapter is to discuss the nature of the disease perspective and find out how appropriate it is for explaining child abuse and forming a framework for policy and practice.

Perhaps the most explicit recent statement of this orientation is to be found in an article by Ray Helfer.[2] He describes the development of practice in relation to the identification and treatment of child abuse and outlines a programme for the future by reference to 'a serious disease model'. He draws an analogy with recent progress made in combating cystic fibrosis in children. He says that in the early and mid 1950s children with cystic fibrosis presented doctors with real difficulties but:

> as experience was gained and research progressed, this disease became better understood, and treatment became available to modify the problems and help the children. Early diagnostic methods were developed and the problem began to be recognised at a point when much of the irreversible pathology could be prevented.[3]

With such an orientation it is assumed that the disease is attributable to a particular virus or bacteria which can be clearly demonstrated. Not only can its causal links be shown but its habits, strengths and weaknesses determined so that the disease can be tackled. Other facts about the disease can be established with regard to its point of onset, duration and course, symptoms, impact on other parts of the body and ultimate outcomes ranging from minor discomforts to death. As Giovannoni argues, the features of acute infectious diseases that lend themselves most neatly to this model are:

> a single identifiable organism that can be isolated and understood in the laboratory, populations that can be identified as being at risk of attack from the organism, preventive strategies that are developed on the basis of knowledge about the organism, a disease with a predictable course and duration, and one with sufficiently uniform manifestations that it can be diagnosed with great accuracy.[4]

When this model is applied to child abuse it is assumed therefore that child abuse is an illness of sufficient unity to be put into a diagnostic category in its own right and that the pathology resides primarily in the parents but manifests itself in the relationship with the child. While allowing that in some cases it may be an expression of family stress, it is psychological or interpersonal family factors which are seen as of prime importance in the etiology. There is a defect in the character structure or personality which, perhaps in the presence of added stress, gives rise to physical expression. This orientation thus views the causes of child abuse as residing with the parents and assumes that it occurs 'mainly in the homes of children . . . and involves some acts or inaction by parents or other caretakers'.[5] It starts by asking the question 'What type of individual or family would harm their children?'

How nearly does the phenomenon of child abuse approximate to this model? Is there agreement amongst researchers about the nature of the disease and how it can be defined? Is there a consistency concerning the characteristics of the perpetrators that has been identified? Can it be predicted, prevented and treated?

Problems of Definition

The clarity of the definition is essential for the utility of the disease model. While at one level it is often assumed that child abuse is objectively given and self-evident, upon closer inspection it is apparent that much of the research is based on very variable criteria as to the nature of the phenomenon. There is little uniformity either in the definitions or the use of the terms to denote them. Definitions range in scope from an emphasis on serious physical abuse to emotional maltreatment. They refer variously to the intentions of the actor, the act's effect upon the child, and the criteria that are used to evaluate the act and its effect.[6]

There is no standardised definition of child abuse that has been developed by researchers and accepted by welfare professionals. 'This lack of definition is the most telling simple indicator that the child abuse area is at an extremely primitive level.'[7] Without a standardised definition, research findings are misleading because the same term is used to denote very different phenomena. As a result welfare workers are faced with the impossible task of solving a problem whose magnitude, roots and solutions remain undefined.

As we have seen the definitional boundaries of the problem have broadened, and more recently have focused on the developmental needs of the child. As a consequence the physical aspects of abuse are seen as symptoms of a much more fundamental form of abuse concerned with social, emotional and psychological needs. In many respects the term is not a diagnostic category at all but a political term designed to call attention to the issue[8] and as such is open to wide interpretation.[9] In fact Helfer and Kempe admitted as much when they wrote in 1976 that 'the term "battered baby" has been dropped. When coined fifteen years ago, its purpose was to gain the attention of both physicians and the public. We feel now that enough progress has been made to move on to a more inclusive phrase – child abuse and neglect.' They argue that such a move is important because 'the most devastating aspect of abuse and neglect is the permanent adverse effect on the developmental process and the child's emotional well-being'.[10]

The Characteristics of Child Abusers

Such problems with definition clearly make comparisons between different studies difficult and mean we should not be over surprised if they come up with wide-ranging and often contradictory findings. Proponents of the orientation are not put off by such difficulties and feel that such research has already made enormous progress. Primarily the 'approach aims at identification of personality characteristics of the abusing parent ... in the hope that one might identify those adults who represent a high-risk group for abusive parenting'.[11] While it is admitted that 'many mysteries still surround child abuse', it is argued that the research has already borne fruit for 'we have learned how to recognise it, and perhaps too well, how and when to suspect it ... we are on the way to making predictions about it and to be able to recognise when a baby or child is at risk within the *milieu* of a vulnerable "family"'.[12] However, just how far is there agreement about the characteristics of parents and families where abuse takes place and are we able to predict with any precision? Upon closer inspection there is very little such agreement. Even a cursory glance at the research discloses a bewildering variety and range of factors that have been unearthed.[13]

Initially, much of the research concentrated on trying to identify psychiatric abnormalities in abusing parents, and Steele and Pollock felt that the area revealed a perfect 'goldmine of psychopathology',[14] but it is now recognised that there are no psychiatric categories which are specifically associated with child abusers. Indeed, the general consensus now is that clinical psychopathy is uncommon and is present in only a small minority of abusive parents.[15] More frequently they are described as having a character or personality disorder, though different researchers identify different disorders. Some abusive parents are said to have impaired impulse control, grossly immature personalities, violent impulses and chronic aggression,[16] others have been described as rigid, cold and detached,[17] while in contrast others have shown excessive anxiety, chronic depression and excessive guilt.[18] Similarly, while some studies have stressed the predominance of low intelligence amongst abusers[19] others report a normal range of intelligence.[20]

A number of authors have attempted to develop typologies in which certain characteristics are grouped according to different personality types and the underlying psychodynamic then identified. However, it is not simply that there are competing typologies available[21] but some researchers feel the parents they have studied could not be fitted into any such categories anyway.[22] Gelles[23] reviewing some of this earlier research noted that of nineteen personality traits identified as characteristic of abusers only four were cited by two or more authors:

> It was impossible to determine whether certain psychological factors were causally associated with child abuse, or even in some of the current essays which purport to document numerous psychological traits associated with child abuse, I find profiles of my students, my neighbours, my wife, myself, and my son.

It is not just that research has failed to reveal any consistent patterns among violent parents that practitioners could then take up, but that a 'clearcut psychological distinction between abusers and non-abusers does not exist'.[24]

Recognising the limitations of trying to identify the characteristics of actual or potential abusers according to psychological factors some authors have discussed how certain stress situations are associated with such families. Premarital conception, unplanned, unwanted or resented pregnancies and youthful parenthood have all been identified as features in the life history of abusing parents.[25] A high frequence of illegitimate births or suspected infidelity have also been found and in some cases marriage followed directly as a result of extra-marital conception.[26] Such factors are all seen to give rise to 'poor mother–child relationships'.[27]

More recently researchers have attempted to identify the characteristics of the children themselves which may put them at greater risk, but again there is little agreement, for while some researchers have found a preponderance of girls,[28] others have found a preponderance of boys[29] and some a rough equality.[30] Again, while the majority of studies indicate a child is most vulnerable between the ages of 3 months and 3 years, Gil in his much larger sample found a broad age range including teenagers, though the form of the abuse differed.

Difficulties in the pre and neo-natal period including low birth weight, prematurity, abnormal pregnancy, abnormal labour or delivery, neonatal separation, mother–child separation in the first six months and illness of mother or child in first year have also been noted.[31] Such findings have led some authors to suggest that a major factor in child abuse is a failure in mother–child 'bonding' because of difficulties or separation at or soon after birth. Again, others have not identified such factors and do not feel that a failure in bonding is significant.[32]

A variety of social stresses have been associated with abusive families in terms of poor housing, financial difficulties, unemployment, physical illness, mental illness, dependency on welfare agencies, and social isolation.[33] Certainly most studies have included a disproportionate number of families from social classes 4 and 5, but with only a few exceptions,[34] authors claim that this reflects a selective bias in the way certain deprived families are more easily identifiable. It has been a consistent argument of this approach, since the initial discovery by Henry Kempe, that child abuse is to be found in all sections and classes in society. Thus while certain social factors may contribute to the stresses experienced by certain families this is not seen as a major or even necessary explanatory factor. It is psychological factors which are of prime importance in the etiology of child abuse.[35]

However, most of the research, particularly in the 1960s and early 1970s, does not meet even the minimal standards of evidence necessary in scientific investigation.[36] The studies do not test specific hypotheses and begin and end as broad studies with relatively untested commonsense assumptions, with little guidance as to how the evidence is to be interpreted.[37] Rarely have researchers defined the factors they are studying such as 'cold, rigid parents', so that the reader can never be sure whether the parties involved give the same meaning to the term as the researcher or even what the researcher means by them. Nearly all the research has been based on retrospective studies so that the factors associated with abuse are only identified after the event, and only a few authors have attempted to improve the quality of their research by the use of control groups. As a consequence there is no way of knowing whether the traits seen as causally associated with the problem are over-represented or under-represented in the population at large. In 1978 Allan concluded her survey of such research by writing:

> The quality of research in the area of child abuse still leaves much to be desired. There has been little attempt to review previous research with a view to formulating and testing specific hypotheses . . . frequently studies seem to start and finish with relatively untested commonsense assumptions. Much of our existing knowledge has been gathered from descriptive studies which lack controls and proper sampling procedures. This has enabled authors to make claims and counter claims about the importance of different variables in the absence of any sustained efforts to discover which are directly and which are artefactually related to abuse.[38]

Now many might argue that the scientific investigation of child abuse is still in very early days and that significant progress has been made since the 1960s and early 1970s, and clearly we need to take account of this. The point, is, however, that it was precisely this sort of research and the assumptions associated with the disease model which provided the framework for the policy and practice developments of the period and the way we try to tackle the problem of child abuse today. Yet it is apparent that the research has failed to provide the results or tools whereby policy-makers and practitioners can act with any confidence.

More recently there have been a number of studies which have made attempts to apply a more rigorous methodology to their research and it is noticeable that the reviews of such research findings are far more qualified and sceptical in their conclusions than previously.[39] Four areas regarding the abusive parent have been the focus of research in the last decade and each directs attention to an assumption which had previously been accepted as 'received wisdom' in the literature, and therefore crucial in the etiology: that (1) the abusing parent was deprived as a child; (2) the abusing parent lacks accurate knowledge concerning childrearing; (3) these parents have a character defect which allows aggressive impulses to be expressed; and (4) socioeconomic stresses are neither necessary nor sufficient causes.

For example the most commonly used explanation as to why some parents abuse their children has been that the parents were themselves abused as children. Explanations in terms of a 'cycle of abuse' are primary.[40] However, while some researchers have found abuse in the childhood of abusers no explanations are offered for abusive parents who have not been abused, and no longitudinal study has reported the extent of the relationship. Those that have reviewed the literature conclude that there is 'little valid evidence to support the theory'.[41] Increasingly it has been recognised that 'stress, particularly socioeconomic stress, is an extremely important variable', and that 'stress overshadows personality variables in importance when discriminating between neglectful, abusive and control mothers'.[42]

All studies now seem to agree that the notion, derived from the disease model, that there is a single or cluster of causal variables of child abuse is not the case. They suggest that it is best seen as the result of multiple interacting factors, including the parents' and children's psychological traits. Not only does the label 'child abuse' include a wide range of different behaviours and manifestations but uniform sets of associations between different sets of variables and different types of abuse have not been established. 'Thus, to say that one is dealing with "multiple causes" oversimplifies the matter. Rather, one is dealing with multiple and diverse effects that are associated with different configurations of the same variables.'[43] The nature and direction of the relationship between the variables and the manifestations of the abuse are not known, so that it is not known which variables are more important than others and in what circumstances. As Cohn and Garbarino[44] have noted, while 'we know something about who abuses and neglects, we don't know why'. Nor do we know when, how often, with what degree of certainty and with what implications for the child. It all seems very rough and ready and a very tenuous basis on which to mount attempts to identify, prevent and predict abuse in families – but this is exactly what the disease model implies. In effect the current state of knowledge is used to predict dangerousness.

Predictions of Dangerousness

In recent years there has been considerable debate[45] about the general feasibility of predicting dangerousness in individuals and families. It is now recognised that research on the prediction of future violence does not instil confidence in either the reliability or the validity of the assessment process. 'Whether one develops "predictor scales" based on as many as 100 variables, employs the results of psychological testing, or relies upon the judgements of experienced diagnosticians, prediction rates rise no higher than two wrong judgements for every right judgement.'[46] The empirical support for the prediction of violence is very poor. Such difficulties lead to the statistical problems of 'false negatives' and 'false positives'. If the rate of violence amongst families is itself relatively low and the accuracy of the prediction techniques is relatively weak, the prediction of violence is itself a dangerous activity because of the number of people who will be wrongly identified (false positive) and those that will be missed (false negative). For example, if the criterion to predict violence is 90 per cent accurate (and no test is available with such a high level or accuracy) and if the rate of violence in the population is one in a hundred, then of one thousand persons tested for dangerousness nine of the ten actually violent will be identified correctly but we will incorrectly identify 10 per cent, or one hundred of the thousand people screened. So for every ten violent people correctly identified there will be one hundred wrongly identified. Clearly this has enormous implications for civil liberties.

Those who oppose such developments generally stress the

importance of the individual rights of the people likely to be subjected to intervention, and hence see the growth of registers and so on in child abuse management as unwarrantable interference. They invariably claim that such measures have not worked, may be counterproductive and even if they do reduce the risk to children that this is more than outweighed by the costs. In contrast many of those who support early interventions and attempts at predictions have a much more sceptical view of parents' rights and often claim any efforts to save abused children are justified. However many of those who have attempted to develop research to prevent, identify and predict abuse will not even recognise that empirically such efforts are very limited. A closer look at three such studies shows the severe limitations.

Hanson, McCulloch and Hartley[47] have carried out a complicated statistical analysis on the findings of the Birmingham Child Abuse Study[48] in order to establish whether certain clusters of variables occurred together. Sixty-seven variables were identified which distinguished abuse from control cases, after both age and class had been taken into account. As a result a number of little groups of two or three variables emerged but did not 'seem to have far reaching implications'. However four large clusters were seen as far more significant. The largest cluster of variables hinged on the link between mother's unmarried status and the absence of the child's natural father. A second cluster had to do with the mother's psychological state, but drew in her relationship to the child and outsiders. A third cluster was based on the link between the mother having few social activities and having few opportunities to be free of responsibility for the child. The final cluster was concerned with the father's relationship with his parents.

For all their technical sophistication Hanson *et al.* have to admit that there are severe limitations in using such findings as a basis for action and applying their findings to the individual case: 'of the 62 possible adversities considered in the exercise ... possessing a score of 15 or more adversities here is a *fairly good* indication that we are dealing with a case of child abuse; though the occasional mistakes *may be made.*[49] The authors also recognise that 28 of 134 index cases of abuse were just like the controls in having fairly few adversities. In an attempt to deal with this they say that 'there are some characteristics which never occur in the control sample, so that *we might be able to say* that if there are under 15 adversities, and if such and such a characteristic is found, *we can be fairly sure* we are dealing with child abuse'.[50] Qualifications like 'fairly good', 'we might be able to say' hardly provide a firm foundation for identification and prediction, and in the end the authors conclude that 'the matter of identification must be left to the now familiar methods of vigilance and medical *opinion*'.[51]

Henry Kempe and his colleagues in Denver, who continue to be the main protagonists of the disease model, are far more optimistic and confident about their claims and they argue that they have evidence that abuse can be identified, predicted and prevented: 'Is there a way we can tell which parents are at risk and need help *before* their children arrive at the hospital terribly injured, or even dead? Based on our studies, the answer is yes.'[52] They have carried out a prospective longitudinal follow-up study for two years of a cohort of 350 informed and consenting mothers having their first or second baby at Colorado General Hospital.[53] Mothers of premature babies and babies needing to be taken from them for intensive care were excluded.

The parents were interviewed before the birth and a note was made when a 'danger signal' was identified. Danger signals included: when a mother seemed to be denying the pregnancy or when she was depressed about it and fearful of the delivery:

> Likewise, we noted when the parents said they felt this baby was going to be one too many; or when they themselves came from an abusive or neglectful background; or when they were living in overcrowded, isolated, unstable, or otherwise intolerable conditions; or when the mother's husband and family were not supportive to her and she had no sympathetic friends; or when the parents seemed overconcerned about the baby's sex or performance.[54]

The second screening procedure was identical except that a seventy-four item questionnaire was substituted for the interview.

The third phase was to observe the parents' reactions in the labour and delivery rooms. The nurses took notes on what each mother said, did, how she looked and how the father reacted.

Often videotapes were made of mother and child interactions and delivery-room staff were encouraged to provide anecdotal information. The final phase consisted of observing the families in the first six weeks of the child's life.

By the end of this process the researchers had four separate and rather long lists of negative reactions or circumstances out of which to create ratings that might be effective predictors of abuse or neglect against which could be set a number of positive ones. Of the initial cohort of 350, one hundred mothers were rated as 'high-risk' and a low-risk group of fifty was selected as a control. Kempe and his colleagues then evaluated under five headings how far they were able to predict abuse, based on a follow-up visit to the mother in fifty randomly selected high-risk families and twenty-five low-risk families, between seventeen and thirty-five months later. First they say, there were twenty-two indications of 'abnormal parenting practices' in the 2 high-risk groups compared with only 2 in the low-risk group: 'Of the fifty families we visited in the high-risk group, twenty showed signs of "abnormal parenting practices" while none of the low-risk group did.'[55] There were five cases of 'failure to thrive' because of deprivation in the high-risk groups while there were none in the low-risk group. In the first seventeen months of life twenty-two children in the high-risk groups had at least one accident requiring medical attention while there were only four in the low-risk group. Eight high-risk children had been reported to the Central Child Abuse Registry, and no low-risk children. Ten high-risk children and no low-risk children failed the Denver developmental screening test. And finally, all low-risk children were living in their 'biologic home' but eight high-risk children were either in foster care, permanently living with relatives or had been legally relinquished. Perhaps not surprisingly it is claimed that the results showed 'we could predict with remarkable accuracy which families were at risk'.[56]

On the basis of these findings it is said that the most sensitive predictions had been gathered from the labour ward and delivery room observation phase which had made 76.5 per cent correct predictions; the questionnaire had been 57.5 per cent correct; the prenatal interviews 54.4 per cent correct; giving a combined predictive accuracy of 79 per cent.

According to the definition of abuse used 75 of the 95 children abused out of the total population of 350 had been successfully predicted. Thus there were only twenty missed (false negatives). This gives an incidence of abuse of 28 per cent at a predictive accuracy of 79 per cent. Thus for every person correctly identified another one will be mislabelled. Kempe and his collagues do not mention this factor of false positives.

Perhaps more strikingly, the definition of abuse is enormously broad and all-inclusive. It includes 'indications of abnormal parenting practices'; children who had 'at least one accident requiring medical attention'; children who had failed on the Denver developmental screening test; children who had been reported to the register; and children who had shown signs of 'failure to thrive'. Such a definition is much broader than earlier conceptions of the problem and is probably very different to the conceptions held by most professionals and members of the public as to what constitutes child abuse. Commenting on this, Montgomery has suggested that by strict criteria, only those eight cases where abuse had been reported to the Central Child Abuse Registry should have been treated as child abuse. If this definition is taken the predictions are only 8 per cent accurate, or 92 per cent wrong.

This much narrower definition of abuse was used in a more recent predictive study with very different results.[57] Like the Kempe study above it is one of the few pieces of prospective research on prediction.

A checklist of predictors was applied to the maternity notes of all non-Asian women delivered under consultant care in Bradford during 1979 when they were discharged from the maternity unit.[58] 2802 maternity case-notes were screened and 511 families (18 per cent) were predicted as being 'at risk'. The researchers make some very optimistic claims for their findings for:

> the current commitment to the computerisation of maternity data means that a checklist such as ours, if effective and useful, could be applied with little extra effort. In fact our checklist did predict a group more likely to abuse their children. Two-thirds of all the recognised abuse in our population occurred in the 18 per cent predicted at risk.

It sounds very attractive but upon closer examination it appears that these global statistics actually mean that out of the twenty-eight out of the population on the child abuse register 66 per cent (seventeen) were in the high-risk group. The opposite of this of course is that 483 did not appear on the register – an horrendous false positive. Now I am clearly not claiming, as the authors are not, that the register is in any way an indicator of the level of abuse, but it is the nearest we have of the officially recognised rate in a particular area. One has to be very sceptical about such predictive techniques when we get such findings.

Admittedly the researchers found a similar pattern when they looked at other indices of care, which Kempe regards as abuse, such as 'failing to thrive', 'admissions with trauma', 'post-natal death rates', numbers attending casualty, admitted to hospital and immunisation rates. We should not be surprised that certain sections of the population will be over-represented in such indices, nor that they might have been identified previously as at risk, but to claim that such indices are then some criteria of child abuse is a gross distortion. In fact the authors admit that 'although we seemed able to predict which families would have parenting problems, the rate of serious injury to their children was no higher than that in the not at risk group'.[59] What none of the studies do is analyse their findings in terms of class or social situation. Social structural factors are never held constant when comparing control and high-risk groups.

Prevention and Treatment

The goals of the disease model are not only clear but, in theory, measurable. For the success of preventative and treatment efforts can be assessed in terms of its incidence and prevalence. Certainly if there are two populations who suffer from the disease and only one is treated you would anticipate the incidence and prevalence of the disease in the treated population to decrease. However, there are very few studies which attempt to evaluate the success of interventions into child abuse. Those that do cast serious doubt on the efficacy of such efforts.

As part of their predictive study Kempe and his colleagues attempted to evaluate the success of interventions which were particularly designed to prevent child abuse. The original mothers who were rated as 'high-risk' were split into two groups. Half were to receive the routine follow-up services, and half intervention 'designed to counteract what we felt were abusive tendencies'.[60] This special intervention included 'close watching and care by a single paediatrician assigned to the family', detailed observation and discussion in the hospital, 'thereafter he would see the child every two months', close telephone contact, regular health visitor contact and 'where necessary he would refer the family to other medical facilities or mental health clinics'.

The results on follow-up showed no statistical differences of incidence or prevalence between the two high-risk groups on the basis of: Central Child Abuse Registry reports; indications of 'abnormal parenting practices'; accidents; immunisations; Denver developmental screening test scores. However five children in the high-risk normal intervention group required inpatient treatment for serious injuries, compared with none in the special intervention group. The authors argue therefore that 'although the interventions in our study did not change abnormal patterns of parenting, they did stop children from being seriously injured'.[61] Not all the research has been as optimistic however.

The focus of special intervention in the study by Lealman *et al.* in Bradford was in terms of a specialist intensive social work input provided by a project social worker. Of the 511 predicted to be 'at risk': 103 were put in the High Risk Intervention Group (HRI) and contacted by the project social worker. 209 were placed in the High-Risk Non-intervention group (HRN): and 199 in the High-Risk Social Work group where families were already receiving social work suport. The researchers conclude, somewhat reluctantly, that while the project social worker helped HRI families with a whole range of problems and may have helped prevent things getting worse 'we have no statistical evidence to support the view that intervention improved parenting practice'.[62] As they point out, their findings are the same as the Denver findings, except that the latter had a difference in the number of children receiving serious injury, but as the Bradford researchers note 'no evidence is presented that all five were abused'.[63]

More generally, the United States Office of Child Development has been conducting the first wide-scale evaluation of treatment programmes. Their preliminary findings from five such programmes were not very encouraging, for (1) only a small proportion of cases (5 per cent) dealt with by the various agencies were serious – resulting in hospitalisation, permanent injury or death; (2) the much advocated multi-disciplinary approach had not demonstrated its benefit or justified its cost; (3) in the majority of programmes (85 per cent) intervention was directed solely towards the adult members of families; and finally (4) it was premature to discuss what constituted good care management while the very nature of the dynamics of child abuse remained in question.[64] Such findings hardly constitute success.

However, such evaluative research is very rare. Despite the rapid growth of registers, case conferences, area review committees, special units, child abuse specialists and so on since the early 1970s, we have still not seriously evaluated the disease model on which such developments have been based. The research that has been carried out only makes one more sceptical of the whole approach and the assumptions which inform it. At a minimum we must agree with the conclusions of the Bradford researchers that 'to suggest that prevention is straightforward is to underestimate the complexity of this difficult social and medical phenomenon'.[65] But increasingly it seems that the application of the individual disease model to child abuse is quite inappropriate and fails to provide the basis for tackling the problem.

The Positivist Method

The critical empirical evidence presented so far seems sufficiently decisive to cast very serious doubts upon the disease model, but at the conceptual level even more fundamental criticisms are necessary. The model and its proposals for action are heavily dependent on the conceptual apparatus of positivism. Positivism's essential assumption concerns the unity of scientific method, so that the premises and approach of the physical and natural sciences are applied to human action and society. While there are many varieties of positivism evident in the social sciences our main concern is with 'individual positivism' where it is admitted that while a range of different influences might contribute to the creation of the problem it is in the individual that the fundamental predisposition is situated.

The approach assumes a scientific, neutral stance whereby society and human action is comparable to a natural organism. It is assumed that human action is determined or caused by certain identifiable objective factors. As a result the study of child abuse is reduced to the examination of antecedent factors, or their indicators and correlates. If we can then stop or modify the antecedent factors we can stop or modify the problem. What we need to do is discover certain laws and regularities which can then be applied in everyday practice in order to identify, predict and prevent. In the process the objectivity of the scientiest, *vis-à-vis* the natural scientist, is acclaimed and there is an attempt to analyse and present the data in a hard, often quantified, way.[66]

The social world is presented and analysed as if it was a reified laboratory 'out there' in which individuals can be manoevred according to their best interests in some detached way. It is assumed that child abusers are acted upon by certain factors or causes beyond their control and they are neither responsible nor rational. The abusing parent is seen as a 'victim' and is denied conscious self-determination. The primary focus is on the abuser, and it is assumed that explanations of the incidence, nature and prevalence of child abuse can be deduced from studying the parents.

In treating the human being merely as a neutral medium through which antecedent factors come to expression, the approach ignores the issue of meaning. However, human action takes place in a context which must be interpreted by all concerned. Human beings are not simply determined but actively construct their social worlds. They act in a world of meaning which is inseparable from their biological nature.

The notion of objectivity rests on the assumption that there is a moral consensus in society and that everyone agrees not just that child abuse is a problem but just what the nature and dimensions of the problem are. But as we have seen, definitions, even within the disease model, differ on this. Such an assumption is further undermined when we recognise the very different child rearing norms that exist across society.[67] It thus falls back on the view that the scientist is able to develop value-free criteria and that the medical and welfare practitioner is able to apply these in a neutral way. Scientific research and professional practice are seen as independent from wider political, economic and social influences. Research and practice is reduced to the technical.

By ignoring the situational aspects of abuse a whole range of important issues are excluded. There is a real failure to understand the social aspects and processes involved and to locate the phenomena in any kind of social structure. Wherever social factors are mentioned, e.g. poverty, housing, unemployment, they are discussed as factors impinging upon the individual. In reducing explanations to the individual the model is unable to provide or even contribute to a social theory of child abuse. Even though many commentators feel that certain sections of the population may be more visible and therefore more liable to identification as abusers, the social reaction to abuse is seen as unproblematic. Much of the research is based on actual or suspected cases of abuse and there is a serious failure to analyse the processes by which it is identified and labelled on the part of the family, the community, the professionals and the wider society.

The positivist almost always evades the role of the wider society and the state. But as I have shown, child abuse is not a naturalistic category – nothing is 'naturally' child abuse. It is only child abuse if it has been proscribed in a given society and if the control agencies act in such a way as to enforce that proscription. For example it is not the case that all intentional physical violence to children in this country is proscribed as child abuse, corporal punishment is seen by many as legitimate. The approach has great difficulty in providing an explanation of where the norms and rules have come from whereby we have begun to see certain behaviour as abusive. In assuming that there is a moral consensus in society the manner in which concern about child abuse has grown in recent years is seen as natural, benign and humanitarian and reflecting the advanced stage of civilisation that we have reached.

Conclusions

Even though there are enormous empirical and conceptual problems with the disease model of child abuse there is no doubt that it has had an important influence on debates in this country about the best way of approaching the problem, developing priorities and allocating resources. In focusing exclusively on the abusive parent it has legitimated practices which 'blame the victim'.[68] Essentially parents are studied in terms of what is wrong with them, so that abuse is seen as a problem with certain parents who are unusual, or different to the normal. Abuse results from some individual or family defect and so must be remedied by particular means or exceptionalist solutions which are tailored to the individual case.

In the process other parents are seen as normal and the wider society is not seen as problematic. In arguing for exceptional solutions to exceptional problems scientific approval is given to the wider society in its current social arrangements and the non-abusing majority can absolve themselves of any guilt or responsibility for the problem. Some commentators[69] have suggested that the individualistic values of our society mean there is a culturally based tendency to attribute the causes of problem behaviour to the individuals concerned and to assume they are different and abnormal.

The disease model legitimates the role of a variety of health and welfare professionals who are seen as experts on such exceptional problems, and devolves to them the responsibility of 'doing something about it'. It also reinforces the view that such experts have or can develop the technical know-how to monitor, control and ameliorate in a very individualised way. Yet as we have seen, the model on which such techniques are based is empirically flawed and fundamentally misconceived. The research has failed to provide the results whereby abuse can be predicted and identified with any precision, so that health and welfare practitioners are being asked to do a job for which the basic tools do not exist.

Of course this is exactly what has happened. Children have continued to die and the scandals have continued because practitioners, particularly social workers, are not carrying out the job which they are required to do and which they claim they can fulfil successfully. I have argued that practitioners have been subjected to considerable critical attack from the 'New Right'. While it has been the disease model which has dominated debates on child abuse and provided the framework for thinking, policy and practice it has been increasingly subject to critical conservative interpretation.

June Lait, commenting on the child abuse scandals and the role and approach of social workers, has suggested that there should be 'a contracting and clearer focus in social work activities, and a recognition of the impossibility of *preventing all sin and unhappiness*'.[70] As we have seen, the failure to prevent child abuse has provided the opportunity for the New Right to restructure child care policy and practice according to a more controlling, prescribed view of state welfare and a more pessimistic view of human nature. Again, June Lait has argued that prevention:

> in the context of baby battering, may be an impossible activity, and that the only way officials can protect children from battering or severely neglectful parents is to establish that an offence has been committed and prevent another by removing the child from the threatening environment. Possibly there *cannot* be, certainly there *is* not, a single piece of evidence which establishes that social work intervention, short of removal, has prevented child abuse.[71]

Thus the shortcomings of the disease model mean that it has been increasingly interpreted both in theory and practice according to far more conservative principles. The emphasis continues to be the individual but they are seen to have far more responsibility for their actions and the causes of the problem are seen to lie in personal morality, the decline in traditional loyalties and lack of discipline. To solve the problem coercion should not be a marginal factor but a central part of the control of child abuse. This can be undermined if there is any laxity in the exertion of authority. Child abuse will never be eliminated by idenification, prevention and treatment techniques if these are not used in an authoritative, decisive manner and the law is not seen as central to the process. Thus while much of the language used is still in terms of the disease model, the way the problem is thought about and responded to is qualitatively different to the way it was conceptualised in the early 1970s for example in the work of the NSPCC Battered Child Research Unit.

Not only has the disease model been proved inadequate and been laid open to recent reformulation, it has lead to certain myths about the problem which have acted as a 'smokescreen' for developing more progressive and effective measures. As Newberger and Daniel have said 'we look at child abuse as a phenomenon originating in the psychology of individuals, frequently ignoring the social and cultural realities that frustrate our treatment of particular families and impose formidable obstacles to the prevention of child abuse'.[72] We need to move beyond the disease model if we are going to overcome the current problems and resist the New Right assault. While I do not wish to question the malignant effects of abuse it is vital we question the 'singularly intense focus on abuse without regard to the matrix in which it flourishes'.[73] It is to this matrix and the social situational aspects of abuse that I will turn in the next chapter.

7

Poverty, Social Structure and Child Abuse

The disease model of child abuse, with its emphasis on individualised treatment, cure and prediction, is the dominant paradigm in research, policy and practice. Child abuse is conceptualised as a pathological phenomenon with roots in the personality or psychodynamics of abusing parents. While social factors are taken into account these are seen in terms of the characteristics or factors associated with abusive individuals or families. The model ignores the social arrangements in which people live, and denies that social and economic factors have any responsibility for the problem. In the process it fails to explore the social context in which abuse arises. This leads to two major lacunae. It fails to recognise the importance of inequality and the sense of frustration, repression and aggression that results: by concentrating on dangerous people it ignores dangerous conditions. And it blinds us to the abusive but non-individualistic practices of industrial, corporate and government agencies. In seeing abuse as being manifested and caused at the individual level we do not critically analyse the abuse that institutions, organisations and the wider society practise and legitimate.

The central argument of this chapter is that social and economic factors play a crucial role in child abuse and that there is a great need for policy and practice to address the social context of abuse rather than the individualised identification and treatment of the parents concerned. In the process it is important to develop a theoretical framework whereby such policies can be constructed. However, because the disease model is so dominant in Britain, it is to the USA we have to look for alternative approaches which are sympathetic to a more sociologically grounded explanation of the problem.[1] While there are important variations in the different sociological explanations, they all argue that, for a variety of reasons, certain families are put under severe social and economic stresses which predispose them to abuse and to be officially labelled as such.

Perhaps the clearest demonstration of the need to develop such an approach has been suggested by Pelton in his discussion of the 'myth of classlessness'.[2] He points to the statements in most research, particularly that emanating from Denver, that imply that the problem occurs without regard to socioeconomic class and that it is distributed proportionately among the total population. Pelton demonstrates that this is not the case and that there is substantial evidence of a strong relationship between poverty and child abuse and neglect. While all the available statistics lead to the conclusion that the lower socio-economic classes are disproportionately represented among cases known to public agencies, it is usually suggested[3] that the social processes whereby cases are identified is biased against the poor, for 'poor people are more available to public scrutiny, and likely to be known to social agencies and law enforcement agencies, whose workers have had the opportunity to enter their households'.[4] It is claimed therefore that the class distribution of reported cases does not reflect the real distribution of the problem. Pelton provides three reasons why such arguments should be rejected.

First, while the increased public awareness has led to far more known cases of abuse and neglect in all social groups, the proportions from the different social classes have changed very little, and failed to increase the proportion of reports from above the lower classes. Secondly, child abuse and neglect is related to degrees of poverty even within the lower social classes, so that the highest incidence of the problem occurs in families experiencing the most extreme poverty.[5] And thirdly, even amongst the reported cases the most severe injuries have occurred in the poorest families.[6] He demonstrates that the vast majority of the fatal victims of abuse and neglect are from poor families. He thus concludes that child abuse and neglect is strongly related to poverty both in terms of prevalence and of severity of consequences. This is not to say, however, that the problem does not occur in other classes and groups.

Pelton argues that the myth of classlessness has played a key role in supporting the psychodynamic orientation to the problem and legitimating the medical model of treatment:

> It supports the prestigious and fascinating psychodynamic medical-model approach and, by disassociating the problems from poverty, accords distinct and separate status to child abuse and neglect specialists. The myth holds that child abuse and neglect are not, for the most part, mere aspects of the poverty problem,[7] [and in the process diverts attention from the class related problems of poor households and in encouraging people] to look for personal defects in poor people, it has made it easier to decide to remove children from parents than to provide concrete supportive services within the home.[8]

The Ecological Perspective

An increasingly popular attempt amongst US writers and researchers for developing a more comprehensive framework and explanation of abuse is in terms of the ecological perspective. Gabarino and Gilliam[9] believe that 'child maltreatment' is an indicator of the overall quality of life for families and is concentrated among people who 'have the least going for them economically, socially and psychologically, and who thus comprise high risk families'. The rationale for this view emerges from an ecological approach to the problem, 'one that systematically deals with the interaction of person and environment'. By 'ecological' they mean the way the organism and its immediate environment affect and respond to each other:

> This process of mutual adaptation and accommodation means that the terms of the equation that produce behaviour are always shifting, sometimes subtly, sometimes drastically. It means that in the case of maltreatment the intimate relationships between the child and the parents cannot be accounted for or understood without understanding how the conditions surrounding the family affect interaction between child and parent.[10]

While they are concerned with physical abuse they feel the most important issue is the threat to the normal development of the child, hence their use of the term 'child maltreatment'. Echoing the more recent conceptualisations of Henry Kempe and changes in this country, they argue that the central issue is not physical abuse but the overall pattern of parent-child relations and their impact on the child's social, intellectual and moral competence. By focusing on 'developmental damage' they attempt to draw the study of abuse and neglect back into the mainstream of issues in human development.[11]

It is argued that the special contribution of the ecological perspective is its appreciation of place and that it is based on the proposition that behaviour and development arise out of mutual adaptation of person and environment within an 'ecological niche'.[12] A child's environment can be understood as a series of settings, each nested within the next broader level from the family to the society – akin to Russian dolls.

The central principle in this analysis is to identify situations in which the conditions of life conspire to compound the deficiencies of vulnerable parents. While the approach does not attempt to refute the importance of psychological factors it tries to move beyond an individualistic orientation to focus jointly on social support and social control. It is argued that the 'neighbourhood' is the ecological niche in which families operate and is one of the principal places where such conditions can be located, for psychological deficits are usually complemented by a series of social deficits. It is suggested that these cluster around inadequate support for the parental role and isolation from relationships that provide nurturance feedback. Parental vulnerability is compounded by a lack of contact with family support systems so that social isolation is seen as the 'weak link' that is responsible for abuse and neglect. Thus child abuse 'may be described as a form of situationally determined incompetence in the role of caregiver. It stems from the combination of social stress and a relatively low level of skill as a caregiver.'[13]

Garbarino argues that his research demonstrates[14] that high-risk families tend to be clustered in neighbourhoods that are 'socially disrupted'. He compared neighbourhoods with high rates of officially reported child maltreatment with neighbourhoods that had low rates and concluded that the former were characterised by: low levels of 'neighbourly exchange'; residential instability and transience; restricted interaction amongst children; deteriorating housing; poor relations with institutions such as schools; and a 'pervasive pattern of social stress'. All these 'social deficits' were associated with 'economic deficits'.

In practice the ecological approach to child maltreatment begins by plotting cases on a map which identifies clusters of cases geographically, according to neighbourhoods. Garbarino has suggested that five variables are closely correlated with maltreatment in attempting to predict in which neighbourhoods abuse would be most prevalent. These are: percentage of households with incomes less than $8000 a year; percentage of households with incomes greater than $15 000 a year; percentage of female-headed households; percentage of married mothers (with children under 18) in the labour force; and percentage resident less than one year.[15]

It is thus argued that the quality of the neighbourhood should be a central issue in preventing child maltreatment and that planners should avoid concentrations of families with high needs and low resources. Such segregation tends to produce 'social impoverishment' unless there are countervailing forces at work. It is also important to generate these 'natural' neighbourhood support systems and teach community organisation skills.

Gabarino is particularly keen to overcome social isolation and the privacy of nuclear families[16] and wants to encourage better integration of welfare professionals into the neighbourhoods they serve and the families they work with. This means reorganising the delivery of services around neighbourhoods, and locating offices in the high-risk areas and promoting continuity of service.

Thus the ecological perspective, while critical of the individualised disease model of policy and practice, does not attempt to discredit but to complement it. It makes little contribution to what can be done with particular families in everyday practice, for its emphasis is upon developing ideas for policy and planning. In this respect some of its suggestions echo the Barclay Report support for community social work and its favourable discussion of the use of community networks and patch.[17] However, in arguing against the value of family privacy it is recommended that 'intrusive monitoring networks' should be established, particularly among 'populations prone to abuse'. Similarly there should be greater legal support for intrusion by concerned neighbours and professionals to monitor parenting for 'families do not own their children, they hold them in trust for society'.[18]

While the ecological perspective tries to move away from individualistic explanations of child abuse its attempt to construct a social account of the problem is very partial. The analogy with biological ecology, and its emphasis on the internal mechanisms of neighbourhoods implies that people who live in the neighbourhoods do so because of certain personal characteristics or because of some natural process of social development. In attempting to identify certain neighbourhoods as more likely to contain problems of child maltreatment according to criteria of 'social impoverishments' it is suggested that certain neighbourhoods are socially disorganised and pathological,[19] while others are healthy.

In such areas, it is suggested, social relations are rudimentary, community cohesiveness is undermined, mistrust abounds and social isolation is prevalent. Where there is such dislocation it is implied that internal disorder and indiscipline is evident. People are neither effectively curbed nor can they curb one another so that it is difficult to implant moral habits. Individuals and families do not know each other, develop few ties with the area or with each other and are loath to intervene in the affairs of others. Thus the explanation for the problem is located primarily *within* certain neighbourhoods which are seen as lacking in certain crucial respects and which require special treatment, development and support.[20]

The biological analogy is skewed in certain crucial aspects, for neighbourhoods and communities are not ecological systems but are regulated and influenced by processes unknown to the biologist. When neighbourhood networks do emerge they are usually shaped by influences other than simply the occupation of a shared geographical area.

Increasingly it has been argued that the notion of community is a fruitless explanatory concept and should be replaced or at least complemented by those of class, race, gender

and political economy.[21] Thus instead of looking inward to
find the causes of child abuse primarily in communities,
neighbourhoods and families it would be more productive to
demonstrate how political, economic and historical forces can
account for social deficits and child maltreatment. This is not
to say that the insights of the ecological perspective should be
abandoned but that we need to be aware of it shortcomings.
While never stated explicitly the perspective can be seen as
consistent with certain thinking in this country, and is
expressed in the Parliamentary Committee on Violence in the
Family and other policy documents.[22] Rather than emphasising individual pathology, social pathology is emphasised.

The Socio-Cultural Approach

Since the early 1970s Murray Straus, Richard Gelles and
Suzanne Steinmetz have been carrying out research in the
USA and attempting to develop a theoretical model for
understanding violence in the family rather than the particular
problem of child abuse. They argue that 'research and treatment on the problem of abuse ought to forsake the search for
one general definition of abuse, and focus on the distinctive
acts of violence and non-violence'.[23] As their work has pro-
ceeded they have moved to what they call 'a radical sociological perspective',[24] for they no longer feel that social factors are
only one of the sets of factors which account for intra-family
violence along with non-social factors such as neurological
defects, personality traits and mental illness. They are convinced that at least 90 per cent of the violence which takes
place in US families grows out of the very nature of the family
and the larger society, rather than individual aberrations.
Following their findings in a national survey they argue that
violence is a pervasive and common feature of US family
relations and that violence towards children, rather than being
an abnormal form of behaviour, typifies the nature of adult-
child relations.

Their national survey of family violence[25] defined violence
as 'an act carried out with the intention or perceived intention
of physically hurting another person'. A national probability

sample produced 2143 families of which 1146 had children living at home aged between three and seventeen. Using a series of questions called the 'Conflict Tactics Scales' respondents were asked to consider items in three groups: (1) use of rational discussion and argument (discussed the issue calmly; got information to back up your side; brought in [tried to bring in] someone to help settle things;) (2) use of verbal and non-verbal expressions of hostility (insulted or swore at the other; sulked or refused to talk about it; spited the other; threatened to hit or throw something at other; threw, smashed, hit, or kicked something); and (3) use of physical force or violence as a means of managing the conflict (threw something at the other; pushed, grabbed, shoved the other; slapped or spanked; kicked, bit or hit with a fist; hit or tried to hit with something; beat up the other; threatened with a knife or gun; used knife or gun). Those interviewed were presented with these eighteen items in that order and asked what they did when they had a disagreement with the child both in the previous year (1975) and in the course of their relationship.

The milder forms of violence, what Straus *et al.* call 'normal violence', were the most common. They estimate that at least 58 per cent of all American children are spanked in a year and at least 71 per cent spanked or slapped at some time; approximately 13 per cent of children are hit with objects each year and 20 per cent at some point in their lives, while approximately 5 per cent of children have something thrown at them at least once a year, and double this at some point while growing up.

Even though the most dangerous forms of violence, what they call 'abusive violence', were least likely to occur, the figures demonstrate that approximately 3 per cent of children are kicked, bitten or punched by their parents each year, while 8 per cent have a parent do this at some time in their lives. Slightly more than 1 per cent of children are beaten up by a parent each year and 4 per cent are beaten at least once while growing up.[26] Every year one child in 1000 faces a parent who threatens to use a gun or knife, while nearly 3 per cent have grown up with a parent who threatened them with a gun or knife in their lifetime.

Children whose parents were violent to them experienced

violence more than once.[27] Children having something thrown at them had it happen on average 4.5 times in the year, while those who were pushed, grabbed or shoved had it happen 6.6 times during the year. Spankings and slappings occurred on average 9.6 times a year, while the average of kicks, bites and punches was 8.9 times a year and children were hit with objects 8.6 times. For those who were beaten this was repeated an average of 5.9 times during the year. From this it is extrapolated that if all the items that have the highest probability of injuring or damaging a child (kicks, bites, punches, beatings, threats with or use of a gun or knife) are combined:[28]

> Almost four out of every hundred children (3.6 per cent) are at risk of serious injury each year because of their parents using at least one of these dangerous forms of violence. Assuming that any of these acts has a high probability of causing harm to a child victim, *between 1.4 and 1.9 million children* were vulnerable to physical injury from their parents the year of the study.[29]

From this they write that their findings show that child abuse, far from being rare, isolated events is a chronic condition for many children. They argue that their research indicates that violence towards children is an extensive and patterned phenomenon in parent-child relations. More generally they maintain that physical violence between family members is a normal part of family life in most societies, and in US society in particular.

The research has also attempted to identify the social factors that are associated with violence towards children and lends much support to Pelton's argument. They stress however that their profile is not intended to be used for predicting child abuse, as this would result 'in millions of instances of false labelling'. While it was found that parents at all income levels used severe violence towards their children the distribution was far from equal. They found that there was an inverse relationship between income and parental violence so that those with the lowest incomes had the highest rate of violence and families with incomes of over $20 000 had the lowest. The poorest families had rates of abusive violence that were twice that in the highest income groups.

Similarly manual workers had rates of abusive violence towards their children that were 45 per cent higher than where the breadwinner was a white collar worker. In part this relates to the differential incomes between blue and white collar workers. They also found that unemployment was significant in that in families where the breadwinner was unemployed the rate of physical violence was 62 per cent greater than for other families, while in homes where the breadwinner was only working part-time the rate of violence was nearly double that where the breadwinner was in full-time work.[30]

They also attempted to assess how far family stress increased the likelihood of child abuse.[31] They found that stress experienced by the very poor and those earning over $20 000 had no effect in increasing the probability of physical abuse, but for those earning between $6000 and $20 000 increased stress did increase the risk of abuse. As they point out, stress is a normal part of life for the poor so that not only is physical abuse already high, but it would require far more extreme stress to make any real impact.

In trying to explain child abuse then, Straus and his colleagues start from the premise that violence in families far from being abnormal and pathological reflects a combination of normal processes and situations and arises from the interaction of culture, social organisation and social learning.[32] In attempting to establish why the family is the most physically violent institution that most individuals will encounter it is argued that it is in the family that most people learn to be violent. The distribution of violence results from the cultural norms and values concerning violence in different groups and classes. They argue however that physical punishment is seen and experienced by most family members as normal so that the family provides the primary arena where children observe and receive an explicit training in violence.

It is further argued that certain taken-for-granted cultural norms legitimate such forms of violence in families where they would not be so easily accepted in other areas of society.[33] Most family violence does not enter public consciousness because it is seen as 'normal violence' in the sense that it is seen as acceptable. In general, it is argued, the rule in the family is that if a child is doing wrong and will not listen to reason there is an obligation to use physical violence in the form of hitting. There is an implicit distinction between 'ordinary' spanking, pushing and slapping and 'real' violence and in general, violence to children within the family is permissible as long as it does not result in wounds which need medical attention. However, harm or injury invariably depends on contingencies extraneous to the behaviour such as aim, size, strength, luck, physical condition and environment. This is certainly so for older children. There is an implicit tolerance or permission for family members to use forms of violence on each other which would not be allowed elsewhere.

The prime reason why those at the bottom of the socio-economic ladder have a culture which is more pone to violence is seen to reflect the structural realities which they experience. Essentially the existence of more violence towards children in the lower social classes emerges in response to more fundamental forces in terms of physical and social environment and social organisation.

It is argued that the large proportion of each day spent with family members, while it in part explains the high incidence of violence, cannot account for the high ratio of intra-family violence compared with violence experienced outside the family. The way the family is organised is seen as having unintended consequences for helping to produce violence. There is a wide range of activities and a mixture of ages and sexes which increase the potential for conflicts, while the strength of feeling in such conflicts is likely to be greater than if the same disputes arose elsewhere. Child membership of a family is involuntary and children are not able to terminate or fundamentally restructure such relationships, for family membership carries with it an implicit right to influence the behaviour of others, particularly children by parents. There is a real lack of any alternatives for most family members. Compounding the age and sex differences is the fact that family statuses and roles are assigned primarily on the basis of biological characteristics rather than on the basis of interest and competence.

Like Garbarino they argue that the normative, kinship and household structure increases the privacy of the family and insultes it 'from both social controls and assistance in coping with intra-family conflict'. Similarly it is argued that family relationships are unstable as they are continually undergoing major changes arising from processes inherent in the family life cycle, such as child-birth, maturation of children and ageing, as well as the stresses already noted concerning unemployment and income:

> Families are expected to provide adequate food, clothing and shelter in a society which does not always give families the resources necessary to do this. Also stressful is the expectation that families bring up healthy, well-adjusted, law-abiding and intelligent children who can get ahead in the world. The stress occurs because these traits, and the opportunity to get ahead, are all factors which are to a greater or lesser extent beyond the control of any given family.[34]

Thus Straus, Gelles and Steinmitz argue that the explanation of violence towards children lies in the combined effect of the high level of family conflict; the training in violence and the link established between violence and love by physical punishment; and the implicit cultural norm which gives the parent the right or obligation to hit children if they are not doing as they are told. They attempt to identify a number of 'normal' processes and situations which can be said to cause such violence.

One area which these writers, particularly Gelles,[35] have drawn attention to is that the way a family comes to public attention and is recorded as abusive depends on a variety of social processes and contingencies. Not only does it depend on whether the violence leads to any damage to the child but how and if it comes to the notice of the public agencies. Whether an event is regarded as 'abuse' depends on definitions of what is acceptable and within normal bounds.

A recently published British research project has looked at these processes.[36] Dingwall, Eekelar and Murray have carried out a sophisticated ethnographic examination of how front-line agency staff 'confront, identify, investigate and report instances of suspected maltreatment of children'. They looked at what agency staff consider to be mistreatment, how they come to that conclusion and what they and others then do about it. The roles of hospital accident departments, child health clinics, health visitors and social workers were crucial.

Throughout they argue that the social processes by which decisions are made depends essentially upon moral rather than technical criteria. The core dispute is political, for it is concerned with the point at which intervention in the family may be justified and the form that intervention might take. They conclude that there are far more situations of abuse and neglect available than are ever chosen, but that there is a complicated system of bias built into the process which filters moral character:

> in such a way as to hold back some upper-middle and 'respectable' working-class parents, members of ethnic minorities and mentally incompetent parents while leaving single women and the 'rough' indigenous working class as a group proportionately most vulnerable to compulsory measures. This effect is achieved by tests which are not class-biased in any simple or overt sense but which various social groups are differentially able to meet.[37]

As I will show in the next chapter, my position and approach departs significantly from Dingwall, Eekelaar and Murray on some central areas. However, what they clearly demonstrate is that official definitions of 'abuse and neglect are the products of complex processes of identification, confirmation and disposal rather than inherent in a child's presenting condition and, at least in some sense, self-evident'.[38] It is not simply that the most deprived sections of the population are more likely to be subjected to the stresses which contribute to the problem but that they are more likely to be selected for 'compulsory' intervention by the state rather than any other form of intervention or support.

Structuralist Accounts

The most critical commentator of established policy and practice is the American David Gil. Through his research and more recent forceful analysis he has attempted to shift the ground rules for discussions about child abuse and neglect and construct a debate which is far more radical in its implications.

Much of his earlier research has subsequently been supported by the work of Straus *et al.* and his explanations of the problem have been echoed in part by others. But perhaps more than any other writer he attempts to locate child abuse in a political economy which places primary explanatory significance on the social and economic structure and the values and social processes that support and legitimate it. He demonstrates that the position of families in the socio-economic hierarchy is crucial for the degree of stress and frustration encountered by families in different positions in the social structure. Inequality via the experience of poverty and social isolation is seen as the primary determinant of abuse.

Gil's conclusions are based on his nation-wide study in 1967 and 1968 to provide a comprehensive demographic picture of child abusing adults and their victims.[39] The operational definition used in the survey included only incidents of child abuse which resulted in physical injury of some kind.

A standardised reporting form was developed for use by central registries of child abuse in each state. Approximately 6000 cases were studied in 1967, with a new and slightly larger sample in 1968. A sub-sample of 1380 abusive parent were also analysed for more detailed socio-economic data. The results demonstrated quite clearly that child abuse was more likely among lower-class parents, for over 48 per cent of the abusers had an annual income under $5000, while the proportion of all US families under that income level was 25.3 per cent. The results also showed that abusive adults tended to be poorly educated. Summarising the characteristics of the families reflected by indicators of educational achievement, occupational position and status, income and assistance status, number of children and housing, Gil concludes that families with a low socio-economic background were over-represented, especially among non-white families.

Gil also conducted a household survey with the National Opinion Research Corporation and found that 3 per cent of the sample personally knew families involved in incidents of child abuse in the year preceding October 1965. From this he extrapolates that between 2.53 and 4.07 million adults in the USA knew of at least one case of child abuse. This would be an upper limit, as some cases would be known to more than one respondent. It is certainly above the incidence suggested by Straus, Gelles and Steinmetz.

In the sample of children an attempt was made to assess the seriousness of the physical injuries reported (this disregarded possible emotional aspects) and were considered 'not serious' in 53.3 per cent of cases, 'serious, no permanent damage expected', in 36.5 per cent of cases, 'serious with permanent damage' in 4.6 per cent and fatal in 3.4 per cent. Thus 90 per cent of the reported incidents were not expected to leave any lasting physical effects on the children. From this Gil argues that:

> the scope of physical abuse of children resulting in serious injury does not constitute a major social problem, at least in comparison with several more widespread and more serious social problems that undermine the developmental opportunities of many millions of children in American society, such as poverty, racial discrimination, malnutrition and inadequate provisions for medical care and education.[40]

Even if allowance is made for under-reporting, especially of fatalities, physical abuse is not seen as a major case of mortality and morbidity in the United States.[41]

Elizabeth Elmer's research lends considerable support for this line of argument.[42] She compared seventeen abused children with seventeen children who had suffered accidents eight years after all were originally examined and matched according to age, race, sex and socio-economic status. A second comparison group, matched according to the same variables, consisted of children with no recorded history of abuse and no reported accidents resulting in hospital treatment before the age of one year – the process by which the other two groups were chosen. The study was designed to identify possible physical, developmental and behavioural differences between the groups in an attempt to identify the longer term consequences of abuse. It was hypothesised that the abused children would score lower than the non-abused across a range of variables including height, weight, language development, intellectual functioning, emotional development, school achievement, aggressive behaviour and poor self-concept.

However, few differences were found and these were minor

and inconsistent. All the children showed developmental and social problems and appeared depressed, anxious and fearful. At first the researchers were 'disbelieving' and made various attempts to check the methodology and rework the data. In the end, however:

> it was impossible to avoid the conclusion that abuse as one method of deviant child care did not appear to make a significant difference, at least in the population under study. In addition, our clinical observations had shown unanticipated pathology among most families in all the groups and evidence of considerable psychological damage in many of the children. What could be the common factor contributing to these widespread difficulties? We believe this factor is membership of the majority in the lower social classes, which connotes poverty and all its well-known companions: poor education, menial jobs, inadequate housing, under-nutrition, poor health and environmental violence.[43]

More recently Elmer[44] has returned to the issues highlighted by her research and compared her conclusions with those of Martin and Beezley[45] who are from the Denver school and have also followed-up a group of abused children. Like those evaluated by Martin and Beezley, her follow-up children appeared incapable of enjoying themselves or of being caught up in the excitement of play or fun. Martin and Beezley assumed the characteristics were specific to abused children, but had no control groups to compare with. In contrast Elmer saw the same behaviour in all her groups (abuse, accident and comparison) and 'deduced that we are learning more about lower-class children in general, and less about abused children in particular'.[46]

In more recent years Gil has developed a far more radical perspective. He has criticised traditional definitions which see child maltreatment as occurring and having its primary genesis within families, for he defines child abuse[47] as: 'inflicted gaps or deficits between circumstances of living which would facilitate the optimum development of children, to which they should be entitled, and their actual circumstances, irrespective of the sources or agents of the deficit'. Thus Gil argues that any act of commission or omission by individuals, institutions or the whole society, together with their resultant conditions which 'deprive children of equal rights and liberties, and/or interfere with their optimal development, constitute, by definition, abusive or neglectful acts or conditions'. Child abuse can be manifested at both the institutional or societal level as well as within families, but rarely are they seen as legitimate for discussion within debates about the nature, size and causes of child abuse. But the activities of schools, institutions, unemployment, social security systems, racial discrimination, class differentials have far more deleterious effects upon the life chances and development of children than the traditional concerns of the child abuse literature, policy and practice. For example the higher rate of neonatal mortality among children in social classes IV and V is not seen as abuse, nor is the pharmaceutical industry seen as having any complicity in the maiming of children from poorly tested anti-depressants or contraceptives.

Not only can abuse be manifested at different societal levels but it must not be assumed that because the abuse is identified at one level, usually with the individual/family, that it should be explained at that level. Its genesis may reside elsewhere in the social structure. Gil suggests that whether, and to what extent, human needs are met depends upon the society's policies concerning resources, work, production and rights and the social philosophies which shape them. So that when a social arrangement consistently frustrates the human needs of large sections of the society energy which is blocked by 'structural violence' might erupt as 'reactive, personal violence by individuals and groups'. In the process families act as agents of structural violence:

> It follows from these propositions that if violence is to be overcome in a society and its families, obstructions to the unfolding of human potential need to be eliminated, and the institutional order needs to be transformed into a non-violent one, conducive to human self-actualisation in which all people can freely meet their intrinsic biological, social and psychological needs.[48]

The key analytical focus for Gil has increasingly become the structural obstructions to human development, including: the development and control of resources; organisation of work and production; socialisation; the distribution of rights; and values.

David Webb has underlined the significance of some of these arguments. He suggests that failure to break with the assumption that child abuse is only to be found in the family is politically useful to a society which does not want to consider a comprehensive social policy towards children and in the process constructs social workers as being responsible for the problem. Ideologically the way the problem has been constructed blames the parents and social workers and absolves society and the state from issues of social distribution.

Similarly, explanations of child abuse need to establish underlying structures and mechanisms and not just patterned regularities. Such underlying mechanisms may only become evident by taking seriously unobservable entities and processes which go beyond straightforward appearances:

> Checklists of factors, such as debt, social isolation, difficulties in 'bonding' which may be predictive of child abuse, must also be conceptualised sociologically. The adequacy of such accounts must be judged in terms of how well they explain the phenomenon and not necessarily in relation to their predictive potential.[49]

Webb uses the example of early marriage which is often noted as a contributing factor in child abuse. But early marriage itself reflects particular class and gender divisions in society which exclude certain people from significant life chances. As a consequence while early marriage might be associated with child abuse both reflect processes which are not readily observable. However, if such processes are ignored we are at risk of 'blaming the victim' and privatising what are essentially 'public ills'.

The analysis provided by Gil, and that by Straus, Gelles and Steinmetz, argues that child abuse can only be adequately explained in the social structure of age, class and gender.

Class and Child Care

While little attempt has been made in this country to develop a perspective which emphasises the importance of social structure in explaining child abuse, there have been a number of commentators who have more widely demonstrated the influence of poverty, social deprivation and economic factors on the quality of child care in families.[50] There is now considerable evidence of the statistical association between a lack of money and other indices of disadvantage. Children in poor families experience actual shortages of food, clothing and household equipment and are subjected to the absence of luxuries, treats and holidays and suffer poor nutrition and severe budgeting.

Estimates of the number of people living in poverty depend on the definition used and how it is measured.[51] However, around a quarter of the population in Britain live in households with an income at or below 140 per cent of the supplementary benefit rate. This totals over 14 million people, of which about a quarter are children. By the end of 1983 over 7 million people, including nearly 2 million children, were dependent on supplementary benefits. Similarly, 1.8 million households are living in physically unsatisfactory housing conditions in terms of overcrowding, shortage of amenities or general unfitness. Of children under five, over a quarter live in houses which lack one or more basic facility, a similar number live in houses which lack sufficient internal space and a tenth live in houses which are so structurally deficient as to constitute a health hazard.

The various research projects carried out under the auspices of the SSRC/DHSS programme of research into transmitted deprivation[52] have provided detailed evidence of the manner in which poverty not only shapes families' living standards and social status but puts them at greater risk of ill health, poor housing, low educational performance, greater official delinquency and a variety of child care problems. For example, Mildred Blaxter concluded her review of the research on the health of children by writing that:

> the inevitable conclusion of this review is that there is overwhelming evidence that adverse social factors are associated with health disadvantage in the children's future . . . a great deal of effort has gone into the task of proving, again and again, that these socially-associated differences in the health status of children do exist; almost as if this were something that society did not wish to believe.[53]

Similarly, the Black Report accumulated considerable evidence to demonstrate the close relationship between inequality and health. Not only did the report find that material deprivation affects physical development in young children but that ill-health contracted in childhood can dog an individual for life. Mortality and morbidity rates for infants and children reflect class differentials as does by far the largest cause of death amongst children – accidents. Between 1968 and 1974 10 877 children died from accidents. The report argues that:

> it is impossible to escape the conclusion that in the context of childhood the most straightforward of material explanations is capable of providing a simple chain of causation by which the pattern of health inequality is illuminated. Households in occupational classes IV and V simply lack the means to provide their children with as high a level of protection as that which is found in the average middle-class home.[54]

Poverty, social deprivation and economic disadvantage are important in influencing the quality of child care standards in families. Certainly children who enter state care come disproportionately from families who experience inadequate income, poor housing, single parenthood, unemployment and homelessness.[55] All reasons associated with wider structural inequality. For example, the local authorities[56] with the highest rates of children in care are just those with the highest indices of social deprivation. In March 1981 Southwark had 22.67 children in care per 1000 aged under eighteen, Lambeth 20.26, Hackney 19.13 and Manchester 17.45, while Warwickshire had only 4.67, Surrey 4.02 and Solihull 1.07.

Fuller and Stevenson argue that 'one should be increasingly cautious about attributing their entry into care to the consequences of personal "inadequacy" or "maladjustment" in natural parents'.[57] There is a direct relationship between economic hardship and emotional deprivation for poverty modifies attitudes, personalities and behaviour. Apathy, depression and a sense of helplessness are amongst the feelings that families often report resulting from their struggle to manage financially. In fact the greatest fear for many families, particularly single parents, is that their financial difficulties and debt will lead to their children being taken into care. As Brown and Madge recognise, this is rooted in the material existence for:

the monetary consequences of poverty, which include disconnection of fuel supply and acute shortages of cash to buy food or clothe children adequately, must create situations where children are not properly cared for in a material sense. And the psychological consequences of chronic anxiety and despair are hardly conducive to happy child-rearing.[58]

Wilson and Herbert have shown how poverty forces parents into a style of child-rearing that they are not happy with, and how they adapt to failure by lowering their expectations. There is a self-perpetuating relationship between poor social environment and personal attributes which reinforce each other so that chronic stress:

> may result in feelings of failure, total loss of self-respect, or even paranoid feelings of persecution, and these states of mind in turn may lead to loss of motivation, suicidal actions, or aggressiveness and homicidal tendencies. When family failure eventually leads to contact with the Social Services it is not surprising that in many cases personality attributes are seen as the main 'causative' factor.[59]

Thus social and economic stress, which is directly related to the structure of inequality, has direct consequences for the well-being of children in poor families. People feel their poverty more when it affects their children and they are invariably more humiliated by their failures when they affect their dependents. Such problems are reinforced by the fact that society has articulated expectations of family life, and performance in child care is closely monitored. Poor parents are very aware of this.

Conclusions

In this chapter I have argued that if we are to develop our understanding of child abuse and really want to do something about the problem we must give serious attention to the social structural factors involved. It is not adequate to simply assume that the problem is like a disease which requires prevention, identification and treatment.

At the same time it is important to recognise that such social structural factors are often presented as the unseen background knowledge to the individual situations faced by practitioners. Similarly we cannot simply assume that efforts to eradicate the problem should only be directed at the macro level. I have given numerous examples of the way in which structural inequality has direct implications for the everyday experience, stress and hardship faced by many children and families. We cannot deny those experiences. So that even though child abuse is structurally induced, practitioners have a vital role to play in helping to alleviate the resultant suffering. It is to the implications of this perspective for practice that I will turn in the final chapter.

8

Reformulating Policy and Practice

The central aim of this book has been to locate child abuse in its political context. I have analysed how definitions and responses to the problem have been subject to the professional, organisational and scientific interests involved and changes in the economy and political culture. The concern has been to trace the way the collective definition has been constructed and to demonstrate how certain assumptions, conceptions and theories of the problem have influenced and contributed to policy and practice.

However, not all groups have had equal power to influence the process. The 'ownership' of child abuse has been contested at various times by sections of the medical profession, the NSPCC and other welfare professionals. More recently however the media and the state, in the guise of certain civil servants and politicians, have been crucial. I have argued that the way the problem has been explained has placed responsibility for its genesis on individuals and families and responsibility for its identification, control and reduction on social workers. As a consequence whenever things are seen to go wrong those who are held up for public scrutiny and admonition are the parents and social workers concerned.

I have also demonstrated that these developments have had implications for policy and practice that are much wider than the more prescribed problem of child abuse. It has encouraged a style of social work with families which is more defensive, less prepared to take risks, and relies more on statutory interventions.

The way that the problem has been constructed draws attention not to the structural determinants of child abuse but to the individual ones. It is individual patterns of behaviour, individual personalities and family relationships which are seen as central and not the economic and socio-cultural processes which direct and mediate such patterns of behaviour. Thus prevention is concerned with identifying potential abusers and rehabilitating families in an individualised way. It is the concept of individual responsibility, whether of the parent or the social worker, which is continually propounded.

I have attempted to show that individualised disease-orientated explanations are not only inadequate but fundamentally misconceived. Thus not only do present approaches blame the victim, they inhibit understanding and substitute unrealistic behavioural expectations. We are in danger of instructing people to be individually responsible at a time when they are probably least capable as individuals of controlling their environment and social situation. There is a tendency to assume that individual actions and family relationships reflect the problems of a homogenised affluent society, and in the process obscure the reality of class and the impact of social inequality on child abuse. As a consequence the direction of policy and practice has concentrated on the child as the victim of particularly unusual family circumstances, and the focus has been on rescuing children from situations perceived as dangerous.

Such an approach has acted to deflect attention from the more serious deficiencies in welfare provision for all children and families and implies that help is only available in situations of extreme severity or crisis. The only state response to families and children in need becomes one that is investigative, selective and controlling.

In contrast I have argued that child abuse is strongly related to class, inequality and poverty both in terms of prevalence and severity. This is not to say that the problem does not occur among other groups and classes, nor that when it does occur it does not have severe consequences. However, locating the problem in terms of social structural factors has important implications for the way we define the problem, the way we explain it and the best way of doing something about it. For solving the problem requires a realignment in social policy which recognises the necessity of attacking the social, economic and cultural conditions associated with the abuse.

The State, the Family and Child Abuse

The problem has thus been constructed with strong moralistic overtones which support a paternalism whereby it is assumed that child abuse is one of the worst, if not the worst, manifestations of the decline of the family and the social order more generally. It is not simply that the problem is defined in individual, disease terms but that the state is seen as politically neutral and beneficent and has a responsibility, delegated through the community, and mediated through its welfare professionals to act in situations where standards fall below socially accepted norms. It is assumed that the state acts in 'the best interests' of the family, particularly the child. Such paternalism, both in theory and practice, in the field of child care has been subjected to severe critical appraisal in recent years from very different political perspectives. Superficially it seems that such critiques have many things in common.

It is argued that the state does not necessarily act in the best interests of children and families and that welfare professionals possess far too much ill-defined, discretionary power. Furthermore, that there is little scientific knowledge about abuse and neglect so that certain families can be subject to unwarrantable intervention which can be biased and prejudiced. In the process they have few rights to support their interests and their civil liberties are undermined. Not only is it argued that intervention does not work but that the costs and consequences of intervention, particularly where it involves removing the child from its parents, often outweigh the risks of leaving well alone. As a result it is suggested non-intervention is often the best form of 'action'. In many respects the critique and policy suggestions of the radical non-intervention lobby in crime and delinquency have increasingly been reflected in critiques of child abuse and neglect. It is implied that the Leviathan State has intervened unwarrantably into the private arena of the family.

The proposals for change suggested by the libertarian left are remarkably similar to those outlined by the libertarian right. For example Justice for Children,[1] perhaps the most vociferous representative of the former in this country, suggest a new direction for intervention in the lives of children and their families and recommend a series of principles which they believe will greatly reduce the number of cases coming to court, provide a higher quality of care and protection to children brought to court and generally improve the nature of state intervention in families: (1) the principle of respect for family autonomy recognises there is wide diversity of views and life-styles which vary over time and in different classes, races and religious groups; (2) the principle of voluntary services which seek to support families and keep children at home; (3) the principle of limited intervention in the lives of children and families means that the criteria authorising a referral to court should be strictly defined and limited to (a) where a child has suffered physical harm or neglect which has been inflicted non-accidentally by his parents; (b) where a child has been sexually abused by his parents; and (c) where the child has been abandoned by his parents; (4) the principle of the least restrictive alternative means that the applicant would have to show the need for compulsory intervention and would have to demonstrate that the intervention proposed would be beneficial to the child; (5) the principle of the parties' right to legal representation; and finally (6) the principle of visibility and accountability of decision-making in order to limit discretionary powers and provide firm guidelines for decisions at each stage.

Essentially these principles aim to limit the ways welfare workers and the state intervene in cases of abuse and neglect, protect the privacy of the family, improve the rights of the parties involved and subject the process far more to the rigours of legalistic due process.

Such arguments and recommendations have been similarly expressed in the more recent work of Goldstein, Freud and Solnit[2] which is underpinned by an essentially conservative view of the family. *Before the Best Interests of the Child* discusses those harms to children that should constitute a statutory definition of 'abuse and neglect', warranting investigation of and coercive intervention against the parents. It also proposes standards for deciding what action to take after a finding that a child has been abused and neglected and makes suggestions regarding the procedures in adjudication. Ironically perhaps, Goldstein *et al.*, whose earlier book[3] has often been used to legitimate more wide-ranging and coercive state intervention, advocate perhaps the most narrowly defined grounds for intervention of any current commentators on the problem. Goldstein *et al.* would limit state intervention in cases of child abuse and neglect to four situations:

(1) The death or disappearance of both parents, the only parent or the custodial parent – when coupled with their failure to make provision for their child's custody and care.

(2) Conviction, or acquittal by reason of insanity, of a sexual offense against one's child.

(3) Serious bodily injury inflicted by parents upon their child, an attempt to inflict such injury, or the repeated failure of parents to prevent their child from suffering such injury. They argue that no intervention should be based solely on 'neglect' or 'emotional harm' and that intervention to protect a child from physical abuse should occur only when the parent, through acts or omissions, causes or tries to cause 'serious bodily injury' to the child. The authors would not permit intervention in what are now the great bulk of abuse cases, that result in bruising or minor injuries, unless such a beating was an attempt to inflict more serious injury. Nor would they allow intervention solely to protect a child from emotional harm.

(4) Refusal by parents to authorise medical care when (i) medical experts agree that treatment is non-experimental and appropriate for the child and (ii) denial of that treatment would result in death, and (iii) the anticipated result of treatment is what society would want for every child.

Throughout Goldstein *et al.* argue that the views of judges, doctors and social workers should not be substituted for the views of parents, for they find no reason to believe that they can make better decisions. In fact they argue that decisions other than life and death are only 'preferences for one style of life over another' and that neither law nor medicine provides 'the ethical, political, or social values for evaluating health care choices'.

This perhaps surprising non-interventionist stance is thoroughly consistent with the premises that informed *Beyond the Best Interests of the Child*. Again it is asserted that a child needs unbroken continuity with an adult who is his or her 'psychological parent'. This premise leads them to be very wary of any state intervention that might disrupt the relationship unless the child is suffering from extreme dangers. Also Goldstein *et al.* believe that an adequate psychological relationship between child and parent can only be maintained in:

> the privacy of family life under guardianship by parents who are autonomous ... when family integrity is broken or weakened by state intrusion, needs are thwarted and his belief that his parents are omniscient and all-powerful is shaken prematurely. The effect on the child's developmental progress is invariably detrimental.[4]

This emphasis on the need for family privacy is seen as crucial and they are as wary of intervention leading to supervision (or surveillance) of the family as they are of intervention removing the child. They are also distrustful of state intervention because it offends their firm belief in 'individual freedom and human dignity' and because the state does not have the resources and sensitivity to intervene in the 'fragile, complex interpersonal bond' between parent and child, nor is it able to respond to the changing needs of children. Because of their concern that every intrusion is harmful, they believe that a policy that always errs on the side of non-intervention is most likely to benefit children most.

As Michael Freeman has suggested[5] 'this is the philosophy of extreme liberalism, of an individualism which treats all rights as if they were private property'. While it can accept the night-watchman state of classical liberalism, limited to the functions of protecting everyone against violence, theft and fraud, and to the enforcement of contracts it is not a state committed to any notion of social justice, or equality. However, while they advocate a much reduced role for the state this is not to say it should be weak or soft. Goldstein *et al.* argue that when

intervention does take place it should be authoritative, swift
and decisive – it is a strong state. For although they restrict
intervention to extreme cases, when intervention is necessary
they advocate that when a parent has inflicted or attempted to
inflict serious bodily harm on a child, parental rights should
always be permanently terminated. They argue that:

> parental maltreatment leaves psychological scars which endure long
> beyond any physical beating and preclude a child from regaining the
> feeling of being safe, wanted, and cared for in his parent's presence – the
> very emotions on which his further developmental advances need to be
> based.[6]

The values and recommendations for policy and practice are
consistent with a New Right political economy and may well
prove attractive in a period when Thatcherism is attempting to
restructure the relationship between the family and the state.

In many respects, particularly in the current state of child
care and child abuse work, Goldstein *et al.*'s analysis and
recommendations are appealing in that they seem to recognise
certain difficulties and tensions and provide recommendations
which would clarify policy direction and practice. It is important however that we recognise the inherently conservative
thrust of this work and some of the false premises on which it is
based.

It is assumed that the family is a private arena which has
always constituted the core social unit, often resisting the
encroachment of the wider society and the state.[7] Goldstein *et
al.* have an over-simple view, in which the family is auton-
omous and in general external to state regulations. However,
the idea that the family is a private domain is a socially
constructed myth for it is the 'object' of both direct and
indirect state regulation.[8] The myth acts to obscure this
regulation and helps maintain the family as the main agent of
care and the state welfare services as a residual casualty system.
As Walker has argued[9] the state regulates family life explicitly
through the socialisation of education, health care and social
security provision. Primarily this is confined to the preparation
of human capital and to the maintenance of married women's
dependence on men:[10]

But to conceive of this 'intervention' in terms of one or two isolated instances is to misunderstand the complex relationship between the family and the state and the role of ideological hegemony in the reconstruction of 'normal' social relations. The state's influence over the pattern and direction of family life is exerted more forcefully through non-intervention in certain functions and through the explicit and implicit rationale for this non-intervention.[11]

As a consequence the boundaries of the family and the state are established not through statute but through the normal pattern and duties of family relations. It is inconceivable that the capitalist state would provide universal childcare facilities for example. The freedom and privacy of the family is thus a myth, for it is dependent upon the family's relationship with the state and thus takes on a particular form of freedom and privacy.

While Goldstein *et al.*'s argument would attempt to firm up this socially constructed division between the family and the state, the conception of the family they have in mind is not necessarily based upon the blood-tie and biological kinship. Barrett and McIntosh[12] have suggested that the desirability of child-rearing based on the presence of two parents, whether natural or surrogate, has come to supersede the desirability of children being raised by their own kin. During the nineteenth and early twentieth centuries it was accepted that a child who was illegitimate, orphaned or deserted would be assimilated into the extended family – perhaps by grandparents:

Now, however, an ideologically correct representation of parent-hood and the family is seen as far more important for successful child-rearing than biological ties of kinship. In this sense, as far as child-rearing is concerned, we now attach less weight to families themselves but much more to an ideology of familialism.[13]

Goldstein *et al.*'s emphasis on 'psychological parents' supports this shift, while legitimating a reduced role for the state and an expanding role for the family. There is clearly a danger that the sort of radical critiques of current child care policy and practice as espoused by Justice for Children can be assimilated into such a conservative position.

Reconstituting Social-Democratic Child Protection

Robert Dingwall, John Eekelaar and Topsy Murray have recently developed what they call a middle ground on issues of child protection. This has been related to their research which I referred to in the last chapter.[14] However, it is important to recognise that their findings and recommendations are hardly those of detached social scientists for their methodology, interpretations and ideological position are closely interrelated.

Through the use of participant observation and loosely structured interviews with people in health and welfare agencies they examined how agency staff confront, identify, investigate and report instances of suspected mistreatment of children. They show that it is inferences made about the moral character of family members which is the critical factor when decisions are made to identify a case as mistreatment and to use the law to intervene. They argue that at every stage of the decision-making process there is a preference for the least stigmatising interpretation of the available information and the least overtly coercive possible disposition. Assessments are said to take place under an aura of the 'rule of optimism' whereby parents are seen as honest, competent and caring. The two types of events which lead to statutory action were 'parental incorrigibility', where parents persistently failed to cooperate with the welfare agencies concerned, and 'failure of containment', where concern about a family moved beyond the control of a small group of front-line workers or they felt their own resources and skills were exhausted. Drawing on the work of Gelles they then suggest that one consequence of this 'rule of optimism', is that the number of official allegations of mistreatment is far smaller than the actual size of the problem, which may afflict up to 20 per cent of the children in England.

While the research provides interesting insights into the decision-making process, it is important to be aware of the ideological position it attempts to legitimate. The authors are at pains to dissociate themselves from what they characterise 'chic radicals', such as Justice for Children, who they say see child protection agencies as 'rapaciously scouring the homes of the poor for children to seize',[15] and the 'heavy-handed paternalists', such as Alfred White Franklin, who assume that child welfare should be an absolute social priority requiring the rescue of all innocent children from inadequate or evil parents.

They try to develop a middle ground – what they call a social democratic position. Thus while their personal conclusions are that agency staff are over-respectful of parental liberties and that there should be more state intervention, they argue that the current situation arises because of the inherent limitations placed upon the agencies concerned which results from the bargain struck in a liberal democracy between individual autonomy and state control. They feel that their middle-ground position is superior because unlike others, which emanate directly from a single unified theory, theirs has developed from a grounded empirical base and therefore reflects the world as it is.

They make it plain that they do not see it as their role to question whether the social structure plays any part in causing abuse, for 'while it may be possible to conceive of forms of social organisation which would, as it were, design out mistreatment, these do not seem to represent realizable alternatives at this point in history'.[16] Similarly, because they are only looking at the social processes whereby abuse is identified, they never attempt to analyse what causes the abuse in the first place.

Thus their recommendations for policy and practice are limited to modifications to the present statutory framework and agency procedures. Not only that, but by never asking the question 'what causes the problem?' they slip into a position of assuming that the prime responsibility lies with the parents themselves. As one critical commentator of their work has written 'according to this view, the vital thing is to rescue children from situations of risk. Little attention is paid to the family and social dynamics which created the problem or to ways of reducing the risk while keeping the family intact.'[17] The central concern becomes not just how and why certain cases become selected for statutory treatment but why there are not far more, and by implication that there *should* be far more.

In part this arises from the way the research was carried out. Initially the focus was on court hearings, the organisation and presentation of evidence and the disposal decisions. It became apparent however that this would cast very little light on which cases were officially labelled as abusive, for it is a rare occurrence for a care order not to be granted once the case goes to court.[18] It was only at this stage that it was decided to undertake participant observation within the health and welfare services to assess how agency staff identified such cases in their everyday practice.

They then came across cases which according to the medical and social criteria were the same as those already studied in the court setting. But it is as if they take as their implicit definition of mistreatment and what to do about it from the court. It is not surprising therefore if they later ask themselves why more cases are not statutorily acted upon.

In taking such a narrow, legalistic conception of mistreatment they give little attention to other forms of welfare work with families. It seems that the only response Dingwall, Eakelaar and Murray consider legitimate where there is concern about a child is in terms of statutory intervention. In the process they discredit any other type of work with families as being soft or not in the child's interests. This is clearly a value position and one to which many, particularly social workers, would not subscribe. It gives no serious role to prevention or voluntary work with families or attempts to avoid an adversarial relationship.

At the same time, by simply providing an insight into child protection decision-making in the late 1970s at a micro-level, they fail to provide any serious analysis of the important changes in the increase in place of safety orders, increased reliance on statutory control over children in care and the other important shifts in policy and practice I drew attention to in Chapter 5. It is not adequate to say 'these figures could indicate that parents have become less compliant or reflect the increasing elaboration of inter-agency consultations, which reduces the likelihood of containing marginal cases'.[19] Both may be contributory factors but they fail to explain why this should be the case in the 1970s in Britain. Dingwall, Eekelaar and Murray do not see it as part of their task to consider radical alternatives to current policy and practice.

Towards a Positive Practice

How then can we construct a framework for practice which attempts to be progressive and which takes seriously the structural factors associated with abuse?

In essence there needs to be not only a fundamental reconceptualisation of child abuse but a new form of relationship between the family and the state. These two issues are closely related and together would form the basis for a different type of welfare practice. It is crucial that we stop defining child abuse as a pathological problem affecting a few individuals and families which can be predicted in some scientific and technical way. Child abuse is primarily associated with the stresses and insecurities of certain deprived sections of the community which arise primarily from structural inequality. Therefore if we are serious about the problem we have to look to far more wide-ranging forms of social reorganisation than has even been put on the agenda. The individualisation of familial units, the cultural legitimacy of violence in families and the power relations involved all require radical change.

At present debates take place in terms of the 'rights of children' and the 'rights of parents' and what is the appropriate boundary and standard for state intervention in 'private' family life. The terms of these debates need to be recast. In reality the idea of parental rights has grown up with the notion of parental responsibility for rearing the children required by the labour market and the state. Parents are held responsible not only for producing hard-working, law-abiding and 'well-adjusted' citizens but for any social problems such as child abuse that may arise. 'In this context we should be striving to shift the parameters of the debate away from rights and towards responsibilities, away from *"whose"* responsibilities and towards responsibilities *"to do what"*.'[20]

It is important that we aim towards collectivism and away from individualism in the tasks currently allocated to the sphere of private family life. In a socialist society the private market would disappear and there would be a significant shift away from the main current alternatives of either bureaucratic state provision or the privatised nuclear family for caring for the dependent sections of society.[21] The responsibility for caring for children would be carried primarily by a system of democratic, decentralised, community-run provisions. They would consist of a combination of local mutual aid and nationally provided resources which would be subject to local democratic control. Such developments would ensure women were not left with the prime responsibility for child care and would be supportive of moves towards equality between women and men and the breaking down of the distinction between home and work.

It is not that we simply need an expanded role for the state but that the social relations which it reflects should be democratic and play an active and supportive role in bringing up children. Any attempts to increase the choices available, in order to provide alternatives to the existing patterns of family life, should also indicate current developments in policy and practice. As Peter Moss has suggested:

> the provision of more diverse and flexible care arrangements, to meet the increasing diversity of family life, and to help reconcile the demands of childcare with the demands of equality of opportunity, poses one of the most sensitive and important tasks facing all those concerned with the development of social policy.[22]

He suggests three interim strategies which might encourage such diversity and flexibility in childcare: (1) the encouragement of reciprocal arrangements of care, advice and general support between care-givers and others in the community which would build upon existing networks and arrangements but would support self-help groups and other forms of community development; (2) the development of flexible state forms of childcare provision which would be responsive to care-giver needs and available on demand. This would complement the growth of informal and reciprocal arrangements; and (3) measures to give fathers more opportunity to give time to their children and more generally facilitate the combining of employment and parenthood.

Primary Prevention

Our efforts to prevent child abuse should aim to change the social factors which are disproportionately represented

amongst abusing families. Rather than being primarily concerned with trying to identify abusive families and provide
individualised treatment we need to concentrate our energies
on primary prevention strategies and wider social reforms.
Child abuse must not be seen in isolation from the social
stresses and insecurity experienced by many children and
families and cannot be separated from the range of children's
policy issues and the attack on social deprivation. In attempting to meet the needs of all children and families, and not just
the selected few, we can be more assured that we will be
tackling the problem at hand.

Initially therefore we need to consider the principles of a
primary prevention policy for families which would reduce the
general levels of poverty, stress, insecurity, ill-health and bad
housing. Coussins and Coote[23] have identified six criteria by
which family policies should be measured. They should: (1) be
designed to break down rather than reinforce the artificial
division of labour between women and men; (2) be built on
freedom of choice; (3) recognise that children are our most
precious resource and that everyone has an obligation to them,
whether parents themselves or not; (4) be based on maintaining and expanding the social wage and community facilities
under local control, such as eating places, social centres and
laundries; (5) recognise the rights and needs of children within
families as well as those of the family as a unit; (6) recognise
the additional financial pressure on families with dependent
children, and restore and protect the resources of these
families.

Judged against such criteria, developments over recent
years, particularly since the election of the Conservative
Government under Margaret Thatcher, we have retreated
further into a situation where not only is poverty and deprivation becoming more widespread but those who experience such
problems are held responsible for their plight:

> All the evidence is that the numbers in poverty have increased, that the
> burden of taxation on the poor has got heavier, that cuts in services and
> benefits have hit them hardest. The costs of four years of Thatcherism
> have been heavy and the poor have borne more than their fair share of
> these costs. They have suffered from neglect, from policies of deliberate
> hostility and from a casual disregard of the cumulative impact of policy.[24]

For example, since 1979 the number of people dependent on a more stringent supplementary benefit has risen by 50 per cent to over 7 million. The number below pension age on supplementary benefit has more than doubled, while the number of children being brought up by families dependent on supplementary benefit will have virtually doubled to 1.9 million by 1983/4. It is families, particularly amongst the unemployed, who have been put in the greatest hardship.[25] The welfare state is in the process of being restructured in ways which increase rather than reduce the prevalence of child abuse and neglect. It seems likely that this process of restructuring will continue. The leaked report from the Government Family Policy group[26] illustrates that the central aim is to put independence and personal responsibility back into family life by the re-domestication of women, an increasing role for the family in looking after its dependents and the reduction of the state's role in welfare to the provision of minimal standards. It will be a residual, harsh and stigmatising service – a return to Victorian values. There is no mention of the nature or consequences of family poverty, deprivation or structural inequality in the report. In this situation it is inappropriate to expect that social work can in any way counterbalance such shifts and be expected to control and reduce such problems as child abuse.

If we are to attempt to tackle the factors associated with child abuse and neglect, the first priority must be a comprehensive anti-poverty strategy. Such a strategy should recognise the need for a more equal distribution of resources. While a reduction in unemployment would be important it is also evident that, in the same way as the present government has redistributed to the rich in a period of recession, it is possible to redistribute in favour of the less well off. For example Peter Townsend[27] has calculated that the share of national disposable income going to the poorest 20 per cent of the population in 1980 could be doubled by extracting less than a sixth of the share of the wealthiest 20 per cent. We cannot begin to solve the problems associated with poverty until we try to tackle the problems of inequality and the accumulation of income and wealth by those at the top of the social structure. However it is not simply a question of tackling inequality but also of improving the democratic control and allocation of power, so that individuals, families and communities have more choice open to them and more control over their lives.

As I have demonstrated there is considerable evidence of deprivation amongst young children. The Black Report on Inequalities in Health argues that 'top priority must be given to measures which will enhance family living standards and reduce the high risk of children suffering those forms of deprivation and poverty which inhibit healthy development'.[28]

It is apparent that the present social security system fails to meet the needs of children and families. For example David Piachaud[29] has attempted to estimate the true cost of bringing up a child. After making allowance for food, clothing, laundry, heating, toys and presents, pocket money, the cost of travelling to school, and a minimal allowance for entertainment he demonstrates that the supplementary benefit rate for an eight-year-old is only 64 per cent of the true cost of providing what the rate is intended to cover. His calculations were at the lowest cost.

There are a range of intermediary reforms which could be introduced to tackle the problem. The Child Poverty Action Group have recently argued for a series of modest but practical measures which could enable immediate improvements to be made. The first goal would be to raise the level of child benefit to at least 5.5 per cent of average gross male industrial earnings. This would have equalled a figure of £7 in April 1981. For 1983/4, when child benefit is £6.50, it would give a figure of approximately £9.30. The Black Report recognised the importance of providing resources for those caring for young infants and recommended, in 1980, that the maternity grant needed to be increased to £100. It also recommended the introduction of an 'infant care allowance' at a similar level as for child benefit to be paid to those caring for children under five.[30]

Such measures could be financed by modifications in the tax system. The Child Poverty Action Group has estimated that:[31] the abolition of the married man's tax allowance would save £3.5 billion in the year 1982/83; the restriction of all tax allowances and reliefs to the standard rate of tax would save over £700 million; and the abolition of the ceiling on national insurance employee and self-employed contributions would save £520 million.

Social Services Departments and Prevention

In advocating primary prevention strategies for child abuse we must recognise that social services departments and social workers have been cast in the central role in dealing with the problem. I am not arguing that this in itself is wrong, only that the expectations placed upon them are wholly inappropriate without wide-ranging social reforms. Whether such changes take place or not, social services departments and social workers will continue to play this central role. But rather than attempting to develop their own policies which might foster preventative measures with deprived families, it seems there has been a shift towards approaches which are primarily controlling and rescue orientated.

Yet it was the clear intention of the Seebohm Committee and subsequently the Barclay Committee that social services departments would be a preventive service and support family and community networks. This preventive duty to promote the welfare of children is embodied in Section One of the 1963 Children and Young Persons Act and the first section of the Child Care Act 1980. Many social workers are committed to this element of their role but it seems the philosophy is less evident in the policies of the social services departments themselves. For example, for the year ending March 1981 the total local authority expenditure on preventive and supportive services for families was £5 015 000 out of a total personal social services budget of £1 843 930 000 or less than 0.3 per cent.[32]

Fuller and Stevenson have drawn attention to the growth during the 1970s of specialist fostering and adoption officers and the lack of equivalent social work specialists working in a preventive role with children and families:

> There is no doubt that much effort goes into prevention and rehabilitation by some social workers for some families, but the impression at present is that this is socially and professionally less valued than the work which is being undertaken in relation to substitute care.[33]

Many departments have been introducing new systems for planning for children in care in which if rehabilitation back home is not effected in the first few months then a permanent placement should be sought with foster or preferably adoptive parents. Increasingly the notions of shared care are less in evidence and it is assumed that the social services department is to supplant the family if the parents cannot cope alone. There are increasing indications that the permanent placement model is the one equated most frequently by social service professionals with having a child care policy.

In contrast I believe we need to place these preventive principles at the centre of child care policies and show that the relationship between the department and the family can be a positive experience. The role of the personal social services should be to supplement and support parents in the care they give their children. We therefore need to extend the range of choices available to them. If we recognise that the root of the problem lies in structural factors beyond the control of individuals we are more likely to be able to help them cope with and change their situation than if we see the cause of the problem as arising from the individuals themselves. This is not to say that such preventive work can make good the deprivations arising from poverty and inequality.

One major service which departments could develop, but which in reality has been reduced, is day care. Local authority day nurseries providing all day care were expanded rapidly during the Second World War from 4000 places in 1938 to 72 000 in 1944. However, after the war they were rapidly run down to 30 000 places in 1954 and 21 000 by 1969. This fall has been modified slightly by some provision under the urban aid programme. The total is now about 25 000. Yet in 1976 the total on the priority waiting lists was over 12 000. It is apparent that day nurseries can increasingly only offer vacancies to children 'at risk' either of abuse or neglect, or with special needs. It is often day nurseries which are the first resource considered for closure by departments in a period of financial cutback because there is no statutory obligation to provide them. As a result those that remain are often used as specialist centres to assess and instill parenting skills in families considered 'at risk' of abusing or neglecting their children.

Holman[34] quotes two important examples of the significance of day care for supporting families under stress. In 1979 Devon Social Services Department[35] reported that in the three divisions with the highest rate of day care provision a particularly low proportion of the child population was in care and had been admitted into care during the previous two years. The opposite was the case for divisions with low provision. The report argued that an increase in day care facilities would lead to fewer young children needing to come into care, remaining in care and being at risk of abuse. Similarly Islington Social Services[36] demonstrate that the number of children under two received into their care dropped by 74 per cent in eight years following the development of its day care and education facilities for under fives. It is thus important to develop the universal availability of day care for children.

In addition, expansion in specialist facilities for helping and maintaining families in a supportive developmental environment is vital. The emphasis should be on assisting parents to manage their children rather than monitoring or constraining the adult. In this respect recent interest in the development of Family Centres might prove important in offering skilled help in an environment which does not hold the parents responsible for their situation and difficulties with their children.[37]

It is important that the principles of practice I wish to advocate should inform the philosophy of the whole approach of the personal social services in their work with families, particularly where there are concerns about child abuse. In attempting to work with families in a shared way it is important to establish a partnership whereby all concerned are encouraged to participate actively. This means seeing the nature of local authority care as a supportive and integrative part of helping. In the process the priority should shift to encouraging a voluntary relationship in which parents are allowed to make choices and decisions rather than being subject to a detached form of surveillance and statutory control. Clearly this questions the individualised professional, expert role of social work in cases of child abuse on which many current procedures and practices are based. Policies should be informed by the notion of working 'with' families, rather than 'for' them, and taking seriously the struggles that many experience every day. In terms of Newberger and Bourne's scheme outlined in Chapter 1 (Table 1.1) this means moving away from policies which are primarily concerned with the rescue of children via the use of coercive intervention and punishment towards policies which are more compassionate via the use of voluntary child development services and guaranteed family services.

Implications for Social Work Practice

If some of the suggestions for immediate and medium-term policies to do something about child abuse and neglect appear modest this will certainly seem to be the case for my suggestions for everyday social work practice. Far from being exceptional or obviously radical I feel that many of the principles and methods of practice already well accepted in working with children and families are very appropriate for what needs to be done in the current climate of child abuse work. Of course, whether certain practices are seen as progressive or creative is very dependent on the time, place and professional culture in which they are presented. If what I have suggested about the direction that recent trends in this area have taken is at all valid it is quite possible that practices that might have been seen as only good social work practice twenty years ago take on a new significance in a different political climate.

For example it seems that the emphasis in the late 1950s and during the 1960s in child care practice emphasised attempts to prevent family breakdown. There was a growing concern to help deprived families in the community and recognise the importance of material and environmental factors in putting children 'at risk' of coming into local authority care. However there is little doubt that there was a failure to specify the nature of these environmental factors in terms of political and economic structures. As a consequence social workers were unable to easily respond to the assault on their preventive work which resulted from the moral panic related to child abuse in the 1970s.

It is thus crucial that we recognise how the issue of child abuse has helped bring about a restructuring of the relationship between the family and the state in the particularly sensitive area of social work practice with children and families. We should not see our interventions as being professionally neutral or technical but as subject to crucial political anxieties and realignments which have fundamental significance for the way we carry out our task, and the way it is experienced by the families involved and the wider society. Because social workers play the central role in mediating between families and the state in this area of work they are able to influence the choices available to clients and protect their citizenship rights. In this respect we must not denigrate our ability to involve clients in the process and work 'with' them in a democratic way on their own territory. I feel that in trying to work with families in a partnership we must attempt to establish voluntary, participatory relationships that can support the various parties in often extremely anxious and stressful periods. Far from encouraging social work which is indecisive and woolly an emphasis on voluntarily work with families will encourage all concerned to think through the reasons for intervention and the best way of proceeding. For example, it is often implied that social work with children in care should be planned and consistent, and that serious early consideration needs to be given to permanent exclusive placements either back home, with foster parents or adopters. However planned, consistent social work does not, as I have argued, have to conform to this permanent placement model. It does not follow that social work which attempts to provide shared care and which maintains the active involvement of parents is vague, drifting and not in the best interests of the child. As June Thoburn has illustrated in her research, 'some of the cases in this study support the view of several of the social workers interviewed that children can maintain bonds with natural parents while being given loving care by foster parents or residential workers'.[38]

Similarly David Berridge,[39] in his research on 'ordinary' children's homes has found that children living in children's homes, particularly adolescents, can cope with and indeed, sometimes claim to prefer a system of shared care. Despite their separation from home, parents continue to occupy a special position in their lives and the natural parents continue to be significant psychologically for the development and maintenance of the young person's identity and general adjustment.

This emphasis on shared care is far more in evidence, and in fact growing, in other areas demonstrating that it is a feasible and realistic alternative. A number of social services departments have established schemes for the short-term fostering of mentally and physically handicapped children in order to support the families in their task and give the parents a break. Often once a relationship between the natural family and the foster parents has been established the natural and foster parents then make their own arrangements and place the child themselves even though the local authority pays, sometimes on the basis of joint funding. This is very different to the area of child abuse and neglect and where children are considered 'at risk'. Increasingly it seems that decisions about the permanent placement of children with substitute families are being pursued vigorously and systematically not just for children who have lingered for too long in limbo, but also to sever in a short time connections of children admitted or committed to care, in order that they have exclusive 'psychological parenting'.

However, if social workers are to resist this trend and encourage shared care it means their approach and priorities may have to be re-ordered. They need to cultivate skills and a style which is more personal rather than more detached and official. The problem we should be concentrating on is not how to terminate parental contact, but how to start it and maintain it in a way that helps the child.[40] Many of the current policies surrounding the 1975 Children Act and planning for permanency were based on the assumption that social workers were far too sentimental about the blood-tie and that separation from parents should be avoided at all costs.

However it seems that quite the opposite is the case,[41] and indeed was the case even prior to the Colwell panic, where children were in foster care. Vic George has found in his research that only 3.8 per cent of natural parents were encouraged to see their children.[42] Bob Holman calculated that in over half the cases neither natural mother nor natural father had been contacted by the social workers in a year.[43] Ros Thorpe found that 45 per cent of her sample had not been seen by a social worker for at least two years, 62 per cent of the parents did not know where their children had been sent, and 72 per cent of the children had no contact with their parents.[44] Similarly, June Thoburn found in her research that in nearly half the cases the parents had no way of contacting their child except via the social services office, and were rarely involved in looking at or preparing for any change in placement.[45]

Feelings of guilt, stigma and poor self-image can often prevent parents keeping up contact, particularly when placements are at some distance, the parents are short of money and they have other responsibilities and stresses to contend with. Clearly social workers have a crucial role to play in encouraging such contact, not just by drawing upon their counselling skills but by keeping to a minimum the practical barriers to contact. Help with the basic financial costs of maintaining parental contact via visits to their children in care, by using Section One or Section Twenty Six of the 1980 Child Care Act, can prove vital.

In arguing that the problem of child abuse and neglect should be seen in the context of work with children and families more generally, it is important to recognise that there are some specific anxieties, procedures and practices that apply to this area of work which need to be taken seriously. This is not to say however that the general principles I am advocating here should not be applied to situations seen as 'NAI' or child abuse. In many respects the need is greater if the parties involved, particularly the parents and children concerned, are not to have their basic citizenship undermined.[46]

Both departments and social workers need to be open, explicit and honest in their discussions with families so that they are aware of the reasons for contact, the formal statutory content of that role and the various options open. It is not uncommon for important decisions to be taken without any real involvement of parents and children and in virtual secrecy. They should be told which of their actions puts them at risk of losing their children so that they then at least have some notion of what is expected. Not only will this avoid the spectre of the paternalistic, anxious approach which manifests an over-generalised but unspecific concern, but it will help everyone understand their respective positions. Most of all it should encourage more realistic involvement and understanding on behalf of the clients in the decisions and procedures that may be involved.

It is important that the parents or guardians be aware of their legal rights. Certainly if it seems that action against the parents' wishes, perhaps in the form of an admission to care, is being considered they should be carefully informed of their legal situation and the options open to them. We need to try to avoid a tense, cautious and limited approach, as this is likely to make the anxiety and lack of trust even greater, and in the process heighten the sense of stress in the family. If there is a conflict of interests and differing view of the 'facts' this will not he helped by a benign defensiveness on the part of the worker and a denial of the authority element of the role.

While difficult in the current climate it is important to try to de-mystify the internal mechanisms of the child abuse system and make them more open, accountable and responsive to the views and feelings not only of the parents involved but also, whenever possible, of the children. Often it is assumed by the experts involved that they know what is 'in the best interests of the child' without involving the child in any way. It is a debate between the local authority and the parents, often with the local authority claiming to speak on behalf of the child's best interests.

For example, the case conference can present a serious threat to civil liberties. Information and opinion is shared by numerous professionals and their line managers, many of whom have no direct knowledge or contact with the family. Not only are parents or children rarely present, and have no one directly representing their view (unless the social worker takes on this role), but they are often given no direct feedback of the decisions taken, why and even that their situation was being discussed at all. The conference is seen as a private professional/organisational arena. Usually the emphasis is on to whom, when and how concerns about a child should be communicated and who should take certain responsibilities. The process of decision-making emphasises the questions of whether statutory intervention should be considered and whether the family should be placed on the child abuse register.

Yet the opportunities are available in case conferences for

attempting to understand the stresses the family may be under and sometimes mobilising help of a practical nature. For this process to take place the family must be directly involved. To involve families in this way means considerable groundwork, otherwise they will be little more than defenceless observers. A part of this groundwork includes encouraging the family to clarify their situation and needs and helping them understand how the different professionals' role and interests vary.

In all child abuse work it is important to be precise, focused and factual both in the way work is carried out with families and the information that is shared with other professionals. The decision of who should be informed, how and when of concerns about a family can be crucial as it is easy for workers and families to lose control of information if it is not carried out sensitively and astutely. The use of organisational, advocacy and negotiating skills are often central.

There is always a danger of using euphemistic and all-inclusive terms which can cloud the issues and which can be interpreted in a variety of ways. For example it is not uncommon to hear behaviour being described as 'inappropriate' or 'significant' without it being specified what is meant by that and how the behaviour would need to change. Another euphemism often used is 'permanence' which has taken on the meaning of the child living with another family.

Conclusion

In this final chapter I have attempted to show how an understanding of child abuse based on structural inequality can inform policy and practice. One of the lingering issues is how the problem can be defined. Essentially I have argued that while child abuse is far more prevalent and pervasive than official statistics and many professionals might admit, the ways of attacking it are certainly not in terms of 'more of the same'. If the problem is a structural one we have to attack it at that level. This is not to say, however, that the individual situations we come across do not require often decisive action and a sensitive response. It thus seems sensible at the present time that for the purposes of a longer term strategy the definition of child abuse should be broad and include all forms of child maltreatment at the individual, institutional and societal level. Such a broad definition would help raise public awareness about the needs of children and families. But for the purposes of quick intervention, perhaps on the basis of statutory action, we should take a much more prescribed narrow definition. This would help protect civil liberties and unwarranted intervention into families while ensuring that attention was not deflected from the wider, more crucial issues.

Welfare practitioners, especially social workers, are in a particularly invidious position. It is important to use all possibilities for arguing and demonstrating that child abuse must be seen in a much wider social context and cannot be eradicated by individualised and potentially authoritarian methods. However, there is a vital role for social workers to help alleviate individual and family suffering in their everyday practice, even though these are structurally induced.

Notes and References

Chapter 1

1. See I. Taylor, P. Walton and J. Young, *The New Criminology: For a Social Theory of Deviance* (Routledge & Kegan Paul, 1973); I. Taylor, P. Walton and J. Young (eds), *Critical Criminology* (Routledge & Kegan Paul, 1975); P. Wiles (ed.) *The Sociology of Crime and Delinquency in Britain: Volume Two: The New Criminologies* (Robertson, 1976); D. Downes and P. Rock (eds), *Deviant Interpretations: Problems in Criminological Theory* (Robertson, 1979); J. A. Inciardi (ed.) *Radical Criminology: The Coming Crises* (Sage, 1980); B. Fine, R. Kinsey, J. Lea, S. Picciotto and J. Young, *Capitalism and the Rule of Law: From Deviancy Theory to Marxism* (Hutchinson, 1979); D. Downes and P. Rock, *Understanding Deviance: A Guide to the Sociology of Crime and Rule-Breaking* (Oxford University Press, 1982). M. Fitzgerald, G. McLennan and J. Pawson (eds), *Crime & Society: Readings in History and Theory* (Routledge & Kegan Paul, 1981).
2. However, see S. J. Pfohl, 'The Discovery of Child Abuse', *Social Problems*, vol. 24, no. 3, February 1977, pp. 310–23; R. Gelles, 'Child Abuse as Psychopathology: a sociological critique and reformulation', *American Journal of Orthopsychiatry*, vol. 43, July 1973, pp. 611–21; R. Gelles, 'The Social Construction of Child Abuse', *American Journal of Orthopsychiatry*, vol. 45, April 1975, pp. 659–68 and in this country M. Chatterton, 'The Social Contexts of Violence' in M. Borland (ed.), *Violence in the Family* (Manchester University Press, 1976); D. Marsden, 'Sociological Perspectives on Family Violence' in J. P. Martin (ed.) *Violence in the Family* (Wiley, 1978); R. Dingwall, J. Eekelaar and T. Murray, *The Protection of Children: State Intervention and Family Life* (Basil Blackwell, 1983).
3. For strident examples of this attack see R. Lewis, 'Artful dodgers of the world unite?' in C. B. Cox and R. Boyson (eds), *Black Paper* (Temple Smith, 1977) and more recently the publications of The Social Affairs Unit. For a more measured critique of the role of sociology in social work training see M. Davies, 'What we have to learn about social work education', *Community Care*, no. 343, 15 January 1981; R. Wright, *Expectations of the teaching of social workers in courses leading to the CQSW:*

Consultation Document No. 3 (CCETSW, 1977). Also applied to child abuse, Dingwall, Eekelaar and Murray, *The Protection of Children*.

4. J. Clarke, 'Critical Sociology and Radical Social Work: Problems of Theory and Practice', in N. Parry, M. Rustin and C. Satyamurti (eds), *Social Work, Welfare and the State* (Arnold, 1979); J. Clarke, M. Langan and P. Lee, 'Social Work: the conditions of crisis', in P. Carlen and M. Collison (eds), *Radical Issues in Criminology* (Robertson, 1980).

5. S. Cohen, *Folk Devils and Moral Panics* (Paladin, 1973), p. 12.

6. See Taylor, Walton and Young, *The New Criminology*, and Downes and Rock, *Understanding Deviance*.

7. K. Plummer, 'Misunderstanding Labelling Perspectives', in Downs and Rock (eds), *Deviant Interpretations*, p. 88.

8. R. C. Fuller and R. D. Myers, 'The Natural History of a Social Problem', *American Sociological Review*, vol. 6, 6 June 1941, p. 320; also W. Waller, 'Social Problems and Mores', *American Sociological Review*, vol. 1, 1936, pp. 922–33. For an application of the natural history approach to child abuse see N. Parton, 'The Natural History of Child Abuse: A Study in Social Problem Definition', *British Journal of Social Work*, vol. 9, no. 4, 1979, pp. 431–51.

9. H. Blumer, 'Social Problems as Collective Behaviour', *Social Problems*, Winter, vol. 18, no. 3, 1971; H. Becker (ed.), *Introduction to Social Problems* (Wiley, 1966); A. L. Mauss (ed.), *Social Problems as Social Movements* (Lippincott, 1975); R. P. Lowry, *Social Problems: A Critical Analysis of Theories of Public Policy* (D. C. Heath, 1974).

10. M. Spector and J. I. Kitsuse, 'Towards a Sociology of Social Problems: Social Conditions, Value Judgements and Social Problems', *Social Problems*, vol. 20, no. 4, 1973; J. I. Kitsuse and M. Spector, 'Social Problems and Deviance: Some Parallel Issues', *Social Problems*, vol. 22, June 1975, pp. 584–94. In the second article Kitsuse and Spector argue that the task of social problems theory is to describe and explain 'the definitional process in which morally objectionable conditions or behaviours are asserted to exist, and the collective activities that become organised around these assertions'.

11. See K. Erickson, *Wayward Puritans* (Wiley, 1966) for an interesting example of this.

12. E. Rubington and M. S. Weinberg (eds), *The Study of Social Problems: Five Perspectives* (Oxford University Press, 2nd edition 1977); also M. S. Weinberg and E. Rubington (eds), *The Solution of Social Problems: Five Perspectives* (Oxford University Press, 1973).

13. H. S. Becker, *Outsiders: Studies in the Sociology of Deviance* (The Free Press, 1963).

14. Becker, *Outsiders*, p. 145; also A. Lindesmith, *The Addict and the Law* (Indiana University Press, 1965); C. E. Reasons, *The Criminologist, Crime and the Criminal* (Pacific Palisades, 1974); D. Musto, *The American Disease:*

Origins of Narcotic Control (Yale University Press, 1973); R. J. Bonnie and C. H. Whitbread, *The Marihuana Conviction: A History of Marihuana Prohibition in the US* (University Press of Virginia, 1974).

15. D. T. Dickson, 'Bureaucracy and Morality', *Social Problems*, vol. 16, no. 2, 1968, pp. 143–56.

16. J. F. Galliher and A. Walker, 'The Puzzle of the Social Origins of the Marihuana Tax Act of 1937', *Social Problems*, vol. 24, no. 3, February 1977, pp. 367–77.

17. See T. Duster, *The Legislation of Morality* (The Free Press, 1970); J. Young, *The Drugtakers* (Paladin, 1972).

18. J. R. Gusfield, *Symbolic Crusade: Status Politics and the American Temperence Movement* (University of Illinois Press, 1963).

19. A. Platt, *The Child Savers: The Invention of Delinquency* (University of Chicago Press, 1969).

20. J. Gusfield, *The Culture of Public Problems: Drinking – Driving and the Symbolic Order* (University of Chicago Press, 1981); C. L. Wiener, *The Politics of Alcoholism: Building an Arena Around a Social Problem* (Transaction Books, 1981).

21. J. Gusfield, 'Categories of Ownership and Responsibility in Social Issues: Alcohol Abuse and Automobile Use', *Journal of Drug Issues*, no. 5, 1975, p. 290.

22. S. D. Stein, 'The 'Sociology of Law: Some Comments on Theoretical Paradigms and Case Studies', *British Journal of Criminology*, vol. 20, no. 2, April 1980.

23. A. Gouldner, 'The Sociologist as Partisan: Sociology and the Welfare State', *American Sociologist*, 1968, pp. 103–16; A. Scull, *Decarceration, Community Treatment and the Deviant: A Radical View* (Prentice Hall, 1977).

24. J. Young, 'Thinking seriously about crime: some models of criminology' in Fitzgerald, McLennan and Pawson (eds), *Crime and Society*, p. 293.

25. F. Pearce, *Crimes of the Powerful* (Pluto Press, 1976).

26. P. Bachrach and M. S. Baratz, 'Decisions and Non-Decisions: An Analytical Framework', *American Political Science Review*, no. 57, 1963, pp. 641–51.

27. S. Lukes, *Power: A Radical View* (Macmillan, 1976), p. 22; see also T. Benton, 'Objective Interests and the Sociology of Power', *Sociology*, vol. 15, no. 2, May 1981, pp. 161–84.

28. M. Clarke, 'Social Problem Ideologies', *British Journal of Sociology*, vol. 26, 1975, pp. 406–16, p. 407.

29. E. Schur, *Radical Non-Intervention: Rethinking the Delinquency Problem* (Prentice Hall, 1973).

30. E. Schur, *Crimes Without Victims: Deviant Behaviour and Public Policy* (Prentice Hall, 1963).

31. E. H. Newberger and R. Bourne, 'The Medicalisation and Legalisation

of Child Abuse' in J. M. Eekelaar and S. N. Katz (eds), *Family Violence: An International and Interdisciplinary Study* (Butterworths, 1977).

32. G. Smith, 'The Place of "Professional Ideology" in the analysis of "Social Policy": some theoretical conclusions from a pilot study of the Children's Panels', *Sociological Review*, vol. 25, no. 4, 1977, pp. 843–65.

33. There has been much interest in recent years in the nature of professional ideologies and operational philosophies and the way these relate to the accounts of the professionals involved, particularly in the area of delinquency. See J. H. Marx, 'A Multi-Dimensional conception of Ideologies in Professional Arenas', *Pacific Sociological Review*, Fall 1969, pp. 75–85; P. C. Hardiker, 'Social Work Ideologies in the Probation Service', *British Journal of Social Work*, vol. 7, no. 2, 1977, pp. 131–54; P. Hardiker and D. Webb, 'Explaining Deviant Behaviour: The Social Context of "action" and "infraction" accounts in the Probation Service', *Sociology*, vol. 13, no. 1, 1979, pp. 1–18, D. May and G. Smith, 'Policy Interpretation and the Children's Panels: A case study in Social Administration', *Applied Social Studies*, vol. 2, 1970, pp. 91–8; H. Parker, M. Casburn and D. Turnbull, *Receiving Juvenile Justice* (Basil Blackwell, 1981).

34. For example E. Friedson, *Profession of Medicine: A Study in the Sociology of Applied Knowledge* (Dodd, Mead & Co., 1970); C. S. Stoll, 'Images of Man and Social Control', *Social Forces*, vol. 47, no. 2, 1968, pp. 119–27.

35. See Friedson, *Profession of Medicine*; F. Allen, 'Criminal Justice, Legal Values and the Rehabilitative Ideal', *Journal of Criminal Law*, vol. 50, 1959, pp. 226–32; M. J. Clarke, 'The Impact of Social Science on Conceptions of Responsibility', *British Journal of Law and Society*, vol. 2, no. 1, Summer 1975.

36. This framework has been developed from J. Carter, 'Problems of Professional Belief' in J. Carter (ed.), *The Maltreated Child* (Priory Press, 1974); J. Carter, 'Is Child Abuse a Crime?' in A. W. Franklin (ed.), *The Challenge of Child Abuse* (Academic Press, 1977); Parton, 'The Natural History of Child Abuse', *British Journal of Social Work*, vol. 9, no. 4, 1979.

37. See for example the publications of Justice for Children, The Family Rights Group, The National Council for One Parent Families and the Children's Legal Centre.

38. For example a private member's Child Care Bill introduced in March 1982 unsuccessfully fought to abolish the section 3 resolution procedure and replace it with a juvenile court hearing; to abolish the 'habits or mode of life' grounds for taking over parental rights; to make parents fuller parties to the proceedings; and to give parents a new right to apply for access to their child in local authority care. The last proposal was accepted as an amendment to the Health and Social Services and Social Security Adjudication Act 1983. The proposals concerning section 3 resolutions remain unreformed.

39. A quote from paragraph 3 of the press release dated 27 July 1982 from the Parliamentary Social Services Committee announcing the inquiry into 'Children in Care'.

40. See for example R. Bailey and P. Lee (eds), *Theory and Practice in Social Work* (Basil Blackwell, 1982). J. Hearn, 'The problem(s) of theory and practice in social work and social work education', *Issues in Social Work Education*, vol. 2, no. 2, 1982.

41. S. Cohen, 'Its All Right for You to Talk: Political and Sociological Manifestos for Social Action' in R. Bailey and M. Brake (eds), *Radical Social Work* (Arnold, 1975) p. 76.

Chapter 2

1. M. P. Thomas Jr, 'Child Abuse and Neglect Part 1: Historical Overview, Legal Matrix and Social Perspectives', *The North Carolina Law Review*, vol. 50, no. 2, February 1972, pp. 293–349.

2. See in particular E. Wilson, *Women and the Welfare State* (Tavistock, 1977).

3. M. May, 'Violence in the Family: An Historical Perspective', in J. P. Martin (ed.), *Violence and the Family* (Wiley, 1978).

4. See for example D. Bakan, *Slaughter of the Innocents: A study of the Battered Child Phenomenon* (Jassey-Bass, 1971); F. H. Garrison, *Abt-Garrison History of Paediatrics*, vol. *1* (W. B. Saunders, 1965); S. X. Radbill, 'A History of Child Abuse and Infanticide' in R. E. Helfer and C. H. Kempe (eds), *The Battered Child* (University of Chicago Press, 1968); P. J. Resnick, 'Infanticide', in J. G. Howells (ed.), *Modern Perspectives in Psycho-Obstetrics* (Oliver & Boyd, 1972); S. Smith, *The Battered Child Syndrome* (Butterworth, 1976).

5. Radbill, 'A History of Child Abuse and Infanticide', p. 4.

6. Smith, *The Battered Child Syndrome*, pp. 7–8.

7. May, 'Violence in the Family: An Historical Perspective', pp. 136–7.

8. C. Norton, *English Laws for Women in the Nineteenth Century* (1854); C. Norton, *A Letter to the Queen on Lord Chancellor Cranworth's Divorce Bill* (Longman, 1855); M. Kramnick (ed.), *Wollstonecraft: Vindication of the Rights of Woman* (Penguin, 1975). Also G. Mitchell (ed.), *The Hard Way Up: The autobiography of Hannah Mitchell, suffragette and rebel* (Virago, 1977).

9. I. Pinchbeck and M. Hewitt, *Children in English Society vol. 1* (Routledge & Kegan Paul, 1969).

10. S. West, 'Acute Periosteal Swellings in Several Young Infants of the Same Family, Probably Rickets in Nature', *British Medical Journal*, vol. 1, 1888, pp. 856–7.

11. J. S. Heywood, *Children in Care: the development of the service for the deprived child* (Routledge & Kegan Paul, 3rd edn 1978).

12. H. Perkin, *The Origins of Modern English Society, 1780–1880* (Methuen, 1969).

13. E. Shorter, *The Making of the Modern Family* (Collins, 1976); E. Zaretsky, *Capitalism, the Family and Personal Life* (Pluto Press, 1976).

14. J. Donzelot, *The Policing of Families: Welfare versus the State* (Hutchinson, 1980).

15. P. Ariès, *Centuries of Childhood* (Penguin, 1962). Also D. Hunt, *Parents and Children in History* (Basic Books, 1970); L. DeMause (ed.), *The History of Childhood* (The Psychohistory Press, 1974).

16. See M. Anderson, 'The Relevance of Family History' in C. Harris (ed.), *The Sociology of the Family: New Directions for Britain* (Sociological Review Monograph no. 28, 1979).

17. See H. Hendrick, *Kept from History: Aspects of the Status of Children Part 1 and 2* (Justice for Children nos. 22 and 25, 1981).

18. P. Thane, 'Childhood in History', in M. King (ed.), *Childhood, Welfare and Justice* (Batsford, 1981).

19. Shorter, *The Making of the Modern Family*, p. 256.

20. Thane, 'Childhood in History', p. 11.

21. Shorter, *The Making of the Modern Family*, p. 5.

22. Donzelot, *The Policing of Families*, p. 55.

23. W. Norton Grubb and M. Lazerson, *Broken Promises: How Americans Fail Their Children* (Basic Books, 1982).

24. Pinchbeck and Hewitt, *Children in English Society vol. 1*, ch. 11.

25. May, 'Violence in the Family', p. 139.

26. May, 'Violence in the Family', p. 150

27. J. Walvin, *A Child's World: A Social History of English Childhood, 1800–1914* (Penguin, 1982).

28. Walvin, *A Child's World*, pp. 21–2.

29. The increase in concern about the level of violence in the nineteenth century was explicitly expressed in May 1874 when the Government commissioned an inquiry into the law on brutal assaults which revealed a general consensus among police and judicial authorities about the serious level of violent crime, ascribed mainly to drink, and which recommended the need for harsher punishments. See May 'Violence in the Family', p. 149.

30. G. Stedman-Jones, *Outcast London* (Clarendon Press, 1971).

31. Walvin, *A Child's World*, p. 18.

32. See G. Pearson, *The Deviant Imagination: Psychiatry, Social Work and Social Change* (Macmillan, 1975), and G. Pearson, *Hooligan: A History of Respectable Fears* (Macmillan, 1983).

33. The work of Mary Carpenter illustrates the increasing concern at the

time. She argued that juvenile delinquency usually originated in parental neglect so that in effect pauper, vagrant and criminal children aged under fourteen could all be classed together. Because they were in trouble through no fault of their own they should be trained rather than punished. Mary Carpenter's reformatory movement shows the increasing attempts to understand delinquency in terms of urban life and parental neglect. It therefore argued for the need for preventive work to forestall delinquency, but focused on the parents.

34. A. Platt, *The Child Savers: The Invention of Delinquency* (University of Chicago Press, 1969).
35. Wilson, *Women and the Welfare State*, p. 23.
36. See N. Parry and J. Parry, 'Social Work, Professionalism and the State', in N. Parry, M. Rustin and C. Satyarmurti (eds), *Social Work, Welfare and the State* (Arnold, 1979); R. G. Walton, *Women and Social Work* (Routledge & Kegan Paul, 1975).
37. May, 'Violence in the Family', p. 154.
38. Information from May, 'Violence in the Family', p. 143.
39. According to Margaret May in 1982 the society amalgamated with the Associated Institute for Improving and Enforcing the Laws for the Protection of Women to form the Associated Societies for the Protection of Women. After considerable wrangling with the NSPCC it agreed to refer cases of child cruelty and neglect to the latter and concentrate on adult women.
40. L. G. Housden, *The Prevention of Cruelty to Children* (Jonathan Cape, 1955) p. 30.
41. Parry and Parry, 'Social Work, Professionalism and the State'.
42. See J. Fido, 'The Charity Organisation Society and Social Casework in London 1869–1900', in A. P. Donajgrodski (ed.), *Social Control in Nineteenth-Century Britain* (Croom Helm, 1977); C. Jones, *State Social Work and the Working Class* (Macmillan, 1983).
43. Donzelot, *The Policing of Families*, p. 55.
44. Stedman-Jones, *Outcast London*, ch. 16.
45. For example Samuel Barnett and Arnold Toynbee advocated non-contributory pensions for the respectable working class who had maintained themselves outside the workhouse up to the age of sixty, subsidised public housing, free school meals and free education.
46. J. Eekelaar, R. Dingwall and T. Murray, 'Victims or Threats? Children in Care Proceedings', *Journal of Social Welfare Law*, March 1982, p. 75.
47. Heywood, *Children in Care*, p. 101.
48. For an account of the origins and history of the NSPCC see A. Allen and A. Morton, *This is Your Child: The Story of the NSPCC* (Routledge & Kegan Paul, 1961).
49. Those attending included Lord Shaftesbury, the Baroness Bardett-

Coutts, Cardinal Manning, Dr Barnardo, Lord Aberdeen, Sir Henry Foulter (Mayor of London) and Mr Kegan Paul.

50. To ensure the Bill's passage through Parliament the Society circulated 10 000 copies of a pamphlet, 'Imperial Legislation and Street Children' to every corporation in the country. As a result 87 corporations representing more than 4 million people petitioned Parliament in favour of the Bill. At the same time a letter running to twelve foolscap pages was sent to every MP.

51. Pinchbeck and Hewitt, *Children and English Society vol. 2* (Routledge & Kegan Paul, 1973), ch. 20.

52. Quoted in Pinchbeck and Hewitt, *Children in English Society vol. 2* (Routledge & Kegan Paul, 1973), p. 627.

53. Heywood, *Children in Care*, pp. 103–4.

54. Eekelaar, Dingwall and Murray, 'Victims or Threats? Children in Care Proceedings', p. 68.

55. Heywood, *Children in Care*, p. 93.

56. Quoted in Housden, *The Prevention of Cruelty to Children*, p. 36.

57. May, 'Violence in the Family', p. 163.

58. G. Searle, *The Quest for National Efficiency* (Oxford University Press, 1971).

59. E. J. Hobsbawm, *Industry and Empire* (Penguin, 1969) ch. 9.

60. B. B. Gilbert, *The Evolution of National Insurance in Great Britain* (Michael Joseph, 2nd edn 1973).

61. The material and arguments for this section depend heavily upon C. Parton, *Liberal Individualism and Infant Mortality: The Infant Welfare Movement in Huddersfield* (MA Thesis, Huddersfield Polytechnic, 1981).

62. Donzelot, *The Policing of Families*, p. xxi.

63. V. MacLeod, *Whose Child? The Family in Child Care Legislation and Social Work Practice*, (Study Commission on the Family Occasional Paper no. 11, 1982) Part 1.

64. Heywood, *Children in Care*, p. 131.

65. R. M. Titmuss, 'Problems of Social Policy', *UK Civil Histories of the Second War* (Longmans Green, 1950).

66. MacLeod, *Whose Child? The Family in Child Care Legislation and Social Work Practice*, pp. 19–20.

67. See for example Wilson, *Women and the Welfare State*, chs 3, 4 and 8.

68. See J. Packman, *The Child's Generation: Child Care Policy from Curtis to Houghton* (Basil Blackwell/Robertson, 2nd edn 1981) particularly ch. 1.

69. Heywood, *Children in Care*, pp. 148–9; Jones, *State Social Work and the Working Class*.

70. Heywood, *Children in Care*, p. 152.

71. B. Jordan and N. Parton (eds), *The Political Dimensions of Social Work* (Basil Blackwell, 1983), p. 3.

72. MacLeod, *Whose Child? The Family in Child Care Legislation and Social Work Practice*, p. 29.

73. J. F. Handler, *The Coercive Social Worker: British Lessons for American Social Services* (Rand McNally, 1973), p. 42.

74. Even prior to the passage of the 1948 Act there were criticisms that the role of the child care service was defined too narrowly and could do little to mitigate deprivation and prevent hardship and admission into care. The stress on the need to keep families together was seen to be legitimated by the work of John Bowlby. It was increasingly argued that the lack of warmth and security that was thought to be characteristic of 'problem families' had deleterious implications for the future. Increasingly ideological and scientific legitimation was given to the link between neglect in early life and later problems and the belief that early intervention was important. See for example T. Stephens, *Problem Families* (Pacifist Service Units, 1946); The Women's Group in Public Welfare, *The Neglected Child and his Family* (Oxford University Press, 1948); J. Bowlby, *Child Care and the Growth of Love* (Penguin, 1953).

75. Ingleby Report, *Report of the Committee on Children and Young Persons*, Cmnd 1191 (HMSO, 1960).

76. Eekelaar, Dingwall and Murray, 'Victims or Threats? Children in Care Proceedings', p. 76.

77. *Crime – A Challenge to us all* (The Longford Report) (The Labour Party, 1964).

78. *The Child, the Family and the Young Offender*, Cmnd 2742 (HMSO, 1965).

79. *Children in Trouble* Cmnd 3601 (HMSO, 1968).

80. For example this was proposed in a debate in the House of Commons on 12 May 1949 and by *The Times* in a Leader article on 22 October 1951 following a number of severe cases. However the Children and Young Persons (Amendment) Act 1952 did modify this criminal approach to cruelty and gave more opportunity to childrens departments to become more involved in cases of cruelty and wilful neglect. It removed the requirement of the prosecution of a parent as a condition precedent for finding a child to be in need of care and protection within the 1933 Act. Under the 1952 (Amendment) Act failure for whatever cause in the parenting function leading to a specified condition in the child became a ground for intervention. Such grounds included that the parent or guardian was 'unfit to exercise care or guardianship or [was] not exercising proper care and guardianship' and 'he was being ill-treated or neglected in a manner likely to cause him unnecessary suffering or injury to health'.

Chapter 3

1. J. Caffey and W. A. Silverman, 'Infantile Cortical Hyperostos: Preliminary Report on a New Syndrome', *American Journal of Roentgenology*, no. 55, 1945, pp. 1–16; J. Caffey, 'Multiple Fractures in the Long Bones of Infants Suffering from Chronic Subdural Hematoma', *American Journal of Roentgenology*, no. 56, 1946, pp. 163–73; J. Caffey, 'Infantile Hyperostosis', *Journal of Paediatrics*, no. 29, 1946, pp. 541–9.

2. See E. F. Lis and G. S. Frauenberger, 'Multiple Fractures Associated with Subdural Hematoma in Infancy', *Paediatrics*, no. 6, 1950, pp. 890–2; M. J. Smith, 'Subdural Hematoma with Multiple Fractures', *American Journal of Roentgenology*, no. 6, 1950, pp. 343–4; H. Bakwin, 'Roentgenographic Changes in Homes following Trauma', *Journal of Paediatrics*, no. 49, 1952, pp. 7–15; G. H. Barmeyer, L. R. Alderson and W. B. Cox, 'Traumatic Periostitis in Young Children', *Journal of Paediatrics*, no. 38, 1951, pp. 184–90.

3. See P. V. Woolley Jr and W. A. Evans Jr, 'Significance of Skeletal Lesions in Infants Resembling those of Traumatic Origin', *Journal of the American Medical Association*, no. 181, 1955, pp. 17–24.

4. S. H. Fisher, 'Skeletal Manifestations of Parent Induced Trauma in Infants and Children', *8th Medical Journal*, no. 51, 1958, pp. 956–60; C. H. Kempe and H. K. Silver, 'The Problem of Parental Criminal Neglect and Severe Abuse in Children', *Journal of Diseases of Children*, no. 48, 1959, p. 528; D. S. Milter, 'Fractures among Children – 1, Parental Assault as Causative Agent', *Minn. Medicine*, no. 42, 1959, pp. 1209–13.

5. See L. Adelson, 'Slaughter of the Innocents: A Study of forty six homicides in which the victims were children', *New England Journal of Medicine*, no. 246, 1961, pp. 1345–9; J. L. Gwinn, K. W. Lewin and H. G. Peterson Jr, 'Roentgenographic Manifestations of Unsuspected Trauma in Infancy: A Problem of Medical, Social and Legal Importance', *Journal of the American Medical Association*, no. 176, 1961, pp. 926–29.

6. See E. Elmer, 'Abused Young Children seen in Hospitals', *Social Work*, no. 5, 1960, pp. 98–102. Also H. Boardman, 'A Project to Rescue Children from Inflicted Injuries', *Social Work*, no. 7, 1962, pp. 43–51.

7. See S. Smith, *The Battered Child Syndrome* (Butterworths, 1976).

8. The American Humane Association is a private charity dedicated to child and animal protection. However, unlike the prevention societies the AHA did not provide a direct service but undertook research, thus providing research and training materials for paediatric and family-focused social workers.

9. See V. De Francis, *Child Protective Services in the United States: Reporting a Nationwide Survey* (Denver Children's Division, American Humane Association, 1956).

10. The Federal Children's Bureau was created by legislation in 1912 to investigate and report upon all matters pertaining to the welfare of children and child life among all classes, though it was not to deal with the welfare of individual children.

11. See G. Y. Steiner, *The Children's Cause* (Brookings, 1976) chs 3 and 4; and B. C. Nelson, 'Setting the Public Agenda: The Case of Child Abuse' in J. V. May and A. B. Wildawsky (eds), *The Policy Cycle* (Sage, 1978).

12. Dr C. Henry Kempe was a noted paediatrician of Denver General Hospital and the University of Colorado School of Medicine. Earlier in his career he had specialised in immunology, where he developed an interest in the behavioural as well as the microbiological aspects of illness.

13. See Nelson, 'Setting the Public Agenda: The Case of Child Abuse', p. 26.

14. See C. H. Kempe, F. N. Silverman, B. F. Steele, W. Droegemueller and H. K. Silver, 'The Battered Child Syndrome', *Journal of the American Medical Association*, no. 181, 1962, pp. 17–24.

15. Kempe, Silverman, Steele, Droegemueller and Silver, 'The Battered Child Syndrome', p. 19.

16. See for example A. F. Philp, *Family Failure* (Faber, 1963); A. F. Philp and N. Timms, *The Problem of the 'problem family'*, (Family Service Units, 1957).

17. See for example C. H. Kempe and R. E. Helfer (eds), *The Battered Child* (Chicago University Press, 1st edn 1968, 2nd edn 1974, 3rd edn 1981); R. E. Helfer and C. H. Kempe (eds), *Child Abuse and Neglect: The Family and the Community* (Ballinger, 1976).

18. For further discussion of how the problem and responses to it have developed subsequently in America see Nelson, 'Setting the Public Agenda: The Case of Child Abuse'. M. Rosenthal and J. A. Louis, 'The Law's Evolving Role in Child Abuse and Neglect' in L. R. Pelton (ed.), *The Social Context of Child Abuse and Neglect* (Human Sciences, 1981).

19. S. Antler, 'The Re-discovery of Child Abuse' in Pelton (ed.), *The Social Context of Child Abuse and Neglect*.

20. See E. Friedson, *Profession of Medicine: A Study of the Sociology of Applied Knowledge* (Dodd, Mead & Co., 1970).

21. S. J. Pfohl, 'The "Discovery" of Child Abuse', *Social Problems*, vol. 24, no. 3, February 1977, pp. 310–23.

22. For example there were five doctors credited with the crucial article 'The Battered Child Syndrome'. Kempe and Silver were respectively heads of the Division of Paediatrics and Radiology at the Children's Hospital, Denver; Brandt Steele was an Associate Professor of Psychiatry at the University of Colorado Medical School and on the staff of the Children's Hospital there; William Droegemueller was a resident in obstetrics and gynaecology at the University of Colorado and the Children's Hospital in Denver; Silverman was in the Department of Paediatrics and Radio-

logy of the Cincinnati College of Medicine and Children's Hospital in Cincinnati.

23. See for example R. Astley, 'Multiple Metaphysical Fractures in Small Children', *British Journal of Radiology*, no. 26, 1953, pp. 577–83. Even though in 1956 Caffey spoke in London of the radiological aspects of the problem in some depth it gave little impetus to the discovery. He went on to suggest that 'early diagnosis' was vital if the 'abused youngsters' were to be removed from their 'traumatic environment' and the wrongdoers 'punished'. See J. Caffey, 'Some Traumatic Lesions in Growing Bones other than Fractures and Dislocations: Clinical and Radiological Features', *British Journal of Radiology*, no. 30, 1957, pp. 225–38. See also British Medical Association and the Magistrates Association, *Cruel and Neglectful Parents* (1956).

24. Leader, 'Welfare of Children', *British Medical Journal*, vol. 2, 28 September 1963, pp. 761–2.

25. D. L. Griffiths and F. J. Moynihan, 'Multiple Epiphyseal Injuries in Babies ("Battered Baby Syndrome")', *British Medical Journal*, no. 11, 1963, pp. 1558–61.

26. Griffiths and Moynihan, 'Multiple Epiphyseal Injuries in Babies ("Battered Baby Syndrome")', p. 1560.

27. Leader, 'Cruelty to Children', *British Medical Journal*, no. 11, 21 December 1963, pp. 1544–5.

28. A personal discussion with Miss Joan Court suggests that Dr Lloyd Griffiths was responsible for coining the label 'battered baby'. It seems Dr Moynihan first came across the issue at a meeting of the South East Metropolitan Orthopaedic Club, at King's College Hospital. Baby twins under a year old who had a fairly classical radiological appearance proved difficult to diagnose. This prompted him to search the literature and he came across Caffey's work. This fostered Dr Moynihan's interest, especially when shortly afterwards he came across three or four similar cases in Guy's Hospital and two more in Kent. Whilst in Manchester he met Dr Griffiths who produced a set of X-rays which were typical of the injuries, and it was from this encounter that the article arose.

29. E. Turner, '"Battered Baby" Syndrome', *British Medical Journal* correspondence, 1 February 1964, p. 308.

30. See A. C. Fairburn and A. C. Hunt, 'Caffey's "Third Syndrome": A Critical Evaluation ("The Battered Baby")', *Medicine, Science and the Law*, no. 4, 1964, pp. 123–6; G. E. Parker, 'The Battered Child Syndrome', *Medicine, Science and the Law*, no. 8, 1965, pp. 160–3.

31. K. Simpson, 'Battered Babies: Conviction for Murder', *British Medical Journal*, vol. 1, February 1965, p. 393. Discussion of the 'syndrome' was also included in R. Roof, 'Trauma in Childhood', *British Medical Journal*, vol. 1, 12 June, 1965, pp. 1541–3; and P. A. Russell, 'Subdural Hematoma in Infancy', *British Medical Journal*, 21 August 1965, pp. 446–8.

32. J. M. Cameron, H. R. Johnson and F. E. Camps, 'The Battered Child Syndrome', *Medicine, Science and the Law*, no. 6, 1966, pp. 2–21.

33. British Paediatric Association, 'The Battered Baby: A Memorandum by the Special Standing Committee on Accidents', *British Medical Journal*, vol. 1, no. 601, 5 March 1966, pp. 601–3.

34. Similar arguments were presented by Dr Fleming the following year, who participated in constructing the BPA memorandum. He argued that the problem of child neglect and cruelty cannot be defined separately and that 'close cooperation between doctors and social agencies is essential at all stages'. It is interesting that Dr Fleming was the Senior Medical Inspector at the Home Office Children's Department at the time, indicating that even at this time there were links between the interested parties in the medical profession and the State. See G. M. Fleming, 'Cruelty to Children', *British Medical Journal*, no. 11, 13 May 1967, pp. 421–2.

35. Concrete evidence for this is that the British Medical Journal Index first included a section headed 'Battered Baby Syndrome' for the period covering January to June 1966 – the period covering the BPA memorandum.

36. See K. Bain, 'The Physically Abused Child', *Paediatrics*, no. 31, 1963, p. 895; H. Boardman, 'A Project to Rescue Children from Inflicted Injury', *Social Work*, no. 7, 1962, pp. 43–51.

37. Elmer, 'Abused Young Children seen in Hospitals'. V. J. Fontana, 'The Maltreated Syndrome in Children', *New England Journal of Medicine*, no. 269, 1963, pp. 1389–94.

38. Friedson, *Profession of Medicine*.

39. Pfohl, 'The "Discovery" of Child Abuse'.

40. See A. Hughes, 'The Battered Baby Syndrome – A Multi-Disciplinary Problem', *Case Conference*, vol. 14, no. 8, 1967, pp. 304–8. B. Kahan, 'Battered Babies', *Hospital Journal and Social Services Review*, 26 January 1968, p. 169; C. Walton, 'The Battered Baby Syndrome', *New Statesman*, 9 September 1966; E. Woolley, 'The Battered Baby Syndrome', *Nova*, October 1967, pp. 78–81; *The Times*, 9 July 1966.

41. See A. Allen and A. Morton, *This is Your Child: The Story of the National Society for the Prevention of Cruelty to Children* (Routledge & Kegan Paul, 1961). One of the authors, Revd A. Morton, was Director of the Society for most of the post-war period until the late 1970s.

42. T. Coleman, 'The NSPCC in need', *The Guardian*, 19 February 1965, p. 14.

43. A. Lapping, 'What use is the "Cruelty Man"?', *New Society*, no. 142, 17 June 1965, pp. 16–17.

44. A. Shearer, 'The NSPCC – In Search of a New Identity', *World Medicine*, vol. 7, 8 March 1972, pp. 17–20.

45. For example in 1956 there had been just over 1000 child care officers in

England and Wales, by 1962 this had risen to 1500 and by 1970 to 3741. Similarly the work of Children's Departments grew with the increased emphasis on prevention following the 1963 Children and Young Persons Act. In the year ending March 1967 234 000 children were referred to Children's Departments of whom 46 000 were admitted to care and 133 000 were helped under Section 1 of the 1963 Children and Young Persons Act. In the year ending 1970 350 000 were referred, 42 000 admitted and 220 000 helped in their own homes. See J. Packman, *The Child's Generation: Child Care Policy from Curtis to Houghton* (Blackwell, 1975, 2nd edn 1981), particularly ch. 4.

46. See Packman, *The Child's Generation.*
47. Lapping, 'What use is the "Cruelty Man"?', p. 17.
48. Much of the information that follows was gained from discussions with Revd Arthur Morton, Miss Joan Court and Mr Ray Castle.
49. For a recent parallel see H. Sharron, 'Surviving on Child Abuse', *Social Work Today*, vol. 14, no. 37, 7 June 1983, p. 4.
50. Articles by Joan Court included the following: 'Battering Parents', *Social Work*, January 1969; 'The Battered Child: (1) Historical and Diagnostic Reflection (2) Reflection on Treatment', *Medical Social Work*, no. 22, 1969, pp. 11–20; 'The Battered Child Research Project', *Child Care News*, July 1969; 'An Historical Review of the American Child Abuse Laws', *Child Care News*, November 1969; 'Battered Babies', *Health Visitor*, December 1969; 'The Need for a Multi-Disciplinary Approach', *Nursing Times*, June 1971; 'Psychosocial Factors in Child Battering', *Journal of the Medical Women's Federation*, April 1970; (with C. Okell), 'An Emergent Programme to Protect the Battered Child and his Family', *Intervention* (Association of Professional Social Workers) Spring 1970; (with W. Robinson), 'The Battered Child Syndrome', *Midwives Chronicle and Nursing Notes*, July 1970; (with A. Kerr), 'The Battered Child Syndrome – a Preventable Disease', *Nursing Times*, June 1971. Articles written by other members of the unit included C. Okell, 'The Battered Child – A Tragic Breakdown in Parental Care?', *Midwife and Health Visitor*, vol. 5, June 1969; C. Okell and C. H. H. Butcher, 'The Battered Child Syndrome', *Law Society Gazette*, no. 66, 1969, p. 9; C. Okell, 'Childhood Accidents and Child Abuse', *Community Medicine*, no. 128, 1971, p. 8. A. Kerr and J. Court, 'Battered Babies', *London Doctor*, no. 3, 1972, p. 2; R. A. Jones, 'Parental Anguish and Child Abuse', *Practice Team*, no. 11, April 1972, pp. 22–4; C. Okell, 'The Battered Child Syndrome – Recent Research and Implications for Treatment', Royal Society of Health Congress at Eastbourne, April 1972, pp. 24–8; R. A. Jones, 'Battering Families', *Health and Social Services Journal*, no. 83, 1973, pp. 13–14.
51. See for example A. K. Skinner and R. L. Castle, *78 Battered Children: A Retrospective Study* (NSPCC, 1969).

52. R. Castle, 'Providing a Service', in A. W. Franklin (ed.), *Concerning Child Abuse* (Churchill-Livingstone, 1975).

53. Okell, 'The Battered Child Syndrome – Recent Research and Implications for Treatment'.

54. See Okell and Butcher, 'The Battered Child Syndrome'.

55. See Court, 'The Battered Child: (1) Historical and Diagnostic Reflection (2) Reflection on Treatment'.

56. Skinner and Castle, *78 Battered Children*; R. L. Castle and A. M. Kerr, *A Study of Suspected Child Abuse* (NSPCC, 1972).

57. For example the British Humanities Index lists only nine articles under either 'children battered' or 'infants battered' between 1968 and 1972. See for example *The Observer*, 'Parents who batter their babies', 17 May 1968, p. 6; *The Observer*, 'My baby cried, so I hit him', 16 June 1968, p. 7; Ruth Ingles, 'Why Parents Batter Babies', *The Observer*, 14 September 1969.

58. See report in *The Times*, 1 October 1969, of the Council of Europe Consultative Assembly in Strasburg which passed a resolution urging governments to take steps to 'curb the ill-treatment of children'.

59. See for example A. N. Guthkelch, 'Infantile Subdural Hematoma and its relationship to Whiplash Injuries', *British Medical Journal*, no. 7, 1971, p. 430; A. S. Mushin, 'Ocular Damage in the Battered Baby Syndrome', *British Medical Journal*, no. 3, 1971, pp. 402–4; B. Harcourt and D. Hopkins, 'Opthalmic Manifestations of the Battered Baby Syndrome', *British Medical Journal*, 14 August 1971; G. Jackson, 'Child Abuse Syndrome: The cases we miss', *British Medical Journal*, vol. 2, 24 June 1972, pp. 756–7.

60. S. Isaacs, 'Neglect, Cruelty and Battering', *British Medical Journal*, vol. 3, 22 July 1972, pp. 224–6.

61. See articles from: (1) child guidance, N. Lukianowicz, 'Parental Maltreatment of Children', *British Journal of Social Psychology*, no. 3, 1968, pp. 189–95; (2) a solicitor, C. Low, 'The Battering Parent, the Community and the Law', *Applied Social Studies*, no. 3, 1971, pp. 65–80; (3) the police, H. Davies, 'Maltreated Children: Early Warning System and Follow-up Scheme', *The Police Journal*, vol. LIV, no. 3, 1971, pp. 193–6.

62. Davies, 'Maltreated Children: Early Warning System and Follow-up Scheme'; W. H. Parry and M. W. Seymour, 'Epidemiology of Battered Babies in Nottingham', *Community Medicine*, vol. 126, no. 8, 1971, pp. 121–3.

63. See J. M. Cameron, 'The Battered Baby, *British Journal of Hospital Medicine*, no. 4, 1970, pp. 769–77.

64. For example, in 1970 Henry Kempe delivered the Windermere Lecture to the NSPCC which demonstrates the similarities and links, C. H. Kempe, 'Paediatric Implications of the Battered Baby Syndrome', *Archives of Disease of Childhood*, no. 46, 1971, pp. 28–37.

65. T. C. N. Gibbens and A. Walker, *Cruel Parents – Case Studies of Prisoners convicted of violence towards Children* (Institute for the Study and Treatment of Delinquency, 1956).

66. T. C. N. Gibbens, 'Violence to Children', *Howard Journal of Penology and Crime Prevention*, vol. 13, no. 3, 1972, pp. 212–20.

67. The only mention of the 'Battered Child' in *Social Work Today*, the journal of the British Association of Social Workers, was in relation to the dismissal of Miss Joan Court as head of the NSPCC Battered Child Research Unit in 1971. (See *Social Work Today*, 21 October 1971, 18 November 1971, 13 January 1972 and 27 January 1972). This dismissal seems to reflect in part the clash of perspectives, between the fast developing professional social work approach, as epitomised by the Research Unit, and the more traditional inspectorial roles in the NSPCC.

68. See Davies, 'Maltreated Children: Early Warning System and Follow-up Scheme'; and Parry and Seymour, 'Epidemiology of Battered Babies in Nottingham'.

69. DHSS, *The Battered Baby*, CM02/70 (1970); DHSS, *Battered Babies*, LASSL 26/72 (1972).

70. Skinner and Castle, *78 Battered Children*.

71. DHSS. *The Battered Baby*.

72. In a personal communication Miss Court has said she spent a great deal of her time initially helping to increase awareness of the problem within DHSS.

Chapter 4

1. The analysis in this section draws closely on N. Parton, 'Child Abuse, Social Anxiety and Welfare', *British Journal of Social Work*, vol. 11, no. 4, 1981, pp. 394–414.

2. A word used to summarise the feelings of social workers in the mid 1970s about this area of work in DHSS, *Social Service Teams: The Practitioner's View* (HMSO, 1978); see also E. M. Goldberg and R. W. Warburton, *Ends and Means in Social Work: The Development and Outcome of a Case Review System for Social Workers* (Allen & Unwin, 1979); D. Howe, 'Division of Labour in the Area Teams of Social Services Departments', *Social Policy and Administration*, vol. 14, no. 2, 1980, pp. 133–50. J. Mattinson and I. Sinclair, *Mate and Stalemate: Working with Marital Problems in a Social Services Department* (Blackwell, 1979).

3. S. Cohen, *Folk Devils and Moral Panics: The Creation of Mods and Rockers* (Paladin, 1973) p. 9.

4. See Bob Holman article in *The Times*, 29 January 1975.

5. S. Hall, C. Critcher, T. Jefferson, J. Clarke and B. Roberts, *Policing*

the Crisis: Mugging, the State, and Law and Order (Macmillan, 1978) ch. 8.

6. This is very common with child abuse for it is claimed: (1) that the identified bruises etc. are symptomatic of much more worrying parental attitudes and parent–child relations; and (2) that the officially identified number of abused children is only a very small number of the real total. For instance, C. Schneider, J. K. Hoffmeister and R. E. Helfer, 'A Predicative Screening Questionnaire for Potential Problems in Mother –Child Interaction' in R. E. Helfer and C. H. Kempe (eds), *Child Abuse and Neglect: The Family and the Community* (Ballinger, 1976) claim that 20 per cent of the parental population have child rearing attitudes and experiences that are so similar to known abusers as to make them indistinguishable from abusers on any dimension except the absence of documented evidence.

7. It is far from apparent that S. Hall *et al.*'s grand theory that moral panics in the early 1970s were part of a wider crisis is valid. Some critics have argued that the actual material selected as proof of the slide into crisis does not add up to anything that was particularly 'exceptional'. See S. Cohen, *Folk Devils and Moral Panics* (Blackwells, 2nd edn revised 1980). Similarly it is my own view that we should not necessarily view this period as unique, for similar developments, with a correlation between crisis and moral panic, seem to have been in evidence in other periods in history. However the nature of the social reaction and the form of the panic have differed. This seems to have been the case in the last quarter of the nineteenth century. For interesting discussions of S. Hall *et al.*'s thesis see D. Downes and P. Rock, *Understanding Deviance: A Guide to the Sociology of Crime and Rule Breaking* (Oxford University Press, 1982) ch. 10; and J. Ditton, *Controlology: Beyond the New Criminology* (Macmillan, 1979) ch. 4.

8. Parton, 'Child Abuse, Social Anxiety and Welfare'; and N. Parton, 'The Natural History of Child Abuse: A Study in Social Problem Definition', *British Journal of Social Work*, vol. 9, no. 4, 1979, pp. 431–5.

9. See A. Shearer, 'The Legacy of Maria Colwell', *Social Work Today*, vol. 10, no. 9, 1979, pp. 12–19, in which it is suggested that the local media helped sustain interest in the case in East Sussex and would not let the problem go away until an inquiry was 'secured' from central government.

10. See note 4.

11. See in particular Sir Keith Joseph's speech to the Pre-School Play-groups Association, 29 June 1972, reproduced in E. Butterworth and R. Holman (eds), *Social Welfare in Modern Britain* (Fontana, 1975); and Sir K. Joseph, 'The Next Ten Years', *New Society*, 5 October 1972, pp. 8–9.

12. Adrian Webb in P. Hall, H. Land, R. Parker and A. Webb, *Change, Choice and Conflict in Social Policy* (Heinemann, 1975), p. 68. A specific

example of this priority was the establishment of the SSRC/DHSS research programme on 'transmitted deprivation' at this time.

13. For a discussion on the nature and implications of the cycle of deprivation thesis for social policy and social work practice see B. Jordan, *Poor Parents: Social Policy and the Cycle of Deprivation* (Routledge & Kegan Paul, 1974); B. Jordan, *Freedom and the Welfare State* (Routledge & Kegan Paul, 1976) particularly chs 10, 11, 12 and 13. B. Jordan, *Automatic Poverty* (Routledge & Kegan Paul, 1981) particularly chs 7 and 8; B. Holman, *Poverty: Explanations of Social Deprivation* (Martin Robertson, 1978).

14. Perhaps most explicitly stated by S. Wasserman, 'The Abused Parent of the Abused Child', *Children*, no. 14, 1967, pp. 175–9. Sidney Wasserman was involved with the Scientific Advisory Committee of the NSPCC Battered Child Research Unit at the time.

15. Quoted from A. W. Franklin (ed.), *Concerning Child Abuse* (Churchill–Livingstone, 1975) introduction.

16. Dr Alfred White Franklin has a long and distinguished career in paediatrics. During the 1960s he was honorary consulting physician at the Department of Health, St. Bartholomew's Hospital; honorary consultant paediatrician, Queen Charlotte's Maternity Hospital; was formerly chairman of the Invalid Children's Aid Association; co-founder and treasurer of the Oastler Club; past president of the British Paediatric Association; president of the British Society for Medical History (1974–7); with a practice in Harley Street. In recent years he has been a central figure in the British Association for the Study and Prevention of Child Abuse and Neglect and its international equivalent.

17. See British Paediatric Association, 'The Battered Baby: A Memorandum by the Special Standing Committee on Accidents', *British Medical Journal*, vol. 1, 5 March 1966, pp. 601–3.

18. Much of the information for this section is taken from personal discussions with Dr Franklin.

19. A. W. Franklin, 'Personal View', *British Medical Journal*, vol. 4, 16 October 1971, p. 167.

20. *Clarke Hall and Morrison's Law Relating to Children and Young Persons* (Butterworths, 9th edn by Margaret Booth 1977 and Supplement 1979).

21. These included Eileen Ring, who had headed the recently instituted DHSS internal committee to discuss the problem.

22. S. Smith, R. Hanson and S. Noble, 'Parent of Battered Child: A Controlled Study' in Franklin (ed.), *Concerning Child Abuse*.

23. J. Mounsey, 'Offences of Criminal Violence, Cruelty and Neglect Against Children in Lancashire' in Franklin (ed.), *Concerning Child Abuse*.

24. Speech to the Annual General Meeting of the Magistrates Association reported in *The Times*, 12 October 1973.

25. A phrase used by Dr A. W. Franklin in a personal communication.

26. See Parton, 'Child Abuse, Social Anxiety and Welfare', where this argument is developed further.

27. J. O'Conner, *The Fiscal Crises of the State* (St James Press, 1973); A. Gamble, *The Conservative Nation* (Routledge & Kegan Paul, 1974); I. Gough, *The Political Economy of the Welfare State* (Macmillan, 1979).

28. For example the law relating to homosexuality was amended in 1967 to legalise sexual relations between consenting adults; the 1969 Divorce Law discarded the notion of 'matrimonial offence' and established 'irretrievable breakdown of marriage' as the sole criterion for divorce; the 1967 Abortion Law enabled women to gain a legal abortion more easily.

29. See R. Wallis, 'Moral Indignation and the Media: An Analysis of the National Viewers' and Listeners' Association', *Sociology,* vol. 10, 1976, pp. 271–95; R. Wallis, *Salvation and Protest: Studies of Social and Religious Movements* (Pinter, 1979); Hall, Critcher, Jefferson, Clarke and Roberts, *Policing the Crisis*; T. Nairn, 'Portrait of Enoch Powell', *New Left Review,* no. 61, May/June 1970, pp. 2–27.

30. See S. Hall, 'Reformism and the Legislation of Consent' in NDC *Permisiveness and Control: The Fate of the Sixties Legislation* (Macmillan, 1980). On the National Viewers' and Listeners' Association, the Festival of Light etc., see D. Cliff, 'Religion, Morality and the Middle Class', in R. King and N. Nugent (eds), *Respectable Rebels* (Hodder & Stoughton, 1979).

31. As depicted in B. Jackson, *Working Class Community: Some General Notions Raised by a Series of Studies in Northern England* (Routledge & Kegan Paul, 1968); M. Young and P. Willmott, *Family and Kinship in East London* (Routledge & Kegan Paul, 1957).

32. In the late 1960s many of the anxieties of the traditional middle classes, which became associated with the New Right, were voiced by Enoch Powell, whose recipe for filling the political vacuum was unmistakably populist in intent. He was one of the few senior politicians at the time who had the ability to tap into this growing feeling of social anxiety and who attempted to return the 'silent majority' to the fold. In doing so he tried to re-establish the 'sense of Englishness' which seemed so important, *vis-à-vis* an 'internal enemy' i.e. black immigrants. While such a scapegoat gave concrete recognition to many popular anxieties, it also helped to restore a popular content to English self-consciousness.

33. A. Gamble and P. Walton, *Capitalism in Crisis: Inflation and the State* (Macmillan, 1976); A. Glynne and B. Sutcliffe, *British Capitalism, Workers and the Profits Squeeze* (Penguin, 1972); Gough, *The Political Economy of the Welfare State*; S. Bolger, P. Corrigan, J. Docking and N. Frost, *Towards Socialist Welfare Work; Working in the State* (Macmillan, 1981) ch. 2.

34. K. Phillips and M. Wilson, 'The Conservative Party: From Macmillan to

Thatcher', and M. Wilson, 'Grass Roots Conservatism: Motions to the Party Conference' both in N. Nugent and R. King (eds), *The British Right* (Saxon House, 1977).

35. Lord Hailsham, *Guardian*, 12 February 1970.

36. 1972 was the year the government and the working class entered on a collision course and more strike days were lost than in any other year since 1919. The conflict in Northern Ireland reached new heights, the year opening with the deaths of thirteen Catholics on 'Bloody Sunday'. The temper of violence seemed to be reflected abroad with the regular news of American bombings in Vietnam, while terrorists groups such as Black September, Bader Meinhof and the Japanese Red Army emerged in what was seen as an international conspiracy, and which captured the headlines in the British media.

37. S. Chibnall, *Law and Order News: An Analysis of Crime Reporting in the British Press* (Tavistock, 1977) ch. 4. Others have also commented on a complementary development in the growth of the concept of 'dangerousness'. See I. Taylor, *Law and Order: Arguments for Socialism* (Macmillan, 1981); A. E. Bottoms, 'Reflections on the Renaissance of Dangerousness', *The Howard Journal of Penology and Crime Prevention*, vol. xvi, no. 2, 1977, pp. 70–96.

38. Taken from Chibnall, *Law and Order News*, p. 76, Fig. 1.

39. See for example Leader 'Caring for Children', *New Society*, vol. 24, no. 55, 7 June 1973, p. 542.

40. See J. Clark, M. Langan and P. Lee, 'Social Work: The Conditions of Crisis', in P. Carlen and M. Collinson (eds), *Radical Issues in Criminology* (Martin Robertson, 1980).

41. What has come to be called the 're-discovery of poverty' was important here. See A. Harvey, *Casualties of the Welfare State* (Fabian Tract, no. 321, 1960); D. Cole and W. Utting, *The Economic Circumstances of Old People*, Occasional Papers in Social Administration, no. 4 (Bell, 1962); D. Cole, 'Poverty in Britain Today – The Evidence', *Sociological Review*, 1962, pp. 257–82; B. Abel-Smith and P. Townsend, *The Poor and the Poorest*, Occasional Papers in Social Administration, no. 6 (Bell, 1965).

42. See in particular D. Donnison, P. Jay and M. Stewart, *The Ingelby Report: Three Critical Essays* (Fabian Society, 1962) and The Longford Study Group, *Crime: A Challenge to Us All* (The Labour Party, 1964).

43. A phase introduced in P. Townsend (ed.), *The Fifth Social Service: A Critical Analysis of the Seebohm Proposals* (The Fabian Society, 1970).

44. For a discussion of the internal politics behind Seebohm see P. Hall, *Reforming the Welfare* (Heinemann, 1976); J. Cooper, *The Creation of the British personal social services, 1962–1974* Heinemann, 1983).

45. R. Bacon and W. Eltis, *Britain's Economic Problem: Too Few Producers* (Macmillan, 2nd edn 1978). Also in *The Sunday Times*, 2, 9 and 16 November and 14 December 1975.

46. For more recent developments of this argument see C. Brewer and J. Lait, *Can Social Work Survive?* (Temple Smith, 1980); D. C. Anderson (ed.), *The Ignorance of Social Intervention* (Croom Helm, 1980); D. Anderson, J. Lait and D. Marsland, *Breaking the Spell of the Welfare State: Strategies for Reducing Public Expenditure* (The Social Affairs Unit, 1981); C. Brewer, T. Morris, D. Morgan and M. North, *Criminal Welfare on Trial* (The Social Affairs Unit, 1981).

47. H. Molotch and M. Lester, 'News as Purposive Behaviour: On the Strategic Use of Routine Events, Accidents and Scandals', *American Sociological Review*, vol. 39, February 1974, pp. 101–12.

48. See for example Social Worker 2 in the Lucie Gates case, 'Savaged by the Press', *Community Care*, no. 445, 13 January 1983, pp. 16–17; A. Hill, 'How the Press Sees You', *Social Work Today*, vol. 11, no. 36, 20 May 1980, pp. 19–20; M. Phillips, 'Social Workers and the Media: A Journalists View', *Social Work Today*, vol. 10, no. 22, 30 September 1979, p. 22; R. Young, 'Social Workers and the Media: A Social Services View', *Social Work Today*, vol. 10, no. 22, 30 January 1979, pp. 10–11.

49. C. Andrews in *Social Work Today*, vol. 4, no. 12, 1974, p. 637; quoted in R. Mawby, C. Fisher and J. Hale, 'The Press and Karen Spencer', *Social Work Today*, vol. 10, no. 22, 30 January 1979, pp. 13–16.

50. But see also R. I. Mawby, C. J. Fisher and A. Park in 'Press Coverage of Social Work', *Policy and Politics*, vol. 7, no. 4, 1979, pp. 357–76; D. Walker, 'Are Social Workers Badly Treated by the Newspapers?', *Social Work Today*, vol. 7, no. 9, 5 August 1976, pp. 292–3; M. Roberts, 'Giving the Public the Right Image', *Community Care*, no. 308. 27 March 1980, pp. 16–17.

51. However, see Chibnall, *Law and Order News*; P. Golding and S. Middleton, *Images of Welfare: Press and Public Attitudes to Poverty* (Martin Robertson, 1982); P. Golding and S. Middleton, 'Making Claims: News Media and the Welfare State', *Media, Culture and Society*, no. 1, 1979, pp. 5–21.

52. S. Hall and T. Jefferson (eds), *Resistance Through Rituals: Youth Subcultures in Post-war Britain* (Hutchinson, 1976) ch. 2; Hall, Critcher, Jefferson, Clarke and Roberts, *Policing the Crisis*, ch. 3; S. Cohen and J. Young (eds), *The Manufacture of News: Social Problems, Deviance and the Mass Media* (Constable, 1973).

53. Hall, Critcher, Jefferson, Clarke and Roberts, *Policing the Crisis*, p. 62.

54. Hall and Jefferson (eds), *Resistance Through Rituals*, p. 76.

55. Chibnall, *Law and Order News*, ch. 2.

56. Chibnall, *Law and Order News*, p. 44.

57. For a discussion of the differential treatment of social work and child abuse by the press see references in note 50 above.

58. Hall, Critcher, Jefferson, Clarke and Roberts, *Policing the Crisis*, p. 61.

59. See C. Anderson, *The Care-Takers* (Bookstall, 1972).

60. Graham Bagnall (born 20 May 1970) died on 28 May 1972. His condition had been a matter of concern since he had been about 10 months old, and at 13 months he had been in hospital 'with injuries consistent with battering'. Three months later his elder brother (then aged 3) was also admitted to the same hospital with suspicious injuries. Meanwhile, Graham had been boarded out in an approved foster home. The possibility of adoption by the foster parents was discussed but rejected by Graham's parents (his mother and step-father) when they understood the implications of adoption. While Graham was in foster care his mother gave birth to her third child, a daughter. Graham was returned to the parents because there seemed to be no grounds for opposing their request. Six weeks later he was found dead in his cot. Subsequently, both parents were convicted of manslaughter. His step-father was 'educationally sub-normal', he had been to Approved School, and was known to have been aggressive/violent on three occasions. A report was published by Shropshire County Council in January 1973, with a supplementary report by Shrewsbury Group Hospital Management Committee in March 1973.

61. S. M. Smith, R. Hanson and S. Noble, 'Parents of Battered Babies: A Controlled Study', *British Medical Journal*, no. 4, 17 November 1973, pp. 338–91.

62. M. Hall, 'A View from the Emergency and Accident Department' in Franklin (ed.), *Concerning Child Abuse*.

63. P. D. Scott, 'Parents Who Kill Their Children', *Medicine, Science and the Law*, no. 13, 1973, pp. 120–6. See also P. D. Scott, 'Fatal Battered Baby Cases', *Medicine, Science and the Law*, no. 13, 1973, pp. 197–206.

64. Smith, Hanson and Noble, 'Parents of Battered Babies: A Controlled Study'.

65. Apart from media entries discussed in the text see also: B. Brandenburger, 'Are We All Kid Bashers at Heart?', *Observer*, 18 March 1973, p. 30; S. Smith and S. Noble, 'Battered Children and Their Parents', *New Society*, 15 November 1973, pp. 393–5; S. Norris, 'Research has Highlighted the Problem of Battered Children', *Guardian*, 3 October 1973, p. 9; D. Tindall, 'Maria Colwell', *Listener*, 22 November 1973, p. 690; J. Goodwin, 'Baby Batterers: Are They Really Villians or Victims?', *Daily Telegraph*, 14 September 1973, p. 17; M. Holland, 'Children at Risk', *New Statesman*, 16 November 1973, pp. 721–2; M. Kellmer-Pringle, 'Every Day Two Children Die . . .', *Observer*, 25 August 1974, p. 18; H. Dawson, 'The Left Alone Children', *Observer*, 11 August 1974, p. 18; 'Tug of Opinion', *The Economist*, 7 September 1974, p. 30; J. Linklater, 'Baby-Bashing', *Spectator*, 10 August 1974, pp. 174–5.

66. A phrase used by S. Smith, 'Correspondence', *British Medical Journal*, 25 May 1974.

67. P. Hartley, *Child Abuse, Social Work and the Press: Towards the History of a*

Moral Panic. (Unpublished M.A. Dissertation, Department of Applied Social Studies, University of Warwick, 1982.)

68. Golding and Middleton, *Images of Welfare*, pp. 89–91.
69. A. Waugh, 'The Lesson of Lucie Gates', *Spectator*, 20 November 1982.
70. Golding and Middleton, *Images of Welfare*, p. 90.

Chapter 5

1. See in particular DHSS, *Social Service Teams: the Practitioner's View* (HMSO, 1978); E. M. Goldberg and R. W. Warburton, *Ends and Means in Social Work: The Development and Outcome of a case review system for social workers* (Allen & Unwin, 1979); D. Howe, 'Divisions of Labour in the Area Teams of Social Services Departments', *Social Policy and Administration*, vol. 14, no. 3, 1980, pp. 133–50; J. Mattinson and I. Sinclair, *Mate and Stalemate: Working with Marital Problems in a Social Services Department* (Blackwells, 1979); A. Holmes and J. Maizels, *Social Workers and Volunteers* (Allen & Unwin, 1978).
2. DHSS, *Child Abuse: A Study of Inquiry Reports* (HMSO, 1982).
3. See DHSS, *Report of the Committee of Inquiry into the Care and Supervision Provided in Relation to Maria Colwell* (HMSO, 1974) ch. 5.
4. Somerset County Council, *Wayne Brewer. Report of the Review Panel* (1977).
5. DHSS, *The Battered Baby*, CM02/70 (1970). Also DHSS, *Battered Babies*, LASSL 26/72 (1972).
6. DHSS, *Non-Accidental Injury to Children*, LASSL (74) (13) (1974).
7. This has been supported by Miss Joan Court, first Director of the NSPCC Battered Child Research Unit, and Social Work Service Officer at DHSS at the time of Maria Colwell and the period up until mid 1977, and Mr Geoffrey Lupton, Principal Officer at the DHSS during the period.
8. *Social Services for Children in England and Wales*, ordered by the House of Commons to be printed 21 December 1976 (HMSO).
9. See DHSS, *Non-Accidental Injury to Children: Area Review Committees*, LASSL (76) (2) (1976).
10. DHSS, *Non-Accidental Injury to Children: Area Review Committees*, para. 10.
11. *Social Services for Children in England and Wales 1973–75* (HMSO, 1976) ch. 5, para. 11.
12. See BASW Working Party Report, *The Central Child Abuse Register* (BASW, 1978) summarised in *Social Work Today*, 21 March 1978, pp. 14–17. The report identifies the rationale of registers as that they: (1) Bring together information about families under stress who seek support from a succession of different agencies and hospitals. This is said to safeguard the child by aiding the detection of a sequence of injuries

which may be considered when assessing NAI and discovering mobile families; (2) can be used to monitor the safety of an abused child who remains at or has returned home; (3) provide a central record against which the support for children and their families by all agencies can be monitored, and can be used to influence resource allocation; (4) can be used for statistical or research purposes in assessing the nature and extent of abuse; (5) can prevent unnecessary duplication of work by identifying the worker currently involved.

13. M. H. Hall 'The Diagnosis and Early Management of Non-Accidental Injuries in Children', *The Police Surgeon* no. 6, October 1974, pp. 16–74; J. Furness 'Bite Marks in Non-Accidental Injuries of Children', *The Police Surgeon* no. 6, October 1974, pp. 75–87.

14. DHSS, *Non-Accidental Injury to Children*, LASSL (75) (29) (24 October 1975).

15. The books recommended were: J. Carter (ed.), *The Maltreated Child* (Priory Press, 1974); J. M. Cameron and L. J. Rea, *An Atlas of the Battered Child Syndrome* (Churchill–Livingstone, 1975); R. L. Castle and A. M. A. Kerr, *A Study of Suspected Child Abuse* (NSPCC, 1972); A. W. Franklin (ed.), *Concerning Child Abuse* (Churchill–Livingstone, 1975); R. E. Helfer and C. H. Kempe (eds), *Helping the Battered Child and his Family* (J. B. Lippincott, 1972).

16. DHSS, *Report of the Committee of Inquiry into the Provision and Co-ordination of Services to the Family of John George Aukland* (HMSO, 1975).

17. DHSS, *Non-Accidental Injury to Children: Proceedings of a Conference held at the DHSS on 19 June 1974* (HMSO, 1975).

18. DHSS, *Non-Accidental Injury to Children: Proceedings of a Conference held at DHSS on 19 June 1974*, pp. 38–9.

19. See *The Times*, 2 October 1974.

20. DHSS, *Non-Accidental Injury to Children: The Police and Case Conferences*, LASSL (76) (26) (1976).

21. DHSS, *Non-Accidental Injury to Children: The Police and Case Conferences*, LASSL (76) (26) paras 8, 10, 15.

22. See for example, First Report from the Select Committee on Violence in the Family, *Violence to Children*, Session 1976–77, ordered to be printed 26 April 1977, vol. II, *Evidence*, pp. 44–58 (HMSO, 1977).

23. First Report from the Select Committee on Violence in the Family, *Violence to Children*, Session 1976–77 ordered by the House of Commons to be printed 26 April 1977, vol. I, *Report* (together with the proceedings of the committee); vol. II, *Evidence*; vol. III, *Appendices* (HMSO, 1977).

24. *Violence to Children: A Response to the First Report from the Select Committee on Violence in the Family* (Session 1976–77), Cmnd 7123 (HMSO, March 1978).

25. *Violence to Children*, Cmnd 7123, para. 104.

26. DHSS, *The Battered Baby*, CM02/70; DHSS, *Non-Accidental Injury to Children*, LASSL (74) (13); DHSS, *Child Abuse: The Register System*, Draft Circular LA/C396/23D, 21 December 1978.

27. *Violence to Children*, Cmnd 7123.

28. DHSS, *Child Abuse: The Register System*, LA/C396/23D.

29. DHSS, *Child Abuse: Central Register Systems*, LASSL (80) 4 (1980).

30. DHSS, *Child Abuse: Central Register Systems*, LASSL (80) 4, para. 1.1.

31. DHSS, *Child Abuse: Central Register Systems*, LASSL (80) 4, para. 2.2.

32. DHSS, *Child Abuse: The Register System*, LA/C396/23D, para. 5.c.

33. The circular included reference to the following research, the nature of which is reviewed in the next chapter: J. L. and R. G. Carpenter, 'Final Results of a Study of infants at risk of sudden death', *Nature*, vol. 268, 25 August 1977, pp. 724–5; M. A. Lynch, J. Roberts and M. Gordon, 'Child Abuse: Early Warning in the Maternity Hospital', *Developmental Medicine and Child Neurology*, vol. 18, 1976, pp. 759–66; M. A. Lynch and J. Roberts, 'Predicting Child Abuse: Signs of bonding failure in the Maternity Hospital', *British Medical Journal*, vol. 1, 5 March 1977, pp. 624–6.

34. Original italics.

35. BASW, *The Central Child Abuse Register*.

36. A phrase used in a letter by S. Smith, 'Parents of Battered Babies', in *Correspondence, British Medical Journal*, vol. 12, 25 May 1974, p. 443.

37. *Report of the Departmental Committee on the Adoption of Children* (Houghton) (HMSO, 1972).

38. For example Malcolm Dean, social services correspondent of the *Guardian* at the time, was an adopter.

39. L. Fox, 'Two Value Positions in Recent Child Care Law and Practice', *British Journal of Social Work*, vol. 12, no. 3, 1982, pp. 265–90.

40. Fox, 'Two Value Positions in Recent Child Care Law and Practice', p. 272.

41. J. G. Howells, *Remember Maria* (Butterworths, 1974).

42. Howells, *Remember Maria*, p. 6.

43. Howells, *Remember Maria*, p. 63.

44. J. Goldstein, A. Freud and A. Solnit, *Beyond the Best Interests of the Child* (Free Press, 1973).

45. See for example: *Practice Guide to the Children Act 1975* (ABAFA, 1976); *Assumption of Parental Rights and Duties: Practice Guide* (1977); *Planning for Children in Long-term Care* (ABAFA, 1977); *Terminating Parental Contact* (ABAFA, 1980).

46. J. Rowe and L. Lambert, *Children Who Wait* (ABAFA, 1973).

47. See for example P. Sawbridge and M. Carrilibe, 'Social Work Tasks in Relation to Placing Children in New Families', in Central Council for Education and Training in Social Work, *Good Enough Parenting* (CCETSW, 1978).

48. B. Jordan, 'Client Participation in Decision Making', *Paper presented to the BASW Annual Conference*, April 1982, Bath.

49. See C. Hussell and B. Monaghan, 'Going for Good', *Social Work Today*, vol. 12, no. 47, 17 August 1982, pp. 7–9.

50. Hussell and Monaghan, 'Going for Good', p. 7.

51. See Goldstein, Freud and Solnit, *Beyond the Best Interests of the Child*; and J. Goldstein, A. Freud and A. Solnit, *Before the Best Interests of the Child* (Free Press, 1979).

52. J. Packman, *The Child's Generation* (Blackwells/Robertson, 2nd edn 1981).

53. See A. W. Tredinnick and A. C. Fairburn, 'Left holding the baby', *Community Care*, no. 310, 10 April 1980, pp. 22–5; A. W. Tredinnick and A. C. Fairburn, 'The baby removed from the parents at birth – prophylaxis with justice', *New Law Journal*, vol. 130, no. 5955, 19 June 1980, pp. 498–500.

54. All figures from *Children in Care in England and Wales* (HMSO, various years).

55. Packman, *The Child's Generation*, p. 183.

56. See N. V. Lowe and R. A. H. White, *Wards of Court* (Butterworths, 1979); S. Maidment, 'Wardship and Local Authorities – The Current Limits', *New Law Journal*, vol. 132, no. 6060, July 8 1982, pp. 667–70; A. Bainham, 'Wardship, Care and the Welfare Principle', *Family Law*, vol. 11, no. 8, 1981. For the figures prior to 1978 see Lowe and White, p. 9. The figures for 1978 onwards can be found in the annual Judicial Statistics.

57. See Packman, *The Child's Generation*.

58. See A. Gamble, 'The Free Economy and the Strong State' in R. Miliband and J. Saville (eds), *Socialist Register 1979* (Merlin, 1979); A. Gamble, *Britain in Decline: Economic Policy, Political Strategy and the British State* (Macmillan, 1981) particularly ch. 5; I. Taylor, *Law and Order: Arguments for Socialism* (Macmillan, 1982) chs 1 and 2; T. Fitzgerald, 'The New Right and the Family', in M. Loney, D. Boswell and J. Clarke (eds), *Social Policy and Social Welfare* (Open University Press, 1983).

Chapter 6

1. Revd. A. Morton, Foreword to R. L. Castle and A. M. Kerr, *A Study of Suspected Child Abuse* (NSPCC, 1972) p. 1.

2. R. E. Helfer, 'Basic issues concerning prediction', in R. E. Helfer and C. H. Kempe (eds), *Child Abuse and Neglect: The Family and the Community* (Ballinger, 1976). For an interesting critical analysis see S. Montgomery, 'Problems in the Perinatal Prediction of Child Abuse', *British Journal of Social Work*, vol. 12, no. 2, 1982, pp. 189–96. See also the discussion

between Ray Helfer and Stuart Montgomery in 'Correspondence', *British Journal of Social Work*, vol. 12, no. 6, 1982, pp. 669–672.

3. Helfer, 'Basic issues concerning prediction', p. 364.

4. J. M. Giovannoni, 'Prevention of child abuse and neglect: research and policy issues', *Social Work Research and Abstracts*, vol. 18, part 3, 1982, pp. 23–31, p. 24.

5. D. G. Gil, Foreword to R. Volpe, M. Breton and J. Mitton, *The Maltreatment of the School-Aged Child* (Lexington Books, 1980) p. ix.

6. J. M. Giovannoni and R. M. Becerra, *Defining Child Abuse* (The Free Press, 1979) ch. 1.

7. E. Zigler, 'Controlling Child Abuse in America: An effort doomed to failure', in R. Bourne and E. H. Newberger, *Critical Perspectives on Child Abuse* (Lexington Books, 1979).

8. R. Gelles, *Family Violence* (Saga, 1979) ch. 10.

9. R. Dingwall, J. Eekelaar and T. Murray, *The Protection of Children: State Intervention and Family Life* (Basil Blackwell, 1983); Giovannoni and Beccera, *Defining Child Abuse*.

10. R. E. Helfer and C. H. Kempe, *Child Abuse and Neglect: The Family and the Community* (Ballinger, 1976) introduction.

11. H. Martin, 'A child-oriented approach to prevention of abuse', in A. W. Franklin (ed.), *Child Abuse: Prediction, Prevention and Follow-up* (Churchill –Livingstone, 1978) p. 12.

12. A. W. Franklin, 'Present pre-occupations', in Franklin (ed.), *Child Abuse: Prediction, Prevention and Follow-up*, p. 4.

13. This section draws heavily upon L. J. Allan, 'Child Abuse; A Critical Review of the Research and Theory', in J. P. Martin (ed.), *Violence in the Family* (Wiley, 1978); J. J. Spinetta and D. Rigler, 'The Child Abusing Parent: A Psychological Review', *Psychological Bulletin*, vol. 77, no. 4, 1972, pp. 296–304; R. D. Parke and C. W. Collmer, 'Child Abuse, an interdisciplinary analysis', in E. Mavis Hetherington (ed.), *Review of Child Development Research vol. 5* (University of Chicago Press, 1975); M. Sheppard, *Perceptions of Child Abuse: A Critique of Individualism* (*Social Work Today* and University of East Anglia, 1982); R. J. Gelles, 'Violence in the Family: A Review of Research in the Seventies', *Journal of Marriage and the Family*, vol. 42, 1980, pp. 873–85; W. N. Friedrich and K. K. Wheeler, 'The Abusing Parent Revisited: A Decade of Psychological Research', *The Journal of Nervous and Mental Disease*, vol. 170, no. 10, 1982, pp. 577–87; J. Vesterdal, 'Etiological Factors and Long Term Consequences of Child Abuse', *International Journal of Offender Therapy and Comparative Criminology*, vol. 27, no. 1, 1983, pp. 21–54.

14. B. F. Steele and C. B. Pollack, 'A psychiatric study of parents who abuse infants and small children', in R. E. Helfer and C. H. Kempe (eds), *The Battered Child Syndrome* (University of Chicago Press, 1968).

15. M. Borland (ed.), *Violence in the Family* (Manchester University Press,

1976); E. Baher, C. Hyman, C. Jones, R. Jones, A. Kerr and R. Mitchell, *At Risk: An Account of the Work of the Battered Child Research Department, NSPCC* (Routledge & Kegan Paul, 1976). But see also S. M. Smith, R. Hanson and S. Noble, 'Parents of battered babies: a controlled study', *British Medical Journal*, no. 4, 1973, pp. 388–91.

16. C. Ounsted, R. Oppenheimer and J. Lindsay, 'The psychopathology and psychotherapy of the families: aspects of bonding failure' in A. W. Franklin (ed.), *Concerning Child Abuse* (Churchill Livingstone, 1975).

17. Baher, Hyman, Jones, Jones, Kerr and Mitchell, *At Risk*; A. E. Skinner and R. C. Castle, *78 Battered Children: a retrospective study* (NSPCC, 1969).

18. M. Lynch, D. Steinberg and C. Ounsted, 'Family Unit in a Children's Hospital', *British Medical Journal*, no. 2, 1975, pp. 127–9.

19. S. M. Smith, *The Battered Child Syndrome* (Butterworth, 1975).

20. C. A. Hyman, 'IQ of parents of battered babies', *British Medical Journal*, no. 4, 1973, p. 739; Baher, Hyman, Jones, Jones, Kerr and Mitchell, *At Risk*.

21. E. J. Merril, 'Physical abuse of children: an agency study', in V. de Francis, *Protecting the Battered Child* (Children's Division, American Humane Association, 1962); H. D. Bryant, 'Physical Abuse of Children: an agency study', *Child Welfare*, no. 42, 1963, pp. 125–30; M. J. Boisvert, 'The Battered Child Syndrome', *Social Casework*, vol. 53, 1972, pp. 475–78; Skinner and Castle, *78 Battered Children*.

22. Baher, Hyman, Jones, Jones, Kerr and Mitchell, *At Risk*.

23. R. J. Gelles, 'Child Abuse as Psychopathology: A Sociological Critique and Reformulation', *American Journal of Orthopsychiatry*, no. 43, July 1973, pp. 611–21.

24. R. Bourne, 'Child Abuse and Neglect: An Overview', in Bourne and Newberger, *Critical Perspectives on Child Abuse*, pp. 8–9.

25. Skinner and Castle, *78 Battered Children*; J. E. Oliver, J. Cox, A. Taylor and J. A. Baldwin, 'Severely ill-treated children in North East Wiltshire', *Research Report No. 4 Oxford Record Linkage Study* (Oxford Area Health Authority, 1974); D. Gil, *Violence Against Children* (Harvard University Press, 1970); Smith, *The Battered Child Syndrome*.

26. Steele and Pollock, 'A psychiatric study of parents who abuse infants and small children'.

27. Baher, Hyman, Jones, Kerr and Mitchell, *At Risk*.

28. J. C. Hotter and S. B. Friedman, 'Child Abuse: early case findings in the emergency department', *Paediatrics*, no. 42, July 1968, pp. 128–38; B. Simons, 'Child Abuse: Epidemiological Study of Medically Reported Cases', *New York State Journal of Medicine*, no. 66 1966, pp. 2783–8.

29. Skinner and Castle, *78 Battered Children*; A. H. Green, 'Child Abuse – Pathological Syndrome of Family Interaction', *American Journal of Psychiatry*, no. 131, 1974, pp. 882–6.

30. S. M. Smith and R. Hanson, '134 Battered Children: a medical and

psychological study', *British Medical Journal*, no. 3, 1974, pp. 666–70; Gil, *Violence Against Children*.

31. E. Elmer and G. Gregg, 'Developmental Characteristics of Abused Children', *Paediatrics*, no. 40, 1967, pp. 596–602; M. Klein and C. Stern, 'Low Birth Weight and the Battered Child Syndrome', *American Journal of Diseases of Children*, no. 122, 1971, pp. 15–18; M. A. Lynch, 'Ill-health and Child Abuse', *Lancet*, 17 August 1975, pp. 317–19.

32. M. Richards, 'Non-Accidental Injury in an Ecological Perspective', in DHSS *Non-Accidental Injury to Children* (HMSO, 1975); N. Rose, *Registers of Suspected Non-Accidental Injury* (NSPCC, 1976); M. Rutter, 'A Child's Life', *New Scientist*, no. 62, 1975, pp. 763–6.

33. Skinner and Castle, *78 Battered Children*; Smith, *The Battered Child Syndrome*; E. Elmer, *Children in Jeopardy* (University of Pittsburgh Press, 1967); Baher, Hyman, Jones, Jones, Kerr and Mitchell, *At Risk*.

34. Smith, *The Battered Child Syndrome*.

35. Spinetta and Rigler, 'The Child Abusing Parent: A Psychological Review'.

36. Gelles, 'Child Abuse as Psychopathology: A Sociological Critique and Reformulation'.

37. Spinetta and Rigler, 'The Child Abusing Parent: A Psychological Review'.

38. Allan, 'Child Abuse: A Critical Review of the Research and Theory', p. 59.

39. See in particular Friedrich and Wheeler, 'The Abusing Parent Revisited: A Decade of Psychological Research'.

40. See in particular S. Wasserman, 'The abused parent of the abused child', *Children*, no. 14, 1967, pp. 175–9; J. E. Oliver and A. Taylor, 'Five generations of ill-treated children in one family pedigree', *British Journal of Psychiatry*, 1971, pp. 473–80.

41. S. Jayarantne, 'Child Abusers as parents and children: A review', *Social Work*, January 1977, pp. 5–9; A. Kadushin, *Child Welfare Services* (Macmillan, 1974); M. Benjamin, 'Abused as a Child, Abusive as a Parent: Practitioners Beware', in R. Volpe, M. Bretton and J. Mitton, *The Maltreatment of the School-Aged Child* (Lexington, 1980).

42. Friedrich and Wheeler, 'The Abusing Parent Revisited: A Decade of Psychological Research', p. 585.

43. Giovannoni, 'Prevention of Child abuse and neglect: research and policy issues', p. 26.

44. A. H. Cohn and J. Garbarino, 'Toward a Refined Approach to Preventing Child Abuse', *National Committee for Prevention of Child Abuse* (mimeographed 1981) quoted in Giovannoni, 'Prevention of Child Abuse and Neglect: research and policy issues'.

45. Particularly see J. W. Hinton (ed.), *Dangerousness: Problems of Assessment and Prediction* (Allen & Unwin, 1981); J. R. Hamilton and H. Freeman

(eds), *Dangerousness: Psychiatry, Assessment and Management* (Gaskell, 1982); A. E. Bottoms, 'Reflections on the Renaissance of Dangerousness', *The Howard Journal of Penology and Crime Prevention*, vol. xvi, no. 2, 1977, pp. 70–96.

46. S. J. Pfohl, 'Deciding on Dangerousness: Predictions of Violence as Social Control', *Crime and Social Justice*, vol. 11, spring/summer, 1979, pp. 28–40, p. 28.

47. R. Hanson, W. McCulloch and S. Hartley, 'Key characteristics of child abuse', in Franklin (ed.), *Child Abuse: Prediction, Prevention and Follow-up.*

48. Smith, *The Battered Child Syndrome.*

49. Hanson, McCulloch and Hartley, 'Key characteristics of child abuse', p. 49, my italics.

50. Hanson, McCulloch and Hartley, 'Key characteristics of child abuse', p. 49, my italics.

51. Hanson, McCulloch and Hartley, 'Key characteristics of child abuse, p. 52, my italics.

52. R. S. Kempe and C. H. Kempe, *Child Abuse* (Open Books, 1978).

53. See also J. D. Gray, C. A. Cutler, J. G. Dean and C. H. Kempe, 'Prediction and Prevention of Child Abuse and Neglect', *Child Abuse and Neglect*, vol. 1, no. 1, 1977, pp. 45–58.

54. Kempe and Kempe, *Child Abuse*, pp. 80–1.

55. Kempe and Kempe, *Child Abuse*, p. 85.

56. Kempe and Kempe, *Child Abuse*, p. 85.

57. G. T. Lealman, D. Haigh, J. M. Phillips, J. Stoan and C. Ord-Smith, 'Prediction and Prevention of Child Abuse – an Empty Hope?', *Lancet*, no. 8339, 25 June 1983, pp. 1423–4.

58. Drawing on previous published work which drew upon retrospective studies a checklist of predictions was drawn up. The major factors were: mother under 20 years at birth of first born; mother booked at antenatal clinic after 20 weeks; mother other than married at delivery. The minor factors were: step-children in the family; psychiatric history; previous referral to social worker; termination of pregnancy requested but refused; complications of pregnancy or delivery; baby admitted to special care baby unit; mother took own or infant's discharge against advice. The studies used were M. A. Lynch and J. Roberts, 'Predicting child abuse: signs of bonding failure in the maternity hospital', *British Medical Journal*, vol. 1, 1977, pp. 624–6; R. R. Gordon, 'Predicting child abuse', *British Medical Journal*, vol. 1, 1977, p. 841.

59. Lealman, Haigh, Phillips, Stoan and Ord-Smith, 'Prediction and Prevention of Child Abuse – an Empty Hope?', p. 1424.

60. See Gray, Cutler, Dean and Kempe, 'Prediction and Prevention of Child Abuse and Neglect', pp. 47–8 for a more detailed description of what this entailed.

61. Kempe and Kempe, *Child Abuse*, p. 86.

62. See note 59.
63. See note 59.
64. A. H. Cohn and M. K. Miller, 'Evaluating New Modes of Treatment for Child Abusers and Neglectors: The Experience of Federally Funded Demonstration Projects in the USA', *Child Abuse and Neglect, The International Journal*, vol. 1, no. 2, 1977, p. 453.
65. See note 59.
66. See I. Taylor, P. Walton and J. Young, *The New Criminology: for a Social Theory of Deviance* (Routledge & Kegan Paul, 1973) chs 2 and 3. J. Young, 'Thinking seriously about crime: some models of criminology' and R. J. Sapsford, 'Individual Deviance: the search for the criminal personality', both in M. Fitzgerald, G. McLennan and J. Pawson (eds), *Crime and Society: Readings in History and Theory* (Routledge & Kegan Paul and Open University Press, 1981).
67. J. Newson and E. Newson, *Four Years Old in an Urban Community* (Allen & Unwin, 1968).
68. W. Ryan, *Blaming the Victim* (Vintage, 1971).
69. S. K. Steinmetz and M. A. Straus (eds), *Violence in the Family* (Harper & Row, 1974); M. A. Straus, 'A Sociological Perspective on the Causes of Family Violence', in M. R. Green (ed.), *Violence in the Family* (Boulder, 1980).
70. C. Brewer and J. Lait, *Can Social Work Survive?* (Temple Smith, 1980) p. 79.
71. Brewer and Lait, *Can Social Work Survive?*, pp. 82–3.
72. E. H. Newberger and J. H. Daniel, 'Knowledge and Epidemiology of Child Abuse: A Critical Review of Concepts', *Pediatrics Annals*, vol. 5, part 3, pp. 140–4.
73. E. Elmer, 'Traumatized Children, Chronic Illness and Poverty', in L. H. Pelton (ed.), *The Social Context of Child Abuse and Neglect* (Human Sciences Press, 1981) p. 212.

Chapter 7

1. But see M. Chatterton, 'The social context of violence', in M. Borland (ed.), *Violence in the Family* (Manchester University Press, 1976); D. Marsden, 'Sociological Perspectives on Family Violence', in J. P. Martin (ed.), *Violence and the Family* (John Wiley, 1978); and R. Dingwall, J. Eekelaar and T. Murray, *The Protection of Children: State Intervention and Family Life* (Blackwells, 1983).
2. L. H. Pelton, 'Child Abuse and Neglect: The Myth of Classlessness', *American Journal of Orthopsychiatry*, no. 48, 1978, pp. 608–17, reprinted in L. H. Pelton (ed.), *The Social Context of Child Abuse and Neglect* (Human Sciences Press, 1981).

3. See in particular for Britain: R. Rose, P. Owtram, J. Pickett, B. Marran and A. Maton, *Registers of Suspected Non-Accidental Injury: A Report on Registers maintained in Leeds and Manchester by NSPCC Special Units* (NSPCC, 1976); S. Creighton and P. Owtram, *Child Victims of Physical Abuse: A Report on the Findings of NSPCC Special Unit Registers* (NSPCC, 1977).

4. Pelton, 'Child Abuse and Neglect: The Myth of Classlessness', p. 610.

5. As suggested by the NSPCC studies in note 3.

6. As demonstrated by D. Gil, *Violence against Children* (Harvard University Press, 1970). Also S. M. Smith, *The Battered Child Syndrome* (Butterworths, 1975), reports that a British study of 134 abused children under five found that the parents were predominantly from the lower social classes and concluded that 'battering is mainly a lower class phenomenon'.

7. Pelton, 'Child Abuse and Neglect: The Myth of Classlessness', p. 613.

8. Pelton (ed.), *The Social Context of Child Abuse and Neglect*, introduction, p. 21.

9. J. Garbarino and G. Gilliam, *Understanding Abusive Families* (Lexington Books, 1980). See also R. Volpe, M. Breton and J. Mitton (eds), *The Maltreatment of the School-Aged Child* (Lexington Books, 1980).

10. Garbarino and Gilliam, *Understanding Abusive Families*, p. 21.

11. Garbarino and Gilliam argue that the systems framework proposed by Urie Bronfenbrenner is the most useful approach to the study of human development. U. Bronfenbrenner, *The Ecology of Human Development* (Harvard University Press, 1979).

12. J. Garbarino, 'An Ecological Approach to Child Maltreatment' in Pelton, *The Social Context of Child Abuse and Neglect*.

13. Garbarino and Gilliam, *Understanding Abusive Families*, p. 29.

14. Apart from Garbarino and Gilliam, *Understanding Abusive Families*, and Garbarino, 'An Ecological Approach to Child Maltreatment', see J. Garbarino and A. Crouter, 'Defining the community context of parent–child relations: the correlates of child maltreatment', *Child Development*, no. 49, 1978, pp. 604–16; J. Garbarino, 'The Price of Privacy in the Social Dynamics of Child Abuse', *Child Welfare*, no. 56, 1977, pp. 565–75; J. Garbarino and D. Sherman, 'Identifying high-risk neighbourhoods', in J. Garbarino and S. H. Stocking (eds), *Supporting Families and Protecting Children* (Centre for the Study of Youth Development, 1978).

15. Garbarino, 'An Ecological Approach to Child Maltreatment'.

16. Garbarino, 'An Ecological Approach to Child Maltreatment', p. 47.

17. National Institute of Social Work, *Social Workers: Their Role and Tasks* (Bedford Square Press, 1982) particularly ch. 13 and appendix A.

18. Garbarino, 'The Price of Privacy in the Social Dynamics of Child Abuse', p. 573.

19. Much of this is reminiscent of the ecological perspective developed by

the Chicago School in the 1930s with its emphasis on social disorganisation and differential association.

20. As with the initial policy of Community Development Projects in Britain in the late 1960s.

21. Recent examples of this critique include A. Walker (ed.), *Community Care* (Blackwells, 1982) particularly chs 1 and 2; M. Clarke, 'Where is the community which cares?', *British Journal of Social Work*, vol. 12, no. 5, 1982, pp. 453–69. See also for a Weberian critique of the ecological approach to the city J. Rex and R. Moore, *Race, Community and Conflict: a study in Sparkbrook* (Oxford University Press, 1967).

22. First Report from the Select Committee on Violence in the Family, *Violence to Children*, Session 1976–77 (HMSO, 1977).

23. R. J. Gelles, 'Demythologizing Child Abuse', *The Family Coordinator*, vol. 25, no. 2, April 1976, pp. 135–41.

24. M. A. Straus, 'A Sociological Perspective on the causes of Family Violence', in M. R. Green (ed.), *Violence in the Family* (Boulder, 1980) p. 8.

25. For a full report on the research and its findings see M. A. Straus, R. J. Gelles and S. K. Steinmetz, *Behind Closed Doors: Violence in the American Family* (Anchor/Doubleday, 1980); R. J. Gelles, 'A Profile of Violence towards Children in the United States', in G. Gerbmer, C. J. Ross and E. Zigler (eds), *Child Abuse: An agenda for action* (Oxford University Press, 1980); R. J. Gelles, 'Violence towards children in the United States', *American Journal of Orthopsychiatry*, no. 48, October 1978, pp. 580–92; R. J. Gelles, 'Violence in the American Family', in Martin (ed.), *Violence and the Family*.

26. According to Straus, Gelles and Steinmetz the term 'beaten up' was defined by its place in the list of violence items. It came after the items dealing with kicking, biting, hitting with a fist, and hitting with an object, and before the items dealing with a knife or gun. Therefore it is something more than just a single event but its precise meaning would vary between respondents.

27. With the exception of being threatened with a knife or gun or having a gun used on them.

28. Gelles, 'A Profile of Violence towards Children in the United States', p. 88.

29. Original italics.

30. These findings very much reflect those from studies in Britain. See for example Rose, Owtram, Pickett, Marran and Maton, *Registers of Suspected Non-Accidental Injury*; Creighton and Owtram, *Child Victims of Physical Abuse*; Smith, *The Battered Child Syndrome*.

31. A modified version of the Holmes and Rake Stressful Life Events Scale was used. See T. H. Holmes and R. H. Rake, 'The social readjustment

rating scale', *Journal of Psychosomatic Research*, vol. 11, no. 2, 1967, pp. 213–18.

32. Apart from references in note 25, see S. K. Steinmetz, *The Cycle of Violence: Assertive, Aggressive and Abusive Family Interaction* (Praefer, 1977); R. J. Gelles and M. A. Straus, 'Determinants of Violence in the Family: Towards a Theoretical Integration', in W. R. Burr, R. Hill, F. Ivan Nye and I. C. Reiss (eds), *Contemporary Theories about the Family: Research-Based Theories*, vol. 1 (Free Press, 1979); M. A. Straus (1974) 'Cultural and Social Organizational Influences on Violence between Family Members', in R. Prince and D. Barrier (eds), *Configurations* (Lexington Books, 1974).

33. See in particular D. J. Owens and M. A. Straus, 'The Social Structure of Violence in Childhood and Approval of Violence as an Adult', *Aggressive Behaviour*, vol. 1, no. 2, 1975, pp. 193–211.

34. Straus, 'A Sociological Perspective on the causes of Family Violence', p. 23.

35. R. J. Gelles, 'The social construction of child abuse', *American Journal of Orthopsychiatry*, no. 44, April 1975, pp. 363–71; R. J. Gelles, 'Community Agencies and Child Abuse: Labelling and Gatekeeping', in R. J. Gelles, *Family Violence* (Sage, 1979); A. W. Frank, 'Therapeutic and Legal Formulations of Child Abuse', in H. H. Irving (ed.), *Family Law: An Interdisciplinary Perspective* (Carswell, 1981).

36. Dingwall, Eekelaar and Murray, *The Protection of Children*. Also A. Lawson, 'Taking the decision to remove the child from the family', *Journal of Social Welfare Law*, May 1980, pp. 141–63; J. M. Giovannoni and R. M. Beccerra, *Defining Child Abuse* (Free Press, 1979).

37. Dingwall, Eekelaar and Murray, *The Protection of Children*, pp. 101–2.

38. Dingwall, Eekelaar and Murray, *The Protection of Children*, p. 31.

39. Gil, *Violence against Children*.

40. Gil, *Violence against Children*, p. 137.

41. In Britain there are various estimates of the incidence of child abuse. The First Report from the Select Committee on Violence in the Family, *Violence to Children*, quotes the evidence received from the Royal College of Psychiatrists and work from Dr Oliver in Wiltshire (see J. E. Oliver, J. Cox, A. Taylor and J. A. Baldwin, *Severely ill-treated Young Children in North-East Wiltshire*, Unit of Clinical Epidemiology, Oxford Record Linkage Study, Oxford Regional Health Authority Research Report, No. 4, August 1974. J. A. Baldwin and J. E. Oliver, 'Epidemiology and Family Characteristics of Severely Abused Children', *British Journal of Preventive Medicine*, no. 29, 1975, pp. 205–221, concluded that:

(1) for each 10 000 children under the age of 4 years in England and Wales 10 will be severely injured each year. (2) 1 of these 10 will die

as a result of the severity of the injury. (3) In England and Wales it is estimated that some 3000 children will be injured each year and 6 of them will die each week. (4) It is much more difficult to estimate the number of moderate or mild cases, since they may not be sent to hospital etc. but as many as 40–60 children in 10 000 will be so injured – or 40 000 children in England and Wales.

The Office of Population, Census and Surveys estimates that out of 10 877 children aged 1–14 years who died from accidents and violence between 1968 and 1974, 417 or 3.8 per cent were homicides. In addition it is suggested that the 2.1 per cent (223) of deaths described as undetermined also included a high proportion of homicides. (See A. Macfarlane and J. Fox, 'Child deaths from accidents and violence', *Population Trends*, no. 12, pp. 22–7, (OPCS, 1978).)

42. See E. Elmer, 'A follow-up study of traumatic children', *Paediatrics*, no. 59, 1977, pp. 273–9; E. Elmer, *Fragile Families: The Aftermath of Infant Trauma* (University of Pittsburgh Press, 1977). E. Elmer, 'Traumatized Children, Chronic Illness and Poverty' in Pelton (ed.), *The Social Context of Child Abuse and Neglect*.

43. Elmer, *Fragile Families*, pp. 83–4.

44. Elmer, 'Traumatized Children, Chronic Illness and Poverty'.

45. H. P. Martin and P. Beezley, 'Behavioural Observations of Abused Children', *Developmental Medicine and Child Neurology*', vol. 19, 1977, pp. 373–87.

46. Elmer, 'Traumatized Children, Chronic Illness and Poverty', p. 206. More recent research in this country has included a control group and claims to have found specific long term consequences arising from abuse. However the control group was only matched for age and failed to match for race, sex and class. R. Calam, 'Five Years after the event', *Community Care*, no. 433, 14 October 1982, pp. 17–18. See also M. A. Lynch and J. Roberts, *Consequences of Child Abuse* (Academic Press, 1982).

47. D. G. Gil, 'Unravelling Child Abuse', *American Journal of Orthopsychiatry*, vol. 45, no. 3, 1975, pp. 346–56. See also Gil's foreward to Volpe, Breton and Mitton (eds), *The Maltreatment of the School-Aged Child*.

48. D. G. Gil, 'Societal Violence and Violence in Families', in J. M. Eekelaar and S. N. Katz (eds), *Family Violence: An International and Interdisciplinary Study* (Butterworths, 1978); D. G. Gil, *Unravelling Social Policy* (Schenkman Publishing, 1973); D. Gil, *The Challenge of Social Equality* (Schenkman Publishing, 1976).

49. D. Webb, 'Sociology', in P. Hardiker and M. Barker (eds). *Theories of Practice in Social Work* (Academic Press, 1981), p. 135.

50. The work of Bob Holman has been particularly significant. See R. Holman, *Inequality in Child Care* (CPAG/FRG, 2nd edn 1980); R. Holman, *Poverty: Explanations of Social Deprivation* (Martin Robertson,

1978); R. Holman, 'The Place of Fostering in Social Work', *British Journal of Social Work*, vol. 5, no. 1, 1975, pp. 3–29. A number of American writers have explicitly attempted to develop class analyses of child care. See B. R. Mandel, *Where are the Children? A Class Analysis of Foster Care and Adoption* (Lexington Books, 1973); S. Jenkins and E. Norman, *Filial Deprivation and Foster Care* (Columbia University Press, 1972); A. L. Schorr (ed.), *Children and Decent People* (Allen & Unwin, 1975).

51. This section draws upon: P. Townsend, *Poverty in the United Kingdom: A survey of household resources and standards of living* (Penguin, 1979); M. Brown and N. Madge, *Despite the Welfare State* (Heinemann, 1982); J. Roll, 'Facts and Figures', *Poverty*, no. 56, December 1983, pp. 8–10.

52. See for example: Brown and Madge, *Despite the Welfare State;* M. Rutter and N. Madge, *Cycles of Disadvantage: A Review of Research* (Heinemann, 1976); F. Coffield, P. Robinson and J. Sarsby, *A Cycle of Deprivation? A Case Study of Four Families* (Heinemann, 1980).

53. M. Blaxter, *The Health of Children: A Review of Research on the Place of Health in Cycles of Disadvantage* (Heinemann, 1981) p. 219.

54. See P. Townsend and N. Davidson, *Inequalities in Health* (Penguin, 1982) pp. 127–8. Also Coffield, Robinson and Sarsby, *A Cycle of Deprivation?*, p. 185; S. Dowling, *Health for a change: The Provision of Health care in pregnancy and early childhood* (CPAG, 1983); Report of the Committee on Child Health Services (Court Report), *Fit for the Future*, Cmnd 6684 (HMSO, 1976).

55. See J. Packman, *Child Care: Needs and Numbers* (Allen & Unwin, 1968); V. George, *Foster Care: Theory and Practice* (Routledge & Kegan Paul, 1970); R. Holman, *Trading in Children* (Routledge & Kegan Paul, 1973).

56. DHSS Personal Social Services Local Authority Statistics, *Children in Care of Local Authorities Year Ending 31 March 1981 England*, Table 1.01 (A/F81/12).

57. R. Fuller and O. Stevenson, *Policies, Programmes and Disadvantage: A Review of the Literature* (Heinemann, 1983) p. 88.

58. Brown and Madge, *Despite the Welfare State*, pp. 160–1.

59. H. Wilson and G. W. Herbert, *Parents and Children in the Inner City* (Routledge & Kegan Paul, 1978), p. 183; H. Wilson, 'Parenting in Poverty', *British Journal of Social Work*, vol. 4, no. 3, 1974, pp. 241–54.

Chapter 8

1. A. Morris, H. Giller, E. Szwed and H. Geach, *Justice for Children* (Macmillan, 1980); H. Geach and E. Szwed (eds), *Providing Civil Justice for Children* (Arnold, 1983). Also L. Taylor, R. Lacey and D. Bracken, *In*

Whose Best Interests? The unjust treatment of children in courts and institutions (The Cobden Trust and Mind, 1979).

2. J. Goldstein, A. Freud and A. Solnit, *Before the Best Interests of the Child* (Free Press, 1979). Michael Wald takes a similar but less prescribed position: M. S. Wald, 'State intervention on behalf of neglected children: A search for realistic standards', *Stanford Law Review*, no. 27, 1975, pp. 985–1040; M. S. Wald, 'Neglected Children: Standards for Removal of Children from their homes, monitoring the status of children in foster care, and termination of parental rights', *Stanford Law Review*, no. 28, 1976, pp. 622–706; M. S. Wald, 'Thinking about public policy toward abuse and neglect of children: A review of "Before the Best Interests of the Child"', *Michigan Law Review*, no. 78, 1980, pp. 645–93; M. S. Wald, 'State intervention on behalf of endangered children – a proposed legal response', *Child Abuse and Neglect*, vol. 6, 1982, pp. 3–45. Interestingly Wald's work is favourably received by Taylor, Lacey and Bracken, *In Whose Best Interests?*, p. 87.

3. J. Goldstein, A. Freud and A. Solnit, *Beyond the Best Interests of the Child* (Free Press, 1973).

4. Goldstein, Freud and Solnit, *Before the Best Interests of the Child*, pp. 8–10.

5. M. D. A. Freeman, 'Freedom and the Welfare State: Child-Rearing, Parental Autonomy and State Intervention', *Journal of Social Welfare Law*, March 1983, pp. 70–91. Also M. D. A. Freeman, *The Rights and Wrongs of Children* (Francis Pinter, 1983).

6. Goldstein, Freud and Solnit, *Before the Best Interests of the Child*, p. 73.

7. A socialist perspective on this has been provided by C. Lasch, *Haven in a Heartless World: The Family Besieged* (Basic Books, 1977) and C. Lasch, *The Culture of Narcissm* (Warner Books, 1979); A conservative one by F. Mount, *The Subversive Family* (Jonathan Cape, 1982).

8. J. Donzelot, *The Policing of Families* (Hutchinson, 1979).

9. A. Walker (ed.), *Community Care: The Family, the State and Social Policy* (Blackwell/Robertson, 1982).

10. See for example H. Land, 'Who cares for the family?', *Journal of Social Policy*, vol. 7, no. 3, 1978, pp. 257–84; H. Land, 'The Boundaries between the State and the Family', in C. Harris (ed.), *The Sociology of the Family: New Directions in Britain*, Sociological Review Monograph 28 (University of Keele, 1979).

11. Walker (ed.), *Community Care*, p. 31.

12. M. Barrett and M. McIntosh, *The Anti-Social Family* (Verso, 1982). Also C. Smart, 'Regulating families or legitimating patriarchy? Family law in Britain', *International Journal of the Sociology of Law*, no. 10, 1982, pp. 129–48.

13. Barrett and McIntosh, *The Anti-Social Family*, pp. 25–6.

14. R. Dingwall, J. Eekelaar and T. Murray, *The Protection of Children: State Intervention and Family Life* (Blackwell, 1983). Also R. Dingwall, J.

Eekelaar and T. Murray, 'Times Change and we change with them?', *Community Care*, no. 465, 16 June 1983, pp. 18–19; R. Dingwall, 'Defining Child Mistreatment', *Health Visitor*, vol. 56, no. 7, July 1983, pp. 249–51; R. Dingwall, 'Working Together?', *Maternal and Child Health*, vol. 8, no. 4, April 1983, pp. 153–7; R. Dingwall and J. Eekelaar, *Care Proceedings: A Practical Guide for Social Workers, Health Visitors and others* (Blackwell, 1982).

15. Dingwall, Eekelaar and Murray, *The Protection of Children*, p. 202.
16. Dingwall, Eekelaar and Murray, *The Protection of Children*, p. 222.
17. M. King, 'The New Child Savers', *Legal Action Group Bulletin*, October 1983, pp. 10–11; and the reply R. Dingwall, J. Eekelaar and T. Murray, 'The New Child Savers – A Reply', *Legal Action Group Bulletin*, January 1984, p. 11.
18. See L. Hilgendorf, *Social Workers and Solicitors in Child Care Cases* (HMSO, 1981).
19. Dingwall, Eekelaar and Murray, *The Protection of Children*, p. 209.
20. Barrett and McIntosh, *The Anti-Social Family*, p. 157.
21. See B. Deacon, 'Social Administration, Social Policy and Socialism', *Critical Social Policy*, vol. 1, no. 1, Summer 1981, pp. 43–66; B. Deacon, *Social Policy and Socialism: The Struggle for Socialist Relations of Welfare* (Pluto Press, 1983); G. Dalley, 'Ideologies of care: a feminist contribution to the debate', *Critical Social Policy*, no. 8, 1983, pp. 72–81; J. Finch, 'Community Care: developing non-sexist alternatives', *Critical Social Policy* no. 9, 1984, pp. 6–18.
22. P. Moss, 'Community Care and Young Children' in Walker (ed.), *Community Care*, pp. 137–8.
23. J. Coussins and A. Coote, *The Family in the Firing Line* (NCCL/CPAG, 1981).
24. R. Lister and P. Wilding, 'The Verdict on Thatcherism', in D. Bull and P. Wilding (eds), *Thatcherism and the Poor* (CPAG, 1983).
25. Figures from C. Walker, 'Supplementary Benefits: the sinking safety net', in Bull and Wilding (eds), *Thatcherism and the Poor*; J. Roll, 'Facts and Figures', *Poverty*, no. 56, December 1983, pp. 8–10; House of Commons, *Hansard*, 38, cd 524W, 11 March 1983.
26. See the *Guardian* 17 and 18 February 1983. For examples of how the members of government who support the importance of the family and the sanctity of marriage fall foul of their own rhetoric see F. Wheen, 'Diary', *New Statesman*, 14 October 1983.
27. P. Townsend, 'An Alternative Anti-Poverty Programme', *New Society*, vol. 62, no. 1038, 7 October 1982, pp. 22–3.
28. P. Townsend and N. Davidson (eds), *Inequalities in Health* (Penguin, 1982) p. 177.
29. D. Piachaud, *Children and Poverty*, Poverty Research Series 9 (CPAG, 1981).

30. Townsend and Davidson (eds), *Inequalities in Health*, pp. 179–80.
31. A. Walker (ed.), *The Poverty of Taxation* (CPAG, 1982).
32. DHSS, Health and Personal Social Services Statistics 1982, Government Statistical Office, Table 2.7 (HMSO, 1982).
33. R. Fuller and O. Stevenson, *Policies, Programmes and Disadvantage: A Review of the Literature* (Heinemann, 1983) p. 55; See also R. Hodgkin, H. Penn, J. Streather and J. Tunstill, 'The Case for Prevention', *Community Care*, no. 483, 13 October 1983, pp. 31–2.
34. R. Holman, *Inequality in Child Care* (CPAG/FRG 2nd edn 1980).
35. *The Association Between Pre-School Provision and Demand on Other Services*, unpublished report of the Director of Social Services, Devon, November 1979.
36. See *Guardian Education*, 'Cutting Back on Care', 16 October 1979.
37. Some examples include: A. Whitehouse, 'We're being allowed to keep him', *Community Care*, no. 459, 21 April 1983, pp. 15–17; C. Warren and J. Adamson, 'What is a Family Centre?' in G. Pugh (ed.), *Supporting parents in the community* (National Children's Bureau, 1982).
38. J. Thoburn, *Captive Clients: Social Work with Families of Children Home on Trial* (Routledge & Kegan Paul, 1980), p. 178.
39. D. Berridge, Developments in Residential Care: Children's Homes in the 1980s. *RCA Annual Seminar*, October 1983, Southport.
40. See Family Rights Group, *Fostering Parental Contact: Arguments in favour of preserving contact between children in care and their families* (FRG, 1982); Family Rights Group, *Accountability in Child Care – Which Way Forward?'* (FRG, 1982); Family Service Units, *Family Involvement in the Social Work Process* (FSU, 1982).
41. See DHSS (Social Work Service) *Boarding Out Regulations* (HMSO, 1982) which established that there was 'widespread disregard' of the Boarding Out of Children Regulations. The report was damning about the present level of social work practice in the area related to visiting, records, reviews and health.
42. V. George, *Foster Care: Theory and Practice* (Routledge & Kegan Paul, 1970).
43. R. Holman, *Trading in Children* (Routledge & Kegan Paul, 1973).
44. R. Thorpe, 'Mum and Mrs So and So', *Social Work Today*, vol. 4, no. 22, 1974, pp. 691–5.
45. Thoburn, *Captive Clients*.
46. The argument in the rest of this section draws on N. Parton and T. Thomas, 'Child Abuse and Citizenship', in B. Jordan and N. Parton (eds), *The Political Dimensions of Social Work* (Blackwells, 1983).

Index